THE PURSUIT OF REPUTATION

THE PURSUIT OF REPUTATION

UNLOCKING THE POWER OF PUBLIC RELATIONS

AMITH PRABHU
SUJIT PATIL

First published by Westland Business, an imprint of Westland Books, a division of Nasadiya Technologies Private Limited, in 2023

No. 269/2B, First Floor, 'Irai Arul', Vimalraj Street, Nethaji Nagar, Alapakkam Main Road, Maduravoyal, Chennai 600095

Westland, the Westland logo, Westland Business and the Westland Business logo are the trademarks of Nasadiya Technologies Private Limited, or its affiliates.

ISBN: 9789357768399

10 9 8 7 6 5 4 3 2 1

Typeset by SÜRYA, New Delhi

Printed at Parksons Graphics Pvt. Ltd

CONTENTS

FOREWORD

Those who are in true pursuit of reputation—for their clients or their own organisations—must be good, honest and caring corporate citizens first.

As the representative of a conglomerate that is over 125 years old and amongst India's earliest multinational business groups, what I treasure most is the reputation of trust that we have earned in that period of time. While businesses are meant to profit, for us at the Godrej group—and I am sure for many others as well—what also matters is purpose, sustainability and good citizenship. Good corporate actions, I firmly believe, can lead to good corporate reputation.

The Pursuit of Reputation is a compilation of almost every facet of public relations (PR) and corporate communications that can help craft reputation. The authors have endeavoured to share practical insights and simple techniques that can be practised by all reputation managers to build corporate and brand status.

In my mind, the PR professional plays a significant role in the workplace today—a role that goes well beyond simply issuing communiques and ensuring that media carries the right message. For one, the media landscape itself has changed very dramatically. Social media has become all-powerful and its impact can create or destroy the reputation of a brand or service. As a result, online reputation management (ORM) has become a key part of the communication strategy of an organisation.

The authors have made a good case around embracing technology for building a reputation. Artificial intelligence (AI) is making inroads into all areas of business, and certainly in PR and reputation management. Routine communiques will be written, perhaps more efficiently, by AI-aided software. Earnings releases, corporate announcements or even basic investor relations will be machine-driven. However, I do believe that the human touch in communications is valuable and can raise the efficacy of any message. I am intrigued with the way the authors have explained the use of creativity, emotions and, most importantly, research and data in creating authentic narratives for a brand.

Another interesting facet that caught my eye is the rise in the influence of folks who have a tremendous following in the digital space. A whole new genre of digital PR has emerged.

Clearly, the craft of communications and public relations has come a long way and to ensure that this trajectory continues, it is critical that the right talent is attracted to the profession. A completely new set of relevant competencies has been brought to the fore by the authors. I feel that developing these can enable professionals to raise the bar even further when it comes to building reputation.

I am delighted that such a comprehensive book on reputation management has been written by Sujit and Amith. From what I have seen and what I know about the authors, I am certain that this book will be that much-needed companion not only for a public relations professional but also for every leader across any organisation serious about reputation.

Adi Godrej
Mumbai, July 2023

PREFACE

Why did we write this book?

Eight months into the pandemic, on a late-night Zoom call, we were discussing the state of the PR profession in India. As well-wishers of the profession, we have always wanted to do something that could benefit those engaged in it. The discussion shifted to the field of corporate communications and how the space has evolved significantly in the recent past. We agreed that the reputation of an organisation has taken the spotlight and businesses are grappling with crafting authentic engagement with their stakeholders. We also felt that there is no comprehensive book that covers the multiple nuances of modern public relations and corporate communications that could be referred to by organisational leaders. The seeds of co-authoring a book were sown and began germinating.

Around the same time, the late Anant Rangaswami, during one of the conversations, nudged us to put together a book that would be a ready reference for anyone who wanted to understand PR better. The three of us got on a call to discuss what the book would look like. Anant's perspective helped us organise our thoughts to put together what you see in the ensuing pages. We will be forever grateful to him.

We believe that there is more to PR than just media relations. We picked up over a dozen concepts that constitute public relations, divided them between the two of us and began our late-night writing binges over the weekends between the Delta and Omicron variants. We also realised that the core of public relations is authenticity and inclusion—the new AI. Therefore, we reached out to over seventy-five leaders from public relations and allied fields to contribute a piece of knowledge to the book. Our aim was to create a sense of community, and almost everyone responded. Therefore, at the end of each chapter, you will see choice expert commentaries by industry stalwarts. As such, the book is a passion project for not just the two of us but several others who contributed, followed through and, in a way, are also co-authors of this book.

What we can guarantee is that the book is a wholehearted documentation of our combined knowledge and over forty years of hands-on experience in building the reputations of large corporations and brands using contemporary thinking and processes. Each topic has been carefully chosen to provide insights and practical tips that are much needed to address the nuances of contemporary public relations for building brand status.

As first-time authors, we are super excited about what we believe is an important book. We are confident that this book will be as relevant to a young graduate as much as it will be to a CEO. It will also be useful for those in corporate communications and public relations consulting and for everyone who has something to do with the public relations space.

We have jointly decided that the proceeds from this

book will go towards the higher education of youngsters who want to make a career in corporate communications.

We look forward to your feedback and hope to incorporate any suggestions into future editions.

1

THE RISE AND RISE OF PUBLIC RELATIONS

Have you ever wondered about how the concept of public relations was born?

On a very philosophical level, the history of public relations is as old as the history of mankind. At the heart of public relations are the fundamental concepts of storytelling, building connections, influencing and enhancing trust. These are the tenets that make civilisations thrive and have always been an inherent part of human nature.

Practically every historical event has had a PR element embedded in it. Whether we refer to mythology or holy books or historical texts, there are PR concepts in them. Our greatest epics, the Ramayana and the Mahabharata, if analysed closely, contain traces of these. It is all about human relations—building trust, framing narratives, telling stories and demonstrating good behaviour. The list can be unending. No one can dispute the fact that Gautam Buddha, Shankaracharya or Kabirdas were all amazing communicators who simplified complex life concepts and delivered them to the common people through different modes. The rock inscriptions of Emperor Ashoka were written in local dialects for easy understanding and effective communication. Even during those days, religious leaders sent their disciples to faraway lands to preach and gather advocates.

The timeless nature of communications

Even if we look at other cultures from different eras, we find similar examples. In 50 BCE, Julius Caesar publicised his military exploits in the first known political campaign biography to shape the opinion of the Roman public into accepting that he would make the best head of state. This document can be regarded as the first public newsletter. Socrates, one of the founders of Western philosophy, believed that effective communication should be based on the truth. Aristotle's *Rhetoric* dealt with the art of persuasion and the shaping of public opinion.

From ancient Egypt to the medieval period, people used various channels to relay important information to each other and help keep citizens notified. These methods of communication form a strong base for what is used today in traditional formats. In 394 AD, for instance, Saint Augustine would deliver eulogies to the emperor and the public regularly to benefit the church. It was akin to hosting a press conference in today's world.

In the Indian context, if we go back about a century in time to pre-independent India, there are significant milestones in the public life of Mahatma Gandhi, arguably the greatest Indian public relations icon of all time. In 1930, he led the Dandi March, which we feel may be one of the most well-planned PR campaigns of all time. This twenty-four-day march lasted from 12 March 1930 to 5 April 1930. Just imagine what would have happened if those people on the march had live-tweeted every minute of the journey! The success of the march can be attributed to excellent communication, plenty of common sense, a strong cultural backbone and being strategically designed to have a large-scale impact. Then, in 1942, the Quit India Movement was another campaign-centric event that had good PR at its core. PR has always existed under different forms with the objective to nearly always manage and influence public opinion. And that continues today.

Gandhi managed to mobilise support on the basis of three simple tactics which can teach any PR professional some interesting ways to communicate.

The first tactic was enabling people to identify with a cause that transcended cultural and linguistic diversity. Gandhi was the first to set the example by embracing the cause: discarding Western attire and adopting a simple dhoti. His second tactic was having a powerful symbol: the charkha, which became the logo of the national movement, symbolising self-reliance. And the third tactic was to manifest his ideas, which he did via events like the Dandi March, which captured the attention of the whole nation. And, of course, what tied these tactics together was his relentless communication via letters, speeches and other traditional means.

His use of such strategies was the critical stepping stone towards the larger goal of attaining complete independence in 1947.

Returning to how this field has evolved, the current form of public relations owes a lot to the pioneers and important historical events which laid the foundation of it as a notable profession.

Around 1584, Sir Walter Raleigh is said to have attempted to send reports about the beauty of Roanoke Island to England in order to attract more settlers. Despite his efforts, his attempt was unsuccessful, as it turned out that the land was swampy. Of course, it also didn't help his case when a large part of the settlers who did visit the island disappeared completely without a trace. Sometimes, PR fails.

In 1773, Samuel Adams, who is considered a master of propaganda, orchestrated public relations for the Revolutionary War while three years later, Thomas Paine wrote the pamphlet *Common Sense*, encouraging people to fight for an egalitarian government in America.

It is said that Basil Clark is regarded as the first PR professional, establishing the first UK-based PR consultancy, Editorial Services, in 1924.

However, it is a well-accepted fact that PR first became a profession when Ivy Lee started working as an advisor to John Rockefeller in 1903. As a publicity expert, he was responsible for managing and improving Rockefeller's reputation. Lee is also believed to be the author of the first-ever press release.

One of the most important names in the field of public relations is Edward Bernays, also referred to as the Father of Public Relations, the author of the influential book, *Propaganda*. His strategies were based on theories of behavioural psychology. Bernays believed that political propaganda used by the governments during World War II could also be used by corporations to influence the customer in subtle ways.

It cannot be ignored that some of the innovations of that era must also have sparked the rise of public relations. Arguably, with the invention of the printing press in 1440 by Johannes Gutenberg, a major cultural and social revolution was set into motion following the massive rise in newspapers, documentation, books, fliers and, of course, propaganda.

The telegraph in 1830, the daguerreotype in 1839 (the first commercially successful photographic process in the history of photography named after the inventor, Louis Jacques Mandé Daguerre) and the telephone in 1876 can also be given a lot of credit for paving the way for mass communication. The invention of the motion picture camera in 1892 and wireless telegraphy in 1896 took things to the next level. And one must consider the impact of long-distance radio communication when it was invented in 1901.

Undoubtedly, thought leaders and innovation have been critical to the sector of public relations. It is also true that the changes that the profession has witnessed in the last decade have been more rapid than the developments of the previous century.

The early years

Public relations, despite having been around for more than a century across the world, gained recognition as a profession in India only after 1950. Around this time, a group of public relations practitioners formed the Public Relations Society of India (PRSI) in 1958 in Bombay (now Mumbai) under the leadership of Kali H. Mody. He led the body till 1960, followed by S. Mandietta, who was president from

1961 to 1965, and F.S. Mulla, who became the president from 1966 to 1969. It was under him that this informal body was registered in 1966 under the Indian Societies Act XXVI of 1961, after which Mulla came to be regarded as the founding member of PRSI.

At the same time, around 1965, another body, the Public Relations Circle, was founded and registered in Calcutta (now Kolkata). It was the first-ever association of professional PR practitioners in eastern India.

In 1968, the first All-India Public Relations Conference was held in Mumbai where the members of the Calcutta Public Relations Council decided to disband at a regional level and merge with the PRSI to strengthen the national body. Another significant contribution of this conference was the adoption of the International Code of Ethics (also called Code of Athens) on 21 April 1968. Mulla was also able to extend the reach of the group by establishing regional chapters in Delhi, Madras and Kolkata.

One of the landmark achievements of this professional body of PR practitioners was to bring together leading international PR experts in Mumbai at the 9th Public Relations World Congress in January 1982, hosted with the active participation of the International Public Relations Association (IPRA). At that time, the PRSI was headed by K.S. Neelakandan, Director of Public Relations with Pfizer Ltd in India and also the Executive Chairman of the PR World Congress.

Though there were several individuals and small companies which started even before that, their PR services had a limited scope in media relations. It was only natural then that the entrepreneurs who offered such services came from a background of journalism which began to be seen as a natural hunting ground for individuals in the still-nascent profession.

The development of public relations in India

The evolution of public relations in India can be a fascinating topic of debate. For this book, we want to stick to discussing its rise in the corporate sector. Following Independence, the progression of public relations can be categorised into three incrementally distinct phases—propaganda for persuasion, publicity for awareness and public engagement.

Globalisation of the Indian economy in the 1990s led to a significant rise in competition. This was due to the deregulation of industries, the entry of multinationals and increased opportunities for foreign direct investment. This led to the need for building positive reputations. With more options available in the market, focus on brand-building was important to gain loyal consumers. Liberalisation certainly triggered the need for professional PR and advertising set-ups that could help manage operations.

These were early times. However, several multinational companies began to realise the power of public relations in terms of hiring a PR firm and employing a dedicated professional to manage their public outreach programme. They wanted to gain a strong foothold in the country and for that, they had to create a conducive reputation and environment. PR consultancies were hired by these multinationals to manage stakeholders and roll out advocacy programmes for influencing government legislation. They also engaged PR experts to help craft responses and narratives to counter their critics and competitors.

Over a period, evolved organisations also realised that there is a distinction between public relations and a few terms mistakenly associated with PR like spin, propaganda, publicity and so on. We would like to make it amply clear that there is no greater fallacy than to associate public relations with such terms!

It is important at this juncture to note that corporate brand reputation is different from product brand reputation and certainly very distinct from branding. Most often, corporate brand reputation is linked to the C-suite and deals with building and protecting organisational status. Product brand reputation and branding are linked to the marketing department and are focused on enhancing the standing of the product.

Corporate reputation relies on several factors. Most important among these factors is how top management behaves during good times and bad. It also depends on the quality of product or service being offered. If the quality is high, it can lead to positive word-of-mouth publicity, which further enhances reputation.

We have also seen multiple layers of evolution in the past decade. Persuasion and authenticity have always remained the cornerstones of a good public relations programme. Powerful storytelling has played a stellar role in building repute for many organisations.

Over the years, the concept of public relations became synonymous with reputation management. A few Indian conglomerates began to rely on individuals tasked with being in-house public relations heads. Over time, the work they undertook involved multiple areas of communications—external, internal, brand, marketing, government communications and more. This led to the coinage of a term: corporate communications.

As technology developed, so did public relations. The increase in reach and the availability of mass media like television, print and radio further helped enhance the efficacy of public relations.

Recent disruptions in public relations

Disruption, in a positive sense, leads to good change. It can affect the way business is conducted, the perceptions of stakeholders and the way corporations act. It requires people to adapt to new ways. Disruption means new thinking, newer ideas and innovations.

So, apart from the pandemic, what can cause disruptions in public relations and corporate communications? Innovative technology, new digital platforms, changing business landscapes, shifting economic conditions or national sentiments?

We feel it's all that and more. And we are witnessing new developments occur every single day.

As we will cover in detail in following chapters, PR has evolved much faster in the past five years when compared to the previous several decades. The advent of new media and technology has transformed the way communication takes place. However, one thing that will probably never change is the fact that good storytelling remains an integral part of public relations. Today, PR is seen by many serious corporates as a strategic function and a certain expertise is sought during business planning. PR has made its transition from a broadcast model to an engagement model. So, a shift from a monologue to dialogue means that instead of just presenting stories, the practitioner must establish conversations with the target group. A digital platform enables this.

The power of influencers is on the rise and managing them has become an additional task. Today, a story can go global in seconds. With most now having the ability to broadcast text, photos, videos and infographics with a click of a button, focus on online reputation management has sharpened. Transparency is the norm today, and releasing the right amount of information with minimal aberrations is something that most PR practitioners are grappling with.

With social media, segment-wise conversation has become a possibility. Today, PR practitioners are expected to cover a story as it evolves and create genuine dialogues around it in real time. The evolution in the last fifteen years has been humongous. If we chronicle it, 'blog' was named word of the year by Webster in 2004. The year 2005 saw the birth of social media with Facebook, YouTube and LinkedIn. The years 2006, 2007 and 2008 were when social media press releases with tags and links debuted and search engine optimisation (SEO) became critical. PR-led digital communications with two-way channels began dominating the limelight in 2009. Following 2010-2011, mobile phones began to offer a variety of services ranging from news, maps, videos, entertainment and much more. The year 2012 was when content took centre stage and by 2013, visual content had become king. With wearable technology making an entry in 2014, people's consumption of information via personalised, engaging formats increased. Following 2015, influencers began emerging in a significant way. These were thought leaders or celebrities who had made a mark in their professions and gained a lot of followers on social networks due to their expertise. Furthermore, in 2016, progressive organisations started setting up digital PR verticals that focused on building networks of influencers to produce stories and spawn engagement in an organic manner as opposed to paying them directly to do so (a prevailing trend at that time). During 2017-2018, we saw incredible growth in the number of influencers in almost every field. Anyone with a significant following on social networks began positioning themselves as an influencer. During 2019–2021, we saw a rise in demand for authentic narratives, regulations in influencer engagement and the calling out of opportunistic content. Today, we are also discussing AI's role in PR, which is quickly becoming a reality. The question is, how many PR consultancies and in-house departments have really adapted to these changes? The ones that have had the ability to do so have remained relevant.

As part of the growing PR ecosystem in the past decade, four things have stood out:

❖ Multiple PR start-ups have been founded.
❖ Several universities have begun offering programmes in PR at undergraduate and post-graduate levels.
❖ Many events and platforms have emerged for the PR fraternity which makes it easier for professionals to come together, share news and celebrate victories.
❖ Marketing-centric media outlets focusing on news from the world of PR have blossomed.

Over time, many companies have realised that the sector of public relations comes under management, with the CEO in the driver's seat of the organisation's PR programme. Many founders of current start-ups have got this right and are

driving most of the stakeholder engagement themselves—
the customers, employees, government bodies, investors,
media persons and any special interest groups relevant to
the organisation.

As observed in many other professions, there are always
grey areas where a few practitioners resort to unethical
shortcuts to make a quick buck. However, the core of PR
in our view is not just being ethical and doing the right
thing, but doing everything right.

The field of PR is expected to witness many more changes
in the future. Firstly, the evolution in the sophistication of
the ecosystem is there for all to see. We are seeing a rapid
rise in individuals who are modern in their thinking and
analytical in their questioning. The ways of the past do not
hold good in the present.

There is, of course, a lot of chatter about how AI will
play a big role in the way brands will communicate with
stakeholders. We are of the opinion that this will affect
all functions of business. However, as long as customers,
governments and other stakeholders remain human, PR
professionals will continue to have a significant role to play.

Over the course of this book, we intend to share our
thoughts on the nuances of contemporary PR approaches
that can help businesses create a niche for themselves,
engage with their stakeholders, build reputations and be in
the public eye. Our objective is to share with the readers
all that we have collectively learnt, experimented with,
pioneered, and worked on while managing PR for some of
the biggest brands in India.

We hope you enjoy reading the book as much as we
enjoyed writing it for you.

∼

The evolution of public relations

May I please begin with a confession? I had always thought of myself as a diehard advertising professional. Even when I started focusing primarily on PR in 1987, I was usually embarrassed to admit that I was a PR practitioner. Unless I was visiting the US, I'd prefer describing myself as an advertising and PR professional. And if my audience looked confused, I'd clarify that I am into marketing communications. More than often, that confused them even more, but nine times out of ten, the subject would change. That's because of the negative perception PR professionals had at the time. Influence peddlers! Wheeler-dealers! Fixers!

I happened to have the opportunity of working for two very different prime ministers from two very different countries and cultures. For one of those assignments, the specific brief was to use PR. And for the other, advertising. But neither of these experiences changed my personal view of PR. Of course, I must admit that not once did I doubt, even for a second, the power of PR. Whenever my conviction was challenged, I'd always quote three strong examples of good PR through advertising: 'In India's Life and Part of it' by Burmah-Shell in the 1950s, 'We Also Make Steel' for Tata Steel by the J. Walter Thompson Company (JWT) in the 1980s and my own case study for the Cement Manufacturing Association in 1986.

When I started my own PR consultancy in April 1987, there was no pool of talent in existence. So, I decided to follow the same route as one I had used very successfully at Shilpi since 1965: to mould budding professionals via internships. However, I faced my first and biggest challenge head-on: the ones who applied assumed that they were applying to an ad agency! Nevertheless, the conversion was almost 100 per cent. PR might have taken off slowly, but in the last fifteen years, its growth has rocketed. I believe it owes this growth to advent of social media.

For my top three tips to communication leaders in the country today, I'd like to echo the advice of my hero and role model, Dr Verghese Kurien:

* Integrity
* Integrity
* Integrity

This was when Rajdeep Sardesai had interviewed and honoured him just a couple of years before his demise. Let me explain: the moral responsibility for communicating the truth (and only the truth) lies far more heavily on the shoulders of PR practitioners than it does on advertising professionals. Don't you agree? It was for this very reason that I hosted a meeting with the CEOs of three other PR firms in 1987. I was bubbling with enthusiasm and fresh from initiating, through the Advertising Club of Bombay, a series of workshops on media planning, language copywriting and self-regulation in advertising—workshops aimed at truly professionalising the business. My plea to my fellow PR practitioners was, 'Let's adapt a model of integrity for a budding profession! Please?' Regrettably, no luck. And the result is for all of us to see: 'FAKE NEWS! TROLLS!' My humble appeal to present-day practitioners remains the same. Let's turn the tide and change course. Today!

Roger Pereira is a public relations pioneer

~

Be agile and creative to disrupt and grow

The communications sector has seen a 360° transformation in the past few decades. Earlier, it had no profession and limited media outlets. There was a handful of national dailies, a few regional ones, some magazines and some business papers. There were no 24/7 news channels, though cable TV had arrived and offered a choice apart from Doordarshan.

Today, media surrounds us constantly and everyone has access to it.

When the economy opened up in the early 1990s, India saw an influx of businesses from all parts of the world. They brought with them the understanding and expectation of public relations, which laid the foundation of the profession. Over the years, it has expanded to cover every stakeholder for an organisation. Digital, creative content, public affairs, crisis, data analytics—all this and more find a place in the mandate, which is why we now use the integrated term 'communications'.

Our profession might have begun at the periphery of a company's consideration, but in the last several years, we have found ourselves playing a more central role.

So, what has remained unchanged? One of the biggest lessons I learnt in my journey as a communicator is that it is one thing to convey a message and another to make someone experience it. Back in those days, immersing the target audience in an experience had much more impact than telling them about it. This remains unchanged today, with the ability to elevate experiences to even more captivating levels.

The second aspect that has remained unchanged is authenticity. You are the message, and so are your actions. People can always see through any sugar-coating. On the other hand, if you are authentic in your communication, you build a loyal audience base that will stand by you even when you are down. This was true then, but it is absolutely gospel today. If you combine authenticity with your organisation's purpose, it crafts a strong connection with your stakeholders.

The third and perhaps the most critical lesson I learnt was that you have to be creative and agile. After India opened up to the world of communications, the profession evolved at a dizzying pace, which is something that continues today. The changes in the last two years alone have been groundbreaking. Only those who have been agile are the ones that have landed on their feet. And only those who are creative will be able to disrupt and grow.

Prema Sagar is Chairperson, BCW India Group, at Genesis BCW and Six Degrees BCW

~

Straight from the heart

With all of you out there reading this book, waiting to earn your spurs, I honestly feel that you guys are a lot savvier and, in a good way, a tad too clever. No naïfs, by and large, unlike so many of us who evolved during an era of uncertainty, flakiness and volatility in the world of public relations. But despite these tremors, by sheer dint of back-breaking, intelligent effort laced with authenticity, and a 100 per cent commitment, passion, humility and true posturing, we, the silver-haired generation, reached the flagpole.

Amith and Sujit, the authors, had an earnest request: write a piece that will endure the passage of time and any generational chasms. So, instead of penning down experiences, I thought of sharing what I had gleaned during my fascinating four-decade-long rollercoaster ride, which has been exciting, challenging and, at times, scary. And all through, reputation has been, and will remain, the defining difference.

One thing is for sure: tectonic technological shifts have drastically shortened the communication cycle. Earlier, you had at least till the end of the day to revert, but nowadays, you barely have a few minutes. This is here to stay. You have to be on your toes 24/7. Access to information has shifted phenomenally, from there being a scarcity of it to a surfeit at a click.

Media dynamics have also changed beyond belief; users on social media are often distrustful and quick to point at fault. The credibility crunch keeps widening if the story is emotive. The resulting myopia can often be personally disruptive, and worse is yet to come. This has been the heart of a grave issue. Reputational damage is the biggest dampener. The best I've managed is to not dignify disparagers with a response—the media is rife with lurid stories that are best ignored. A point to consider—good online myth-busting forums can serve a useful purpose. The shift in media ownership from media moguls to business tycoons has created a knock-on effect.

But on all counts, keep your word. One must always

be impeccable with one's word. If you can't give it, don't, or else you'll have to recoil, wounded.

And finally, make sure your boss has your back. Of course, you have to earn it. I have been most blessed and privileged to have had two exemplary bosses to whom I can hold a candle—Mr Kumar Mangalam Birla and Mrs Rajashreeji Birla.

In life, all of us dream big and want to be happy. After a point, transcend to making a difference for the underprivileged. Make them happy. It is very soul-lifting. You would have served your purpose in life.

So long! Enjoy the journey. For if you do not enjoy the journey, you can never reach the destination. Chillax!

Dr Pragnya Ram is the Group Executive President, CSR, Legacy Documentation and Archives, Aditya Birla Group

~

Prove your statements through actions

Over the past two decades, public relations firms have evolved considerably in response to the changing business environment impacted by a whole range of societal, technology and policy disruptions. The key areas of progress are presented below:

Media relations have evolved into reputation consulting: While media relations still remain a significant preoccupation of PR firms, these entities have evolved into 'reputation consultants' to address a whole range of risks related to status and standing. This evolution has propelled a better understanding of business, the forces of change, their impact on business, reputational risks and consequent solutions.

Solution-thinking now integrates digital tools: In the last five years in particular, the arc of influence has widened to include virtual spaces. As a result, traditional media approaches and tools no longer suffice. Most firms have shifted in this direction. There is now more creativity and innovation in designing integrated solutions.

Defining the problem precedes the solution: These days, there is more conversation with clients and more research undertaken to define the problem before a solution is offered. Social and digital analytical tools now empower practitioners to gain a good sense of the problem at hand, leading to more precise and adequate resolutions.

Services are keeping pace with the times: The services portfolio of PR firms is evolving with changing times. A whole range of digital competencies are being built—from monitoring to analytics, from ORM to crisis support, from creative to performance marketing. Newer competencies such as environmental, social and governance (ESG) communications or risk advisory will soon become commonplace. Similarly, new sectoral practices are being developed in response to emerging opportunities—frontier technologies, mobility, new energy, etc.

New disciplines in PR solutions: Hiring programmes of PR consultancies now look for expertise from a variety of disciplines—risk management, financial policy, sectoral competence, research, ESG, etc. Solutions backed by a wide range of expertise are the need of the hour.

My recommendations to leaders in current times are:

❖ Always remember that public perception of an enterprise is determined 90 per cent by what it does and 10 per cent by what it says. So, prove your statements through actions.

❖ Scrutinise every decision through the lens of public interest. All corporate actions have an impact on some stakeholder or the other. Thus, when managing reputation risks, simulating impact and taking decisions after accounting for the impact on stakeholder interest should become a standard practice. Also, do consider upgrading the Chief Customer Officer (CCO) position to a Chief Experience Officer (CXO) level with a seat at the main table and making them a part of all critical corporate decisions.

❖ Provide adequate resources. Everyone is unanimous that in a volatile world, all other things being equal, risk to reputation is the mother of all risks, and that reputation creates a definite competitive advantage. The question is, are you providing adequate resources to do justice to the task? Managing reputation in a complex, diverse society such as India requires considerable experience, expertise and enterprise.

Madan Bahal is the Managing Director of Adfactors PR

Reputation is what defines how companies are shaped over time

PR is at the heart of how organisations transact with their customers and connect with their stakeholders. In today's age of intense public scrutiny, reputation is at the core of a corporate image. Public perception drives regulatory action and investor confidence towards a sector or a company. Companies are pilloried or cheered based on how responsible and honest they appear compared to peers, a factor that influences business landscapes, employee attractiveness and social and community acceptability. None of these are fungible and together remain the sum and substance of a wholesome corporate reputation, which is also the best insurance one can have during crises.

Having said that, what must be understood is that reputation no longer remains a 'net-positive' concept. Today, the top-line perceptions about tobacco giants, mining majors or big tech companies are largely negative. Yet, they are the richest and most profitable companies and exert the most influence in their sectors. The dichotomy between their public image and their profits is evident and jumps the guardrails of the traditional parameters of a corporate reputation. Comebacks or countervailing actions are not uncommon among such companies as public opinion and regulatory actions grow harsher, impacting stock prices or even pushing the emergence of newer business models—for example, big tobacco diversifying into agri products or big tech firms pivoting to future technologies.

Clearly, reputation is what defines how companies operate and are shaped over time.

Three things that a CEO should bear in mind when it comes to reputation:

❖ Firstly, shareholder value. Reputation is built by how stakeholders view their association with your company. The CEO is often the custodian of shareholder value, which goes beyond just the earnings and listing prices on the exchange.

❖ Secondly, the employees. Employee satisfaction is vital. Loyalty and happiness are important factors in avoiding internal strife and public displays of dirty linen. Good human resources (HR) practices lead to a desirable employee reputation which, in turn, adds to the corporate's image in the public space.

❖ Thirdly, to be seen in the right light by policymakers and regulators, community and social responsibility is indispensable. It means being compliant with the laws of the land as well as being viewed as an organisation that adds value to a country's economy and the social agenda. Being on the wrong side of such issues often invites punitive regulations and policies that can become stumbling blocks to progress.

Dilip Cherian is the Co-founder of Perfect Relations

~

The global impact of reputation

It's heartening to note that almost every single brand we partner with nowadays is invested in thinking big about trust, reputation and how to present itself in the world. It wasn't always this way. What's changed?

The research we've done shows that expectations from consumers and decision-makers to create stability in a world rocked by climate change, social tensions and more are higher than ever. People want brands to make real investments in social causes and work towards social stability. At the same time, there's a delicate balance to maintain. Consumers are more sceptical of purpose-washing and see right through brands making empty statements not backed up by genuine change.

It's a challenging environment for brands to navigate and it's not a time for the faint of heart. The brands that will thrive moving forward will do so by being firmly grounded in their purpose and by truly listening to their stakeholders in order to deliver bold, brave action.

A few things missing in CEOs globally when it comes to reputation management:

❖ I suppose I could start by saying we need more women! Just like expectations have shifted for brands, the sweeping changes of the last two years have transformed expectations for leaders in fundamental ways as well. As a CEO myself, it's a shift I've felt the need for personally and I know that the CEOs I work with feel the same. This profession will strongly benefit from having more women.

❖ It's no longer enough for CEOs to put on a tough face and stay neutral in times of crisis. They're expected to take bold, public stands on big issues like sustainability and social justice, and that means they need to introspect on how to engineer an alignment between their personal beliefs and brand values.

❖ Our research shows there's also a broader circle of influence impacting leadership thinking on topics, including everything from sustainability and income inequality to race and the struggle for human rights. Navigating such influences requires CEOs who are deeply engaged with a diverse group of stakeholders and prioritise under-represented groups, such as women and people of colour. And it's not enough to simply listen to employee concerns—leaders must internalise what they hear so they can anticipate how their actions will impact different stakeholders.

Lastly, CEOs can rise to today's challenges concerning reputation by proactively leveraging their unique power and influence to foster positive change. By connecting and empowering diverse groups—employees, consumers, community members—they can facilitate the creation of the ideas and insights needed to create a better, more just world.

*Melissa Waggner Zorkin is the CEO and
Founder of WE Communications*

2

NOT MARKETING'S STEPCHILD

We were listening keenly to a senior professional who was telling us about his experiences and how he has seen the trade evolve. Years ago, he had joined a leading organisation as its communications head. Just a few weeks into the role, his excitement at joining a glorious organisation started waning rapidly. He mused that the board, while hiring him, had expressed an urgent need for the corporate communications function to play a larger role in enhancing brand perception, engagement with stakeholders and, of course, improving press coverage. He was all set to be the action man, the go-to person and in the thick of things. However, on the first day, on the way to his cabin assisted by the HR manager, he realised that his space was tucked away in a remote corner, quite far from the place where the real action happened. He mentioned with some acridity that this should have given him an indication of things to come. The placement of his workspace itself was a sign of the company's attitude towards PR.

What followed was a serious dose of how the leadership

of that organisation was besotted with only 'positive' headlines, killing 'negative' stories and getting pictures on the front page of *The Economic Times*. They were even clear about the position of the picture! All this without any rationale or planned campaigns. 'Every leader was, in a way, a PR expert when it came to giving guidance,' he said with a caustic smile.

We have heard over the years from many that PR has been treated as the need-based stepchild of marketing as well as the poor, neglected cousin of advertising. The story we were told kind of underlined the treatment that has usually been meted out to PR teams.

You must be wondering whom we are talking about. We are not revealing the name for obvious reasons, but this may resonate with many in the field of corporate communications.

It is important to realise that much has changed now. The pace of development in the past decade has been significant. In a fast-evolving business environment with multiple external stimuli impacting business performance and new, disruptive modes of communications and platforms for data consumption by stakeholders, the operative scope of a PR professional has amplified favourably. Today, evolved corporate communications functions significantly impact multiple levers—reputation, employee retention, crisis mitigation, sales leads, product brands, stock price, stakeholder engagement—and does so effectively.

Then why do several corporate communications professionals seem so apologetic? It cannot be that the profession has not done enough PR for PR the way they have for their organisations.

Why does it so happen even now that in an integrated

campaign, even after a very successful roll-out of a PR programme with brilliant outcomes, the work is overlooked in favour of advertising?

We believe there are valid reasons for this and we think it all boils down to something that we have not done enough of: educating internal stakeholders on the impact of PR.

Familiarity of 'advertising'

Advertising is a concept that is straightforward and commonly understood; any lay person knows that a magazine or TV advertisement is a marketing effort that has been paid for. How many can say the same about PR unless they really understand it? Third-party endorsements are more authentic. However, most will not know what effort has gone into making it happen organically.

Limited attention spans of most leaders

Seriously, let us face it! Leadership wants results and FAST. If an IT company brings out a funny advertisement with actors like Shah Rukh Khan or Salman Khan insisting that the product will change your life, many are going to listen and buy instantly. On the other hand, a PR campaign for the same product will aim to build the brand, establish trends and instill confidence in the customers. The work is slow and steady. Results eventually arrive, but does the CEO have the time to notice?

Seeing is believing!

When people see an advertisement, if it really touches a chord, they tweet about it, post on their social media handles, share it or discuss it at length in social circles. PR outcomes are a slow magic. No press release ever gets discussed by the masses. However, the outcomes in media are more sustainable, take time to build and can be more than just a buzz. Advertising, apparently being 'buzzworthy', gets talked about frequently amongst organisational leaders, but PR is where they run to when a crisis happens.

We feel earned media has an edge over paid media, if adopted and manifested well. However, ambiguity exists in terms of establishing uniform, universally accepted metrics which translate into the larger question of how public relations can demonstrate its value towards the organisation's growth. Hence, it is a pity that most of the time, return of investment (ROI) on millions of dollars spent on advertising is never questioned the way ROI on a fraction of that amount spent on PR is.

Perhaps the importance of a good communications department or a PR campaign is best understood by simply imagining what things would be like in their absence. We believe that large organisations are microcosms of a complex world full of diversity. With various stakeholders across several businesses and geographies within and outside the organisation, enabled by a global information landscape, the PR measurement conundrum can be complicated. Trying to quantify it could be even more so. Can one quantify the cost of reputation saved due to effective PR? Can we assign a monetary value to it or to the frequent crises a PR team mitigates silently, and claim it as the ROI? Well, we have a full chapter on PR measurement. More on this subject there.

Bernays firmly believed that public relations has to be considered a science, that businesses can be boosted by affecting changes in public opinion. He treated his campaigns differently; he never pushed a product by way of typical advertising, but would create demand by changing the opinions of the public, which would boost the sales of the products.

PR is a gradual process that can impact public opinion with the objective of motivating people to take certain actions, such as buying a particular soap or computer brand, preferring a political party or fulfilling any brand objective. We also firmly believe that it is an applied social science that combines sociology, anthropology, psychology, economics and many other areas of study.

Mastering the art of writing POEMS (Paid, Owned, Earned Media Strategies)

Over a period, much has changed.

Traditional media relations can no longer be solely depended upon to make a campaign successful. The past few years have seen a significant dilution in traditional newsrooms and a shift towards new media. Going forward, PR professionals will find themselves increasingly doing work that transcends the traditionally rigid boundaries of paid, owned or earned media. It is a no-brainer that effective storytelling happens at the intersection of such platforms. Using POEMS also indicates that the organisation is placing greater emphasis on the consumer rather than disconnected individual modes which may not be effective on their own. As we reflect on the tactics adopted for various campaigns that we have been studying, we find that the most successful ones had well-integrated elements of POEMS in them.

PR and T-20

To set the context of present-day PR, let's draw parallels with our nation's favourite cricket format: T20! A format that was developed on the basis of a lot of thinking and social savvy. The razzle-dazzle ranging from cheerleaders, DJs and entertainment to the deliberately quirky team names, creative jingles and war cries probably make the audiences forget that they have come to watch a gentleman's game.

Our guess is that it works for the dwindling attention spans of the spectators—same as our public!

This shorter format of cricket is based on attributes such as agility, ownership of the game right from the beginning, real-time analysis of the evolving situation, competition analysis, use of technology and the ability to deliver results under multiple constraints.

Do you see the multiple parallels to the world of public relations?

Short-form content engages more

At the moment, our attention spans are pretty bad. Most of us do not have the patience to bear long-form content and they would probably not bother reading comprehensive articles and reports. The content strategy has to change. Bite-sized, snackable content should be the focus. Repurposing content into different formats, distributing it across multiple channels and using tactics to target audience segments that are appropriate for the brand is key. Welcome to the T20 of PR professionals.

The application of AI in PR is on a rise—data will define success

T20 in cricket is a format where team managers use data to make decisions and formulate strategies based on trends. For instance, in one of the matches, past data suggested that South Africa struggled to face spin, so West Indies used an extra spinner. Data captured over the past ten matches enabled a team to discover the type of balls that make life hell for a particular batsman. Statistics showed that in T20 cricket, teams batting second won more matches. That is the power of data.

The base of artificial intelligence (AI) is also data—colossal amounts of data mining, cognification of data and tracing patterns to predict the next steps. If the data is correct, the chances of decisions going wrong are minimal. So, at a very basic level, with AI around, PR professionals would be able to avoid guesswork and decide on the basis of statistics when to launch a campaign, in which region to pilot it, who to engage with and the best influencers to work with.

Imagine if, during a crisis, your AI-based crisis communication system mines data globally. And then the algorithms, using language processing ability, establish the region- and audience-wise sentiment of the narrative. It would be easier for crisis managers to respond during a tough situation. Let us stretch the imagination further. Today, a lot of digital content, be it social media posts, videos or podcasts, goes unmined. Wouldn't it be beneficial if an AI-based system could process this data and give out indicators of brand health?

AI can enable bespoke messaging with micro-targeting, and that too in innovative ways using virtual reality (VR) and augmented reality (AR) along with the usual channels. It could probably redefine how media conferences or briefings are carried out and for global organisations, AI could help in better localisation of content.

In PR T20, professionals will embrace AI to enhance effectiveness.

Authentic influencers enhance reach for brands

Supporters and fans of T20 cricket play a significant role. Not only in encouraging audiences during a match but also in terms of creating a buzz about the team and merchandising and in building positive narratives. For PR T20, influencers have become important contributors to the brand narrative. However, in PR, authenticity matters the most. We are witnessing a trend where audiences want messages from people they can relate to and trust, not from paid celebrities. This has given prominence to micro-influencers and this trend is expected to grow.

Owning the narrative is essential to building thought leadership

T20 is a format that is encouraging for big hitters! Data has shown that the team that owns the game right from the beginning, either by scoring big or getting the maximum wickets in the first ten overs, calls the shots for rest of the match and is most likely to win.

Likewise, big, authentic narratives owned by brands right from the beginning can propel them into the thought leadership space. However, with the deluge of social media influencers, digital news platforms and fake news, your control over your own brand narrative is limited. An effective way to own, set and control it would be to invest in and develop your own media properties in both online and offline spaces and sustain engagement with customers and influencers.

Social listening has become fundamental

The T20 format of cricket is very dynamic. Every over can create a new situation. Captains need to be agile in decision-making during a fast-changing scenario. The same holds true for a PR professional. We are all witnessing polarising times and have realised that fake news is undeniably prevalent and will persist. PR teams have to take the lead role in combating inappropriate narratives by constantly listening to rants on social platforms and fine-tuning their crisis management tactics accordingly. T20 for PR requires that PR professionals become good listeners.

Celebrations and 'PR for PR' has intensified

T20 cricket is all about celebration and fun after a well-deserved victory, combined with a lot of planning, hard work, agility and implementation. Well, it is the same story for PR folks. In a volatile, uncertain, complex and ambiguous (VUCA) world with multiple external stimuli impacting business performance, and with many disruptive modes of communications and platforms for data consumption by the stakeholders, the operative scope of PR professionals has amplified favourably. Today, they significantly impact multiple levers—corporate reputation, employee retention, crisis mitigation, sales, product brands, stock price, stakeholder engagement and many more. We do see a trend of increased impetus by various trade associations to help PR win the due it deserves.

Pandemics and PR

As businesses, we do not get to choose market conditions and competition or when global crises occur! It took a pandemic to remind us of all that we need to focus on and what really matters to us the most across personal and professional levels.

The dependence of brands on PR to stay connected with their stakeholders has gone up significantly. Challenges have been enormous but organisations that demonstrated agility and boldness in their decisions while effectively communicating with stakeholders have done better than others. We see distinct trends emerging and have tried to articulate some of our observations around staying connected with consumers during challenges like a pandemic, potential solutions and, most importantly, how public relations can enable them.

Communicate with PAUSE (Purpose, Authenticity, Ubiquity, Sensitivity and Empathy)

Purpose, empathy and authenticity are in. Today, regardless of how great a story you tell, if you do not tell it with authenticity, you are never going to build a relationship with your audience. Often, something which is purpose-driven could also be construed as opportunistic behaviour by your target group. A case in point was the distribution of free sanitisers by a respected brand, a move that was called out by certain people as being opportunistic during the pandemic. Tonality matters now more than ever.

The twilight of 'spray and pray' strategy of branded content

Whether for storytelling, crisis mitigation or influencer engagement, without data, you are just going to spray and pray. Also, owing to people's overexposure to fake news and branded content, there is a cognitive ad-blocker that switches on every time a consumer today sees content that looks like a tall advertising claim. Therefore, stories you share with audiences must be factual, data-driven and more inclusive. One way to do this is to use research-based narratives to tell your stories. The truth is that in times of shrinking editorial spaces and rising fake news, media leans towards data-driven stories.

Era of hyperlocal content and micro-influencers

People have always been keen about national and international events. The pandemic, however, made us also focus our attention on hyperlocal news. What is happening closer to home or office? Is there a night curfew or lockdown? Are cases increasing? There has also been a rise in the number of effective micro-influencers who are subject matter experts (not necessarily with a huge following) and wield significant influence. It is a no-brainer that organisations are aiming to enhance their outreach in regional media and in regional languages with a focus on micro-markets with micro-influencers and publications.

Spotlight on direct communication channels

The pandemic directed attention towards direct and owned communication channels. Customer experience and brand ethos is the core of an owned media platform strategy which brings brands, influencers and consumers together to co-create content and engage wider audiences. 'Being heard' is one of the most valued aspects that audiences seek today from brands. We believe one should make audiences the protagonist and not limit engagement to transactional purposes. The audience must feel part of the story.

Time to engage

During uncertain times, emotions run high and brands often get caught up in the thick of things. Corporate and brand behaviour is being watched more closely. An employee's view on social media about the organisation and other issues is as important as what the CEO says. Constant monitoring and appropriate engagement through responses is valuable. If your engagement with your audience is poor, you are bound to be highly vulnerable to getting hurt on the reputation front.

Rise of PR in overall communications mix

With corporate scrutiny at its peak and the increased risk of being involved in a crossfire of media, political parties and trolls, dependency on public relations and reputation management has risen. While governments worked hard to control the pandemic, we feel that the effectiveness would be higher if government machinery had had more psychologists, social scientists and, most importantly, 'communicators', on board. It would have certainly helped in avoiding a lot of chaos and confusion caused by miscommunication and mixed narratives! We see a lot more that PR can own going forward.

We think that PR as a profession has come of age—the pandemic established that the one thing which kept people together was good communication.

A focus on building competencies around the theme above and enhancing the prowess that already exists in our communications arsenal can help us set a positive tone for how we build brands and manage reputations.

~

You scratch my back, I scald yours

There is an incident from the 2022 edition of the Super Bowl LVI. While it was an ad agency on the losing side in this particular case, it offers invaluable lessons on how business leaders could view their strategic communication partnerships differently.

It was Coinbase CEO and founder Brian Armstrong who pressed the trigger on this one. Like most companies spending top dollar on advertising during the Super Bowl, Coinbase, a cryptocurrency company, had also put its best foot forward. However, while gloating over the success of its rather frugal commercial, Armstrong decided to stir up a hornet's nest. He tweeted a thread on the making of the commercial that featured a floating QR code. His words 'no ad agency would have done this ad' hit the agency world where it badly hurts.

However, Armstrong's Twitter thread was based on half-baked evidence. The first person who took on Armstrong was the CEO of The Martin Agency, Kristen Cavallo. Her contention was that the Coinbase ad was based on an idea that had first been presented by her agency.

Coinbase's marketing head rushed to defend Armstrong. The rather lame defence was that the agency and the client had made such a well-coordinated presentation to Armstrong that he had assumed they were also employees of Coinbase.

In the corporate world, intermediaries appear to be largely falling out of favour as digital platforms connect you directly to consumers. From financial services to traditional businesses, firms are pushing for the development of communications through their internal teams based on the belief that they will have a better handle on quality. And CEOs like Armstrong are muscling these agencies over.

If you replace the ad agency with a PR partner, it's very likely that a similar scenario may play out.

Fighting the bush fire

One of the first mistakes that business leaders make is believing that your first-hand engagement with the communications team and PR partners happens only when that piece of unmentionable hits the fan.

Many business leaders are guilty of relegating PR and comms teams to a firefighting function, or viewing them as spin doctors.

The more prudent approach would be to develop a cohesive, long-term policy with a systematic investment strategy that pays rich dividends over time.

Fewer Armstrongs…

Do leaders really believe that better ideas cannot come from external partners? Or do they reshape the external idea so much that it loses all semblance of original thinking? Are such leaders so convinced that their own talent is good enough to deliver the goods and that they can safely bypass the agency in the future?

The magic lies in striking the right notes for the orchestra to play in sync. Common sense, isn't it? Unfortunately, it's one commodity that's often in short supply.

And more Cavallos!

The world of communication and PR badly needs strong leadership that does not kowtow to client expectations in a manner that discourages their employees from bringing original ideas to the table.

Just as business leaders do not need consultancies that will only nod in agreement, consultancies also need to set the right expectations from the beginning.

This is the only way to halt one's march into irrelevance. We don't need a Super Bowl to tell us that.

Prasad Sangameshwaran is Editor, BrandEquity.com
at The Economic Times

Organisational reputation through a journalist's lens

Reputation is a matter of perception and may not always be an objective indicator of what an organisation is doing on the ground. Yet, as the collective view of a significant number of stakeholders about an organisation and its past performance, it can be considered a somewhat fair assessment of where an organisation stands. Organisational reputation entails its future as well—where it is headed and where it is likely to reach. That's how some organisations have the reputation of being conservative and risk-averse, or dynamic, progressive and fit for the future.

Media is a key stakeholder for businesses. Its role in building public perception about an organisation is huge, simply because it is often considered to be a credible source of information. An organisation's standing is the magnet that attracts media persons to engage with or write about it. For instance, if an organisation has a great reputation in a particular area, journalists are likely to seek its opinions on the future performance of the sector or government measures that could enable growth. If an organisation is known for innovative policies, then stories on talent or the workplace may feature the company. And if, on the other hand, any organisation has a poor reputation, be it around compliance or any other aspect, the media may aggravate the situation.

Having said that, in my opinion, journalists do appreciate the fact that reputations are not cast in stone. They usually try to stay objective in their assessment and reporting. So, it is an opportunity for brands to keep enhancing their reputation, but it also means that organisations need to be agile in order to protect their most important intangible asset. As Benjamin Franklin said, 'It takes many good deeds to build a good reputation, and only one bad one to lose it.'

The role of reputation, when a publication is following a brand or business for a story angle, is an important one. While the rationale may differ depending on the story angle, for most positive day-to-day stories, journalists prefer going to well-reputed sources since that lends credibility to their story. It is also about association and recall. For instance, if it is a story about the environment, organisations that are known for their sustainability initiatives are likely to be approached by a journalist as against those that are infamous for wasteful practices. Similarly, in the case of a story about workplaces that support new mothers, a journalist is likely to approach an organisation that is walking the talk on this front as against those that are still thinking of doing something around it.

Advice for a CEO while engaging with editors

Building relationships is valuable in any business. It is the single most important aspect for any sustainable engagement.

It is about mutual understanding. To build meaningful relationships with editors in particular, one has to:

- ❖ **Be authentic:** Authenticity, truth and ethical conduct are the cornerstones of any long-lasting relationship and the foundations of trust and respect.

- ❖ **Be grounded:** Most editors are senior, seasoned, well-informed and humble people who are good listeners and have risen through the ranks. Misjudging them and positioning oneself as someone who knows it all is best avoided. Every engagement with media persons is a golden opportunity to build a positive perception about the organisation and oneself.

- ❖ **Have a point of view:** Having an informed point of view and being able to articulate it succinctly is crucial for any leader. Adding value through one's experience of dealing with a range of client issues or knowledge of various industries is always appreciated. Generic information is of no particular use to media persons.

- ❖ **Walk the talk:** No matter how well one engages in a meeting, ultimately, what is done on ground is what matters. Walking the talk is what drives reputation over time. So, it is extremely important to follow through on words with the right actions—being a responsible business, building trust and demonstrating sustained outcomes. Once this becomes second nature, a positive reputation follows.

Nandini Chatterjee is Chief Communications Officer at PwC India

Rinse and repeat no more

We do not know who needs to hear this, but PR is so much more than press stories and pitches. The writing is already on the wall, but many in the fraternity badly need to change their glasses to be able to read it!

The world of PR has grown to encompass compelling narratives, content, thought seeding, amplification and image building. Yet, we reduce it to 'tangible deliverables' because we are conditioned to see it with our lens—which, over time, have become myopic.

What PR can do for you

PR is still about messaging and storytelling. What has changed is the audience profile, mindset, attention span and consumption patterns. Even a great story passed down generations needs to be revamped to better fit the audience of today.

How PR can do it for you

Use a mix of traditional and contemporary techniques. What was applicable then may not be applicable now. Strategy is effort—and it cannot to be taken for granted! The media world is innovating and reinventing itself faster than we can fathom and consumption patterns change quickly, with audiences spoilt for choice. In a world metamorphosising at breakneck speed, strategy which disseminates information and creates iconic stories takes centre stage.

Trends that we see shaping the next five years

❖ **Value over volume:** Quality over quantity, any day! Bid adieu to quantifying monetary value for press articles—

it'll hopefully become a thing of the past. Even 'paid media' is talking about 'programmatic' and 'outcome-based advertising' and the time is ripe for the PR and communications business to start being accountable for business outcomes, not for coverage volume.

❖ **Textual to audio-visual:** Press releases have to change. Think GIFs, Spotify playlists, ready-to-use graphics and more. 'Optimisation' is the buzzword—not just for dissemination plans but for the content's format itself. Exciting times ahead!

❖ **Emphasis on owned media:** A new focus on creating infographics, podcasts and social media content for clients and partners to build valuable brand narratives. The world is embracing Web 3.0 and 'ownership' will be key.

❖ **From integrated marketing communications (IMC) to integrated communications (IC):** As a PR professional, you need to be an ace at comprehending, pitching, writing, drawing up a social media strategy, driving influencer relationships, understanding content, speaking programmes, driving word of mouth and attracting the right talent (for yourself and clients alike). It's all this and more that leads to creating a halo. So, drop the 'marketing'—it's time to talk integrated communications.

❖ **Using software to ace the game:** Embrace tech and enhance quality. From writing to reaching out, dependence on automation will go up manifold. Soon, one might hear of a Chief Technology Officer (CTO) at a PR firm!

❖ **Content creators:** From direct-to-consumer (D2C) brands to traditional companies, the creator economy has got a big fillip thanks to cheap internet, pent-up creativity amongst Indians and increased digital payment adoption. PR teams will increasingly be curating and reimagining their 'media lists' to work alongside this economy to fuel brand love.

Komal Lath is the Founder of Tute Consult

~

On tone, tenor, timing and earning the right to be heard

In Hans Christian Anderson's folktale *The Emperor's New Clothes*, we learn the lesson that sometimes, the public can be misled. It does not matter whether the emperor is wearing clothes or not, so long as the official narrative states so. But with the digital transformation we have experienced in recent years, there are many voices like that of the child in the story willing to call a bluff and declare that the emperor is, in fact, not wearing anything.

How does this affect our engagement as communications professionals with the brands we work with and the consumers we reach out to? In a fast-paced world that is both big and small, where good can become very good through social media amplification and differences seem to be starker than they might actually be, the tone and tenor of engagement becomes the focus.

My attempt here is to examine this very issue. How we engage on different levels is very different from before. The game has evolved and is not what it was. Therefore, it stands to reason that the rules that underpin it have also changed.

I have mentioned earlier that we as PR professionals have a responsibility that needs to be acknowledged: the responsibility to create communities and foster constructive debate.

This obligation has both ethical and strong business implications. Our clients don't just operate in the communities they serve, they are invariably part of a larger community. Thus, communications professionals need to build empathy and scope for debate into messaging and campaigns.

Our consumers have changed their habits and values; they seem to want to experiment and engage more with different brands due to value consciousness, which has prompted the rise of videos and business messaging even in non-traditional online avenues like alternative e-commerce. Consumers are seeking integrated experiences that merge and allow one to vacillate between the online and the offline.

Most marketers and planners will agree that we cannot operate using the same formulae we have used in the years past. How do we ensure that the stories we tell for our clients resonate in such an unpredictable space? How should brands create narratives and then stay the course when it comes to their larger vision and persona? How should the trust of consumers be garnered and what issues and values should be espoused?

The solution, sadly, is not a one-size-fits-all remedy. However, there are a few rules that can be thought of as comprising the etiquette of engagement which can help foster constructive discourse.

Three Cs need to be kept in mind: conversation, culture and credibility. The first one connotes inducing within your clients a healthy appetite for conversation. 'No comment' statements and other forms of reticence can no longer be employed without reputation being threatened. Companies and communicators that tackle challenges head-on and try to directly engage with their audiences are the ones who earn the trust of clients and consumers.

The second point, culture, or more precisely a shift in culture, requires businesses to drive a conversation-led mindset and calls for clients to relinquish the need to control every aspect of the message. Brands and reputations today are co-created and build a narrative in conjunction with each audience segment.

The third point is one that requires constant effort: credibility. A commitment to transparency and discussion backed by facts will allow people to build long-lasting relationships and reputations. In digital spaces, the scope to deceive is always rising, and communicators must use critical thinking, fact-checking, analysis and other research tools to identify the credibility of a source and the battles they pick. This hurdle can be overcome only with diligence and decency. Decency, in fact, may be the most emphatic statement of defiance the profession can make as it drives home the value of the collective consciousness and intelligent debate.

In a world were both information and disinformation are at our fingertips, communications professionals and brands need to find ways to engage meaningfully and consistently with each other and with the public. In the end, it all boils down to our tone, tenor and timing.

Amit Misra is CEO of MSL South Asia and
South East Asia

3

DIGITAL PR: EARNED SOCIAL MEDIA

Professionals in communications and marketing have been grappling with multiple aspects of 'digital' since it came into being, be it metrics, reach, customers calling out inauthentic paid partnerships or simply the conundrum of how to effectively manage detrimental narratives that sprout up around their brands.

Six out of ten CCOs we spoke to agreed that merely the instant gratification of likes, impressions and reach is what drives their campaigns. Two out of ten said that they look at engagement and click-through rates (CTR) and still grapple with real impact. The remaining two CCOs are oblivious to impact and do digital campaigns either to please their bosses or to be in the reckoning.

If these are the statistics, does that mean a communicator needs to focus on digital media more than traditional? No. But as dependence on print media gradually decreases, PR professionals need to develop competencies related to digital spaces and use their vast experience of running traditional earned media strategies to cross-pollinate ideas and methods to replicate the same for the virtual realm.

Digital PR, a powerful tool in the PR arsenal

Let us delve a bit deeper. If traditional media relations can be classified as 'earned media', we would like to define digital PR as 'earned social media'. It may sound simple but as we build on this definition, a plethora of new opportunities and ways to engage stakeholders emerge.

We would also like to introduce a relevant concept that, knowingly or unknowingly, all PR practitioners aspire for. We call it a 'safety net' for brands or, in this case, a 'digital safety net'. It is that positive presence on social media which gives consumers a reason to believe that the brand is a good citizen. It gives brands the right to operate, increases brand love and enhances the employer brand quotient, among many other benefits. Most importantly, it gives the brand that benefit of the doubt during an adverse scenario or a crisis which can easily get amplified on social media.

Operating in the realm of 'earned social media', we have seen some significant results across multiple projects. The ability to reach a significant number of social platforms through compelling content has become a reality and will only grow further.

During our research, we found that setting up a digital PR vertical can be an exciting process. Based on our interactions with some of the best teams across the country, we discovered that there are seven mantras for fuelling a successful digital PR strategy. Here's a condensed version of the arduous baby steps that some of these corporates took in experimenting with a new process, building networks and relooking at the way they engaged wherein today, they are reaping the benefits.

❖ **Outline a realistic vision:** As a first step, our recommendation is to understand the 'why' of digital PR. Let this not be a 'keeping up with the Joneses' game. You need to set the right end objectives. What is it that you want to achieve out of this vertical? What gap are you trying to bridge and how does it fit in your PR arsenal?

❖ **Identify the landscape and players:** Having framed the vision, it is imperative to recognise all the potential areas where digital PR can be manifested, the constituents of this ecosystem, the carriers, the receivers and, most importantly, the platforms where your stakeholder segments are consuming data. It is not a straight equation. Different stakeholders consume data on the basis of their own demography. Some prefer social media, some thrive on thought leadership blogs and some devour e-news portals. Hybrid media is the first choice for some. The landscape is large and the players are many. It will be a process in itself to prioritise where you want to play so as to maximise your reach. Metrics are important, data plays a serious role and the power of well-informed influencers/advocates who can connect their followers to a brand is unmatched. In fact, just like how PR consultancies maintained databases of journalists, the time has come to start maintaining lists of bloggers and influencers. Doing so is central to a successful digital PR programme.

(These first two steps will help create a base. We call it the laying of the digital pipeline. What flows through this pipeline is a no-brainer. It is data or content—the new oil of this century! Content driven by data and backed by research is seen as authentic and authenticity laced with consistency is one of the key pillars of good digital PR.)

❖ **Curate a content strategy:** Since the landscape is vast and data consumption points for various stakeholders differ, the ability of a brand to reach multiple audiences through their preferred platforms is crucial. Digital PR opens up new vistas of content packaging. Videos, infographics, text, images, GIFs and more can be effectively used to make an impact. The key is repurposing. It is such a beautiful concept; a uniform message manifested through different formats and modes is much more effective in establishing a narrative. The biggest advantage of setting up a content hub is that one can create content that suits the needs of traditional, hybrid as well as digital media. Of course, such proactive content is for flooding social spaces with an aim of creating a positive digital safety net, which also improves your SEO outcomes.

❖ **Establish a standard format for a digital press release:** To bring some sanity to the milieu in which news releases are disseminated in a digital PR era, we recommend a conducive format for a digital press release. Imagine a world where headlines are hashtags and the copy comprises crisp videos or pictures combined with shareable links that lead directly to social media handles. It makes life so simple! Not only does it look great but all the data is also available at a glance for influencers to link to their own platforms. This also gives them the flexibility to pick the elements relevant to their stories.

❖ **Add an offline element:** Digital PR outcomes can be heightened with experiential engagements. At the end of the day, authentic content can be generated by influencers when they actually experience the brands. The purpose comes to the fore, the stories are meatier and the engagement is far superior to a general press conference.

❖ **Create a digital PR mindset:** A change in mindset and a focused intervention to institutionalise the digital PR process can be very useful for teams that are still tuned to traditional ways of earned media processes. We found that the difference between organisations successfully using digital PR and those using it not so successfully lies in nothing but their approach.

❖ **From a nose for news to ears for listening:** Our experience says that while you can set compelling narratives through digital PR, you are sometimes vulnerable to them going awry. Social listening, in this case, becomes necessary. Having followed all the steps above, you might be set to roll out your digital PR blitz. However, for a successful digital PR outreach, ORM is indispensable. With a large prevalence of online platforms, social media kingmakers and the power to frame narratives about brands in the hands of the common man, 'social listening' carries huge significance. There are robust tools available for online and offline listening. Technology makes it possible to track each conversation about a brand. It enables faster responses and two-way communication with consumers and also alerts one in real time in case of any negative feedback. The advantage of these tools is that one can witness the campaign unfold, compare it with an identified peer set, course-correct strategy and analyse the outcomes in real time.

It may all sound easy, especially for veterans in the profession reading this. But when it comes to on-ground implementation, realities start dawning. The traditional PR mindset can be so strongly embedded in an individual that it can become an impediment. It gets further complicated whilst setting expectations with brand managers. The propensity to pay (using advertising) and achieve digital outcomes is high. And if we say that we are 'earned social media', we must first prove that we can deliver even if algorithms go against us.

But it is worth the effort since digital PR can drive narratives authentically. And it is possible if the planning is right. For that, a lead time is crucial. In the traditional format, we have seen teams churning out press conferences with just a day's notice and managing to get the message out effectively. Not so in the case of digital PR, though! Compelling content must be curated, influencers need to be chosen, briefing has to be robust, repurposing has to be of high quality and, most importantly, the right platforms need to be identified to maximise reach and effectiveness. So, to make all this happen, a process of getting briefs in advance, having the PR machinery embedded in the entire planning process of a product launch and co-creation of content needs to be in place. This calls for a cultural change in the way one looks at PR and the need to institutionalise a process with an appropriate expectation setting.

As we now say, digital PR is no rocket science but what goes behind establishing a robust process for your PR arsenal is nothing short of a symphony that involves various streams of communications coming together to play their part in the most perfect manner!

Traditional PR abilities are well-embedded and expertise is available across members of the in-house and consultancy teams. However, even though there are overlaps, we feel digital PR requires focused effort to build a set of skills that have been ignored before. To run a good digital PR programme, PR professionals will have to invest time in enhancing their knowledge of SEO, campaign management and the digital landscape while developing their capabilities around influencer engagement, networking, design thinking and digital measurement, just to name a few.

~

Don't think channels, think audience

News consumption patterns are often determined by channel distribution. This traditional approach frequently brings us up short in our core endeavour to understand our audience. The world around us is ever-evolving, especially with the accelerated pace of digital expansion over the last few years. However, this expansion has also highlighted some significant things which we must not ignore.

Our audience is fragmented

This is something that comes to the fore every now and then, but is rarely looked at with the focus it requires. It is time that, before we think of channels and mediums while mapping news consumption patterns, we understand our audience.

This is a complex territory to map. Over the years, our audience has undergone a series of fragmentations due to multiple factors such as gender, generation gaps, socio-economic behaviours, tastes, interests, likes and much more. This fragmentation has been ongoing and won't stop any time in the near future. We are talking about multiple informed groups of individuals, each seeking content and news in their domains. What then should our focus be?

Understanding and knowing audience persona is important

A deep dive into the changing digital landscape shows that it is not limited to a particular kind of media being prevalent. It is about whom it is prevalent to. For instance, audiences who grew up with traditional forms of media will stay with it, even if they might adapt other forms of media. Similarly, new media and digital tools will keep coming in. Therefore, it might be apt to review how we define our world today. Is it a changed world or simply one that's more branched out, with additional channels on hand?

A world where evolution is a direct indication of fragmentation

Traditional print media existed for over 100 years before broadcast came in, and now we have digital media. However, none of these changed our audience. The audience changed first and then came the channels to cater to them. That is the simple dynamic of fragmentation. It is important to look at communications from this lens. Primarily, it is the only way to stay ahead of the curve and keep track of this development.

For a communications professional, the ability to tell a story has not diminished and will not even in the future. How they tell the story is what will change. Today's content is experiential in the sense that it not only engages audiences but also gets them excited and invested. The future is about how well you can map your audience.

Aman Gupta is the Co-founder of D Yellow Elephant

≈

Going above and beyond

As I began to write this, I am reminded of how a marketer joked to her colleague, 'We are creating more content than our audiences can consume.' Her colleague responded excitedly, 'That's a great topic for our next blog or listicle—we could maybe invite UGC (User Generated Content).' I am also well aware that perhaps a young TikToker (or their Indian equivalent) possibly has more to say on this than us older folks, plus we are trying to write it in a *book* (yes, that old-fashioned way to communicate) about PR and marketing trends. So, no pressure!

But nonetheless, here are some brave predictions for key trends—I am assuming that readers already have social listening and analytics tools in place because that's not a trend, that's now hygiene.

❖ As influencer marketing continues to rise, we know video and interactive content is the way to go and (yes, ironically) ephemeral content is here to stay. What will be interesting is how we find ways to marry these big trends of UGC and influencers to interactive ephemeral content. Companies that experiment and innovate to bring these together, rather than merely creating short-form content, no matter how interesting, will find long-term success. Yes, keeping it short is now another hygiene rule where it's all about headlines, or those fifteen- to thirty-second clips! Though funnily, it's not a new rule—one of the earliest editors I worked with (and it was a magazine based on long-form writing) would say sharply, 'Tell me *where* is the hook, *show me the hook*!'

❖ Social media and content marketing have redefined public relations in a big way, broadening its audiences. As with many of those hot initial public offerings (IPOs)/unicorn brands right now, PR is also now D2C. But unlike marketers speaking mainly to customers, PR professionals must leverage social channels to speak to a multitude of audiences—policymakers, investors, partners, vendors and employees. Those leveraging social media content—UGC reels, stories, infographics and more—across audiences have the opportunity to really find the Holy Grail of never-before reach and credibility.

❖ Social commerce was a trend just waiting to happen. Marketers have always known that call to action (CTA) is the valuable; now, companies are going beyond just UGC to have customers directly interact with the *business* and not just the *brand*.

❖ Experiment across platforms. For instance, looking at emerging audio platforms, finding ways to cross-leverage social platforms and repurpose content, creating UGC with audiences beyond just customers and developing edgy and relevant content that is still safe in a world quick to take offence are just some of the main imperatives ahead.

Minari Shah is the Director of
Corporate Communications at Amazon APAC

Data is what shapes digital strategy

PR has been forced to transform and reimagine the media mix. Today, a large part of India's population are digital natives below the age of thirty-five who have grown up in the physical world. Most market research studies reflect this shift in media consumption behaviour. This involves moving clients to think through more integrated campaigns that can appeal to individuals who are seeking more purpose and reason in every brand they engage with.

From contests and promotions to disruption and engagement, from celebrity influencers to real influencers and from large fans to real users, digital PR has come a long way. Brands need to generate a reason for customers to come to their platforms, stay engaged, keep coming back for more and remaining involved.

Three trends in media that are conducive for digital PR

❖ Data will be the key driver for campaigns that will shape outreach strategy for audiences across demographics, geographies and gender. Data will enable listening, understanding of themes, messages and trends and will drive performance metrics—factors that will be important in understanding how a campaign is effective and relevant.

❖ More tools and more automation will be the way forward for PR. We will have access to information, networks and communities at the click of a button.

❖ The impact of influencers and influencer marketing is substantial. With over half of the world's population on social media platforms, PR professionals have had to adapt rapidly to reach people in this new landscape. What will make this possible more than ever is influencer marketing.

Valerie Pinto is the CEO of Weber Shandwick India

~

The lines between PR and marketing are blurring

There's no one way of getting the digital PR strategy right; what works for one of our customers isn't sure to work for the other. However, mentioned below are a few points that we, as a brand, follow and base our work on.

When we work with influencers, we must ensure that the same message is being communicated and shared by more than one influencer. Why? Because the more people talk about it, the more authentic and real it seems. Much like a breaking news story—if a specific topic is being talked about by only one channel, it sounds less believable compared to when all channels cover the same topic.

The next factor that plays a crucial role for brands and collaborations is the idea of authenticity. With the Advertising Standards Council of India (ASCI) guidelines coming into place, influencers and content creators have to communicate the truth about the product or service and offer honest representations of the claims. This authenticity will drive more credibility to influencers. Watching a video online can trigger the purchase of a mobile phone, for example. In that context, the consumer might think, 'I saw a really cool unboxing video by a content creator which has made me decide that this will be my go-to brand.' In some cases, the unboxing video could play the role of awareness as well, apart from driving mental conversion. The last thing before they purchase the mobile phone will be to check reviews, which is where the brand's website and the sanitation of its e-commerce assets comes into play.

So, if we see closely, if we have more influencers being authentic and really indulging in some immersive and deeply creative content, they are more likely to make an individual engage with the brand. When we come across a new product or service being launched, we look forward to having an immersive experience. This is something that content creators and influencers bring to us. Since creators have to be genuine about their efforts, they tend to get engrossed in what the product or service has to offer, which has rich, creative outcomes for viewers. Organisations should identify appropriate influencers for their brands, the ones who indulge in deep creative tasks that match their brands' tonality so that their work pushes the brands' thought process.

To conclude, the lines between PR and marketing are getting blurred. Almost all that PR companies do currently is paid PR in some form. However, brands do have a chance to opt for traditional PR, which takes times and for which the correct strategy needs to be in place. This can ideally be done by maintaining relations by means of the delivery of the right kind of messages and experiences to media stakeholders.

Harshil Karia is the Founder of Schbang

4

THE DAWN OF INFLUENCERS

One would have to have their head deeply buried in the sand to not have noticed the gradual rise of the influencers. Going by the commonly accepted definition, influencers are persons who affect the decisions of their followers. They have always been around with clout that they have enjoyed because of their thought leadership in the form of traditional celebrities such as film stars, sport stars, religious gurus, politicians or academicians. In his book *The Tipping Point*, Malcolm Gladwell discusses archetypes of people: mavens, connectors and salespeople. Influencers encompass these archetypes. They connect ideas and messages with a lot of people and this what makes them attractive to brands.

Nowadays, there are 'influencers' who have cropped up in almost every walk of life. Whether it is podcasters, vloggers, bloggers or Instagram stars on fitness, well-being, travel, fashion, food and technology, there are all sorts of people whom you look to for advice.

These individuals have one thing in common: huge online followings. Even brands have figured out that winning the hearts of these influencers can also win them the eyes, ears and even the souls of their followers and supporters. The way to the hearts of these influencers is, of course, through their wallets.

And rightfully so. Why run away from the opportunity to promote your products and services through someone from whom a simple recommendation is enough for their followers to consider your product?

Even if the word of the decade (2010–2020) was 'influencer', as per Merriam-Webster, the term itself was first used around the 1600s. The prevalence of influence or using influencers is not new at all. For a century or more, there probably has been no better way to pull consumers towards a product than to get prominent people talking about it, although the practice has never been as widespread as it is today.

So, what has changed now?

The sudden increase in the number of influencers has been majorly due to the meteoric rise of social media and technology. The premise is the same but scale has risen significantly—in terms of speed, reach and the ability to measure impact.

In today's fast-paced world, consumers have developed a cognitive ad blocker of sorts. Trust in advertising is dwindling. People want to hear and read experiences of regular people who have used a product, someone they follow online. This has led to a shift in the power to persuade, from celebrities to influencers.

Today, with the proliferation of the internet and with almost anyone with a smartphone being a potential 'journalist', regional influencers have become highly sought after. They have astounding reach and engagement with their audiences and their followers look to them for new trends and information almost blindly. Regional influencers create content that is relational, culturally closer and seemingly more authentic than someone who is not from the same area.

Increasingly, we have observed that brands, large and small, are realising the benefits of sharper targeting through smaller social media influencers—so-called micro- and nano-influencers. The impact that close-knit communities can provide for hyperlocal markets is unmatched.

Micro-influencers are everyday individuals with an audience between 10,000 and 50,000 comprising a strong community of followers. Let us examine some of the nuances of a micro-influencer—a breed that is probably ruling the roost currently!

❖ **They score on loyalty:** As they themselves are hungry to associate with brands, relationships turn out to be collaborative rather than transactional. If nurtured well, they become long-term advocates. They are easy to deal with and if experientially engaged with the brand, the authenticity of their content shines through.

❖ **Engagement rates are high:** Micro-influencers are generally niche players such as moms' groups, wellness advocates or travel lovers. They have followers who are part of their communities and love engaging with their content. As their posts and content are targeted towards smaller audiences, the engagement rates generally tend to be higher.

❖ **They are relatable:** Big influencers with millions of followers are unapproachable and prone to larger risks.

Micro-influencers, however, are more relatable, seen as friends and are more believable. The level of trust and connectedness is higher.

❖ **They are cost-effective with less administrative hassles:** Reaching hyperlocal markets becomes easier. Most importantly, micro-influencers cost less and, most of the time, work on the basis of barters and associations that are mutually beneficial. The latest trend that we have witnessed is bundling groups of these micro-influencers to reach micro-markets. This is usually more economical than tapping a celebrity endorser or influencer with millions of followers.

The last decade has seen a sudden rise in ordinary persons who have amassed a huge following on some social networks. They refer to themselves as digital creators. We shall refer to them as neo-influencers. They specialise in an area—fashion, food, automobiles, gadgets—and develop an expertise on the subject with interesting posts accompanied by images or videos.

These neo-influencers are of five types—nano-influencers, micro-influencers, macro-influencers, mega-influencers and mainstream celebrities. There are also journalists, loyalists, activists and advocates who play a role in the brand's journey.

Influencers are put into different buckets based on their reach. We will delve into that with a little more detail in this chapter. Let us focus on how one becomes an influencer in order to understand this better. Typically, a person follows their passion and start putting out content using hashtags strategically. In some cases, they write consistent blogs and post regular commentary. Rarely do influencers emerge overnight. They plan this as their mainstream occupation and expect to earn from brands paying them to promote a product to their followers.

For brands, influencers are a double-edged sword. Unlike mainstream media which has a structure and a redressal system, influencers operate as individuals wielding tremendous clout. They are aware that they have the power to make or break a brand. Most of them use that knowledge responsibly, but there are cases when influencers have held brands to ransom in order to extract a pound of flesh.

There are umpteen stories of how companies have had to pay a price because an influencer wanted to blackmail the brand or, in some cases, played up incidents to put brands in a spot. Some years back, a brand manager got a call via the helpline number printed on the packet of a breakfast cereal. The caller said he was a journalist, a stringer with a regional TV news channel, and mentioned that he was in possession of a packet of breakfast cereal which contained a dead cockroach. While the brand manager was confident there was no chance that a dead cockroach could have made its way into a packet of breakfast cereal, there was no way one could refute the caller who insisted that he found it as soon as he cut open the packet to serve himself. He threatened to display it on live television unless he was paid a hefty sum of money. It was amply clear that he had devised the whole thing to make some money.

What does a brand do under such pressure? It either calls the bluff or succumbs. That is a call the leadership must take. Both have pros and cons. In this case, the brand decided to send a regional sales manager to engage with this individual. There were two hours of negotiations because the brand manager was keen to secure the 'contaminated' packet to carry out thorough investigations. The journalist suspiciously refused to relent until there was a commitment that he would be paid. However, from an initial demand of Rs 1 lakh, he came down to Rs 25,000 and the manager finally closed the deal and secured the packet. It later came to light that this journalist had done this before with other brands. Would the company have been as worried if he had not mentioned that he was a journalist? Would the company act the same way if someone on Twitter with 100 followers did the same thing in current times? Hard to say.

The point is that these neo-influencers can be both a blessing and a curse for brands. In India, the ASCI has drawn up guidelines for brands and influencers. The guidelines are the foundation stone for regulated, ethical conduct by both parties in the era of influencer marketing. It will, for instance, become incumbent upon brands to get the influencers they acquire for promotions to sign an undertaking agreeing to disclose to audiences that they are doing this in exchange for some form of compensation.

This, however, strikes directly at the aspect of authenticity that brands want to portray. This is also different from how brands would sign on a celebrity to be its brand ambassador. Here, a celebrity represented by a firm or a manager would agree to offer the brand a certain number of days in a calendar year to do certain things—be present for a shoot for an advertisement, be present at company events with employees, dealers, customers and be available for media interactions. The terms of engagement were crystal clear. For example, consumers, by and large, would be aware that Amitabh Bachchan was endorsing Cadbury's

Dairy Milk. As a fan of the star, they might like the product because of this endorsement. More importantly, customers would link the product to the celebrity and it would help in brand recall.

With the onset of the digital influencer, the lines have blurred. It is important to refer to external outlets and their description of the types of influencers that we have earlier.

Here's a quick breakdown of the main categories:

- ❖ Mega-influencers with more than a million followers
- ❖ Macro-influencers with 500K to 1 million followers
- ❖ Mid-tier influencers with 50K to 500K followers
- ❖ Micro-influencers with 10K to 50K followers
- ❖ Nano-influencers with 1K to 10K followers

Then there is another situation that organisations face: embargoes. An embargo is when a journalist or influencer is given certain information in advance to prepare the content, with the explicit understanding that the information cannot be made public until a specific time and date. However, very often, the information is leaked which can happen because someone deliberately chose to be the first to release the information, or because someone passed the information on to a third party who then shares it publicly. This leads to layered complications for all those involved. Sometimes, the person breaking the embargo could be blacklisted and become vengeful. The situation in such cases is always tricky.

The best policy for brands is to have a robust framework for engaging with influencers, and make all employees familiar with it. Bold brands go a step further and choose to make the policy known to a wider external audience as well.

Influencer engagement is certainly going to be a complex area in the years ahead. It intersects marketing and public relations, which can lead to crossed wires between the two departments. Marketing has traditionally been the department that controls budgets, whereas public relations is usually the one asking for bigger budgets in order to deploy influencers.

And then there are also journalists, activists, analysts, advocates and loyalists to manage. They are influencers in their own right. For instance, advocates are typically former employees or current customers who swear by the brand and talk about it without any reward. They also call out the brand when it falters. These constituents are all an integral part of a brand's journey, and very often help fuel the brand's growth.

Some trends that we predict will be emerge in this space:

❖ Impact of influencers will rise further
❖ Micro- and nano-influencers will thrive
❖ Preference of bundling multiple micro-influencers over one large celebrity influencer will grow
❖ Conquering micro-markets through influence will be widely seen
❖ Influencers will become prominent brand partners, affecting direct sales through live shopping
❖ Employees as advocates and influencers will reach the next level
❖ Snackable and shareable content will prevail
❖ Influencer content will get more data- and authenticity-driven due to regulatory norms
❖ Long-term influencer tie-ups or establishment of influencer squads will take place

❖ Creator-focused marketplaces will emerge
❖ Disclosures of paid endorsements will foster transparency

Importance of due diligence in selecting influencers

As the space evolves, multiple complexities come to the fore. There have been various instances when brands have had to dissociate themselves from influencers who turned out to be problematic. Of course, it seems easy to get an influencer on board. However, if proper due diligence is not done, it can lead to a potential crisis emerging out of a discrepancy between the core values of the brand and the influencer.

There have been serious issues many times when a brand lost credibility because an endorser or influencer was caught in the crossfire between polarising audiences. Such social media carnage is significantly detrimental to the brand.

We feel that deep research is very important when choosing influencers to work with. Audience verification, quality of followers, relevance and geographical presence established through third-party online tools, as well as physical verification, can go a long way. A value match to past reputation, any linkages with inappropriate incidents and stands the influencer has taken on various subjects is important. An influencer's values and opinions are, after all, what a brand buys into in the first place and are a big reason for follower growth. Conducting one-on-one interaction to understand each other better is necessary whilst selecting the individual.

While it is difficult to quantify the amount of due diligence brands can do, it is good to see that they are becoming vigilant in managing influencers, with protocols, contracts, ownership of intellectual properties (IPs) and exit clauses in place.

With the right expectations, collaborative working and an infusion of creativity, authentic content and crisp narratives, an influencer-led campaign can bring immense benefits to any brand.

Influencers and influencer engagement are here to stay. Employees need to be trained well to understand the nuances and to make sure that everyone has a pleasant experience about the entire process.

Influencer marketing 101

With one in two consumers believing *anything* an influencer says online as per Nielsen's Global Trust Report[*] and two out of three consumers trusting influencer messages about a brand more than the company's advertising, according to the Edelman Trust Barometer[†], it's time to tap into influencer marketing.

Our research and experience point to healthy ROIs for most businesses using an influencer marketing strategy. We have seen consumers first-hand across beauty brands, fashion labels, hotels and smartphones actually purchase products because of influencer recommendations. People no longer listen to top celebrities to the same extent they did back in the day. Instead, they trust recommendations from peers. While influencers like Miss Malini first emerged around 2008 in India, the scene began maturing only in 2015. But influencers are still considered a relatively new aspect of brand strategy. Most brands are still refining their influencer policies.

What started out as one-size-fits-all solution (when it was merely about the number of followers) has matured since to factor in finer metrics such as actual engagement in the form of likes, comments and clicks. COVID-19 also

---

[*] 'Getting closer: Influencers help brands build more personal consumer connections', Nielsen, May 2022, https://www.nielsen.com/insights/2022/getting-closer-influencers-help-brands-build-more-personal-consumer-connections/.

[†] 'In Brands We Trust?: 2019 Edelman Trust Barometer Special Report', Edelman Intelligence, 2019, https://www.edelman.com/sites/g/files/aatuss191/files/2019-07/2019_edelman_trust_barometer_special_report_in_brands_we_trust_executive_summary.pdf.

awakened businesses to the power of social media platforms and content creators.

Audience relationship is the most significant factor when considering collaboration with a particular influencer. As UGC is valuable, the quality of content production must also be carefully assessed. With digital disruption coming of age, influencers who have exhibited creativity and good engagement have become strong centres of influence.

Trends in influencer marketing

Authenticity

Real influence is truly about leveraging authenticity because in order to build influence, people need to be trusted, and if your message is being endorsed by less than authentic people, then the audience won't trust your brand. Hence, brands need to mine and work the right influencer(s). Blatantly sponsored posts themselves aren't the problem, nor you do not have to forgo production value to make your sponsored posts feel more authentic. What makes sponsored content authentic is the genuine sense of excitement about the brand and the product exhibition by the influencer.

Niche influencing

We are already seeing influencers carving out niches for themselves. Influencers will continue to develop expertise in their niche or domain, making them even more sought after by brands in those verticals. A point to note is that nano- and micro-influencers enjoy better engagement rates than the superstars of social media across platforms. By focusing on the former, brands will be able to stretch their influencer marketing budgets while still working with influencers who are deeply connected to their audiences.

Brand partnerships

The time is ripe to seek ongoing partnerships (instead of one-off projects) with influencers who share values with your brand. Long-term engagement with influencers will preserve brand loyalty even in times of crisis.

Performance-based deals and influencer commerce will increase

Brands will increasingly expect influencers to deliver on their promises such as a specific number of sales or clicks. Globally, more and more brands deploying influencer marketing are using affiliate campaigns, and we foresee the growth of this in India too. It is already being practised by e-commerce stores.

Content creators become founders and brand owners

Like celebrities who have founded brand labels to leverage their brand equity (such as Anushka Sharma with Nush), influencers are also embarking on the same journey. Make-up artist and influencer Namrata Soni started a beauty line called Simply Nam. Bhuvan Bam has a fashion line with Youthiapa. This trend is expected to grow stronger, and will offer more opportunities for brands to collaborate with socially active natives.

Archana Jain is Managing Director at PR Pundit

~

ASCI—building a trustworthy foundation

As consumers, we are all increasingly engaged with virtual spaces in our daily lives. A massive portion of advertising, too, has followed suit. Artificial intelligence, machine learning and the internet of things (IoT) are deeply embedded in our media space. They affect our behaviour online and are an essential part of our lives. Influencers are also a huge part of this digital frontier. For the last thirty-five years, the ASCI has worked to safeguard the rights of consumers on traditional media platforms like television, print, radio and now digital platforms. According to digital marketing agency Adlift, India's bustling influencer market is estimated at about \$75–\$150 million a year compared to the global market of \$1.75 billion.* As India's influencer ecosystem continues to grow exponentially, ASCI wants to ensure consumer protection in digital spaces as well. The idea is to work with influencers and help them build an ecosystem that has a strong foundation based on trust, responsibility and transparency.

Digital media formats blur the lines between content and advertisements, but ASCI's influencer guidelines have made it a requisite for influencers to disclose paid-for posts. By doing this, influencers not only avoid misleading consumers but they also win their trust by being honest about paid partnerships in the first place. The foundation of the influencer–audience relationship is authenticity, and disclosures are a way to build that bridge further.

As far as the future of influencer engagement is concerned, all stakeholders have responded very positively

---

* https://www.adlift.com/in/influencer-marketing/.

to ASCI's guidelines. We have been pleasantly surprised by their willingness to be a part of this new and positive change. By establishing a highly collaborative approach in developing these guidelines, we are working to ensure that concerns of all stakeholders will be well addressed.

Regulating the internet is a near-impossible job and use of AI is a must if one is to make any kind of dent. ASCI has been deploying technology for this very purpose.

When it comes to brands choosing influencers, some of the main concerns beyond the obvious metrics of reach and engagement should be:

❖ Is there a brand fit and do the influencer's own values, beliefs and approach to content sit well with the brand philosophy? Followers want authenticity from influencers and a brand endorsement that clashes with the influencer's worldview diminishes the value of both.

❖ Is the influencer honest? This may be a very basic question, but the fact is that the age-old adage of honesty being the best policy applies to a modern concept like influencer marketing. If the influencer is honest with their followers in terms of disclosures, it points to a certain moral compass which is valuable for a brand when associating with the individual. If the influencer is willing to mislead their audiences, who is to say what their sense of ethics could be vis-à-vis the brand?

❖ What is the influencer's investment in their own brand? Are they building it by posting interesting and original content frequently? Or are they milking it by posting obviously commercial content? Such factors indicate the longevity of the influencer's own brand.

Net-net, influencer marketing is here to stay and become a mainstream part of advertising campaigns. However, a trustworthy foundation will pave the way for a path with minimal stumbling blocks.

Manisha Kapoor is the CEO and
Secretary-General at ASCI

Maximising the buck invested on influencer-led gigs

On the subject of maximising bang for the buck invested on influencer-led gigs, there are three things to keep in mind:

Embrace the pyramid

When creating a new influencer campaign, envision a pyramid. At the very top, prioritise and place a headliner who will become the face of your campaign. Think of national icons from different walks of life—these will be your lead influencers. Under this, place macro-influencers who are subject matter experts within a specific domain. Next, select a few micro-influencers who are also subject matter experts and can engage your target audience. Finally, complete your pyramid by roping in nano/regional influencers who'll take your campaign to every corner of the country. The pyramid approach to influencer engagement ensures that your campaign receives top-of-the-line mass visibility as well as bottom line-focused group communication.

When it comes to content, the creator knows best

The influencer, and not the brand, should lead the content strategy while creating a campaign. Why? Because creators have a greater understanding of the kind of content that works well. Of course, brands can work together with influencers to ensure that the brand's language is used appropriately to create recall. Simply put, an influencer-first approach to content strategy can enhance reach, recall and ROI.

In a noisy world, you need to shout to be heard

Even if the campaign's content is impressive, it won't make the expected impact unless promoted across the right platforms. To this end, brands should also leverage their budget to devise a full-fledged digital campaign around influencer partnership.

By keeping these three points in mind to select the best influencer for a campaign, brands can cover all their bases and launch a truly impactful and engaging campaign.

- ❖ **Right brand fit:** Choose an influencer whose personality matches your brand promise.
- ❖ **Right campaign fit:** Even if personalities match, you must not choose an influencer unless they are suited to your specific audience.
- ❖ **Historical data:** The influencer's past engagement rates, campaign successes and the content they have been creating are all relevant.

While these rules will help you to broadly plan a successful campaign, you are allowed to experiment. Since we live in times where attention spans are diminishing, we can sometimes bend the rules and create a quirky campaign that generates consumer interest and creates virality.

Kunal Kishore Sinha is the Co-founder of
Value 360 Communications

~

Influencer marketing is now mainstream

Influencer marketing is not a new phenomenon, but has evolved to capture the attention of marketing professions across all organisations. With social media becoming a dominant channel driving brand discovery, consideration and purchasing decisions more actively than ever before, the role of influencers has become prominent.

What makes influencer marketing special is the bond that is forged between the influencer and the consumer, which in turn can translate into a rewarding relationship between the brand and the consumer. This bond has to be one of trust and authenticity for an influencer to retain the power they wield over us, the consumers. In fact, four in ten millennial subscribers feel their favourite influencer understands them better than their friends! Any compromise with honesty in the narrative will only lead to a loss of connection with the audience for both the influencer and the brand.

So, is influencer marketing a passing trend or has it settled into its rightful place in the world of marketing? GroupM INCA's 'India Influencer Marketing Report 2021' projects the space to be currently valued at Rs 900 crore and is further anticipated to grow at a compound annual growth rate (CAGR) of 25 per cent till 2025 to reach a size of Rs 2,200 crore; significantly smaller than those of traditional channels of marketing.[*] However, it is the influencers' ability to connect with their communities in a relatable way that makes influencer marketing a valued marketing intervention.

Irrespective of the type of influencer, their creative and engaging storytelling ability is what creates an audience and a following for them. In fact, anyone can become a social media influencer. Do large brands work only with mega- or celebrity influencers, considering their huge following and fan base? Not really—each influencer category is unique. A brand can choose to collaborate with a mix of influencers across categories for the optimal utilisation of budget and to reach the desired audience segment(s).

Interestingly, in the report, celebrities account for only 27 per cent of influencer marketing spends while other categories account for 73 per cent. It is not surprising that 50 per cent of respondents to the survey for the India Influencer Marketing Report 2021 expressed an intent to increase their influencer marketing spends by 25 to 36 per cent.

From an influencer's perspective, it's important that the brand they choose to represent resonates with their audience and is in sync with their values. For instance, it would not be credible to have a food influencer, who is vegan, promoting a non-vegan chocolate. Likewise, for a brand, picking the right influencer involves an analysis of more than just their follower size—evaluating parameters

---

[*] 'Influencer Marketing Will Be INR 900 CR Market in India By The End of 2021', GroupM India, 17 September 2021, https://www.groupm. com/newsroom/india-influencer-marketing-report/.

like expertise in the subject, attitudes and beliefs, style and tonality of communication, previous brand associations, audience demographics, number of followers, engagement and so on. Data-backed and AI-enabled tools for influencer selection are great, but I believe that we cannot, and should not, underestimate the power of intuitive knowledge.

With advances in technology, the use of virtual influencers is also increasing, and some people are feeling connected to digitally-created characters whose 'personalities' are fictional. They give the creator full control over the messaging with immense possibilities for associations and collaborations. Does a virtual robot sharing its views really impress us? Apparently, it does.

I think a virtual influencer can be the perfect brand ambassador. However, making that persona into a recognised, trusted and loved one is not an easy task, particularly with the responsibility of producing a stream of relatable, topical and engaging content.

To conclude, if I had to pick three top points to be mindful of concerning influencer marketing, they would be:

❖ Lacking clarity on the campaign goals between the brand and the influencers.
❖ Curbing the creative freedom of the influencer such that they cease to sound credible or consistent with the style that won them their audience.
❖ Ascertaining the individual's suitability for the topic and alignment with the values of the brand, ideally basing the selection not only on an algorithm but also using one's intuitive knowledge. Being wary of fake influencers who do not have a real audience.

Madhu Chibber is the Head of
Corporate Communications at HDFC Bank

5

ORM: TIME TO TUNE IN

During a very intense discussion on ORM, some of the best names from Indian PR firms were sharing their experiences on how they had managed some of the biggest online crisis situations in the past. The conversations veered towards how even small incidents or seemingly innocuous but mischievous posts on social media had the potential to create havoc for brands. One of the CCOs of a large global fast-moving consumer goods (FMCG) organisation shared an example of how an incident in a small town turned into a full-blown crisis that had to be addressed on multiple levels, all because it was ignored and taken for granted. Another expert on crisis mitigation techniques shared a story of how a conversation on social media with an aggrieved customer started gathering attention, and how the looming crisis was averted by a timely and empathetic response from his team member. A peculiar issue shared by a PR consultancy head was that of his client who, when searched on the internet, always had articles related to his past misadventures appear rather than what he wanted to project, which was not helping his status at all.

We were all warming up to a serious focus on online crisis control, and several quality ideas were popping up. As ever, the collective intellectual might of this august group was outstanding. One thing that everyone unanimously agreed was that ORM is everything that the term suggests, and much more.

Some said that ORM meant taking control of all online conversations around a brand. Another definition was that ORM is about balancing narratives in social spaces, neutralising misleading trends and ensuring that people respect and support you online. ORM, in short, is about managing the reputation of an entity online, be it a product brand, a personal brand or a corporate brand. Managing includes monitoring and improving how one is viewed online. It includes seeing and analysing what a potential customer, reporter or partner will discover about your brand, your people and your product/service when they perform an online search. Before they ever land on your website or pick up the phone to call you, what will they find when they look for you? And will they like it?

It's a no-brainer that a majority of consumers read online reviews before visiting a business. By simply searching on the internet, they can come up with different perceptions about an entity and whether what's on offer is good or bad. A negative online presence, or even no presence at all, can adversely impact the success of the entity. Whether one is completing a business deal, exploring a partnership or reaching out to media outlets, online reputation counts.

Smart managers ensure that they have set up Google alerts for important keywords. Smarter managers scan the internet from time to time to ensure that they can spot untoward comments about the entity they manage. The smartest managers are the ones who are addressing bouquets and brickbats in real time, online. Employing such tactics in the world of ORM is no longer an option.

Practically all news today appears online. Even a TV channel or a print media outlet has a corresponding website on which most of the content is available. So, if an entity is presented in poor light on the website of a news portal, it will show up unfavourably during an online search.

As they say, prevention is the best cure. Setting up online monitoring tools can alert one to potential issues before they snowball into a crisis.

It is imperative for businesses to develop a strong social media presence for their founders, owners, executives and other leaders. Many businesses are defined by the people who run them. People sometimes search using the names of the chief executive—Tim Cook for Apple or Satya Nadella for Microsoft and so on. Everyone for whom public relations matters ought to learn and understand search engine management and optimisation.

For instance, search for your brand using generic keywords. For example, if you run a five-star hotel in Mumbai, and if someone enters 'stay in Mumbai' as keywords, they should see your hotel as the topmost option when the search engine throws up options. If it does not include it during the first few search results, then your SEO needs to be fixed. SEO is meant to help improve the ranking of an entity organically on search engines. One way to do that is to fix content strategy, and the easiest way to build that is through blogs. Often, having nothing appear for your entity is as bad as having poor reviews. It may make people infer negative things about you, or at minimum, it leaves you open to potential brand attacks. When not much shows up for your name during an online search, it's easy for adverse content to quickly gain traction.

Very often, good behaviour by an entity and its executives can go a long way towards ensuring better online reputation. In fact, public relations or reputation management is largely about behaviour. Therefore, building robust content, connecting meaningfully with stakeholders, living up to the promises made as an entity, supporting causes based on merit, establishing credible partnerships and innovating for the betterment of society crafts a robust status online.

If you are a student reading this, ensure that you are proficient in online reputation management. If you are a chief executive who is reading this, make sure you have budgeted to hire someone who can manage online reputations. Hiring an external company to manage this is always ideal, although, internally, a team member needs to be assigned to handle the external team. If nothing else, the internal team member will liaise with the external company. If your business has competition (and which business does not?), then you will be compared. If your business is in a category that can be reviewed—cars, mobile phones, televisions—then mindfulness is key. If your reviews are being neglected and your customer service team is too small or too busy to handle it, then you are missing an opportunity to manage your online reviews, which could be detrimental to your business. In the current digital world, online reviews are worth their weight in gold. Too many negative reviews can damage an entity, whereas primarily positive reviews can keep new customers coming in. Encouraging loyal customers to share testimonials is also vital.

Social media is a rapidly-growing realm and an integral part of how an entity positions itself. People use it to scope out your social presence and determine whether they want to give you their business or work with you or not. If you're not engaging with them and responding on social media, you're missing out on a huge opportunity to grow your business.

ORM is not a single objective to be ticked off on a list. It is an ongoing process. Like most marketing, it requires constant upkeep and frequent monitoring to see how you're doing. Keeping tabs on how your entity is represented online will only help it flourish in the long term.

To better understand ORM, it is also important to understand the types of media in this context. The model we advocate is based on POEMS: paid, owned, earned media strategies. Of course, shared media is an integral part of this philosophy.

Paid media implies all content, online and offline, that requires payment to feature the name of the entity. This appears on a media outlet owned by a third party. The most common form is advertisements. However, in today's day and age, paying certain individuals in cash or kind to promote a product or say something favourable is also considered paid media. Ads on social media, websites or search engines also come under this category. An innovation that media outlets have created over the years is paid promotions, advertorials, sponsored posts and native advertising. They are all similar, with slight variations in the way they are fashioned and distributed. This type of messaging is straightforward—you have full control over your own placements.

Owned media largely relates to the website and the blog—properties that the entity fully owns and, therefore, has complete control over. In many instances, an in-house journal or a publication created for customers, like an in-flight magazine, are also owned media. Although ORM tasks may seem easier when dealing with the online spaces one controls, keep in mind that one has to establish an all-encompassing ORM process that is foolproof. This means you cannot lie just because you own the outlet, as the truth will always find its way out sooner or later.

Earned media concerns the coverage that your entity receives from external platforms free of charge. This includes media coverage that usually stems from three sources—directly from a media release that is shared, an interview given to a journalist or a contributory article written by a spokesperson. It occurs indirectly when the media outlet is doing a story that also covers other entities in the same space; these are called industry stories. Or if there is an exclusive story on the entity because the outlet sees a valid reason (extremely positive or negative) to give it coverage. Earned media is typically controlled by a credible third party although there are undoubtedly grey areas.

Shared media is anything that is created by users and then shared on social networks. One way to make this as seamless as possible is to ensure that the website mentions all the social embassies that the entity is present on. Earned media should be a focus of all businesses; these sources help craft a positive outlook and build trust with online visitors. The simplest form of earned media is word of mouth, which is what most often forms the basis of all public relations.

While you might have now understood the differences between the four types of media, it is key to appreciate how exactly an efficient ORM strategy can benefit your business. These are six reasons to invest in ORM.

❖ **It ensures awareness creation:** Content available online invariably shows up during a search, which is good for a brand. For example, a continental restaurant with a website and regular blog by the chef will show up when someone is looking for the best pasta in town, making a potential customer aware of the restaurant's existence.

❖ **It influences buying decisions:** The way one appears on the internet affects a customer's final decision. The status of your online reputation is also a business quality check—consumers are reading reviews to determine if the company they will engage with is reliable enough.

❖ **It is virtual word of mouth:** Consumers treat online reviews as personal recommendations and can trust them as much as a tip from a friend.

❖ **Better management of negative reviews:** The internet remembers everything. Well, almost. What people say about your business online is likely to remain there, but you still have a chance to alter a negative opinion about your business. Issuing a carefully worded response can turn an unhappy customer into a loyal fan.

❖ **It attracts potential employees:** An online presence helps future employees make an informed decision about the entity they are likely to sign up for. It also boosts the morale of existing employees, which is an important retention tactic.

❖ **It is helpful for valuable feedback:** Monitoring is a critical part of managing online reputations. One can easily collect some useful insights on customer satisfaction and feedback regarding the product or service as long as you simply pay attention to what customers have to say about your business.

So, how does one ensure that the online presence of a brand or business is something to reckon with? Well, it's not rocket science. A bit of quick thinking, a few tools and a culture of listening and keeping watch is all it takes. Let us see how.

ORM strategy

We believe there are just six steps to enable a robust ORM rollout at your organisation.

❖ **Define your end goal and your 'why':** Ask yourself why you wish to delve into ORM. There could be many answers. It could be that you wish to be admired online, be seen as a leader or maybe just be known for ethical stances or causes. It could be to generate leads, get higher ratings, build an employer brand or anything in the realm of building reputation. The most common response we've heard is a desire to safeguard the organisation from an online crisis. Each aspect needs a different treatment. The end goal is important and, once defined, a bit of agility in correcting it during the ORM journey does work, although essentially, it is a measurable goalpost. Establishing an ORM philosophy that includes multiple objectives can be a bit overwhelming, making it even more important to prioritise your goals. This can be based on the most important driver of your ORM need, the resources required, the impact anticipated and the availability of technology.

❖ **Establish a baseline of your online reputation vis-à-vis a thought-out peer set:** It becomes critical then to figure out what your status is in the online space. Quick research, best done in comparison with your identified peer set of brands, can give a realistic picture of where you stand and what needs to be corrected. Multiple tools are available for doing this. The basic principle of accepting a data-driven reflection of one's brand holds good. We have seen many CCOs assume that their brands are well-respected and have a great resonance with the right target groups, but the reality is often different. But once you know the reality, appropriate tactics can be employed to achieve the desired outcomes. Having a set of baseline indicators—admiration scores, response time, impressions, reach—helps strategise an incremental impact plan. Some parameters that are essential as a part of ORM philosophy:

- *Conversations:* Around the brand and its competitors
- *Tonality:* Positive, negative and neutral sentiment
- *Aspects:* Parameters specific to business (post-sales service, product lines)
- *Sample posts:* Competitor's activations and content
- *Responsiveness:* Response time to queries or rants

❖ **Acquire a holistic content strategy:** It is ideal to establish an ORM strategy through content-building. Our experience says that content that is sharply focused, bucketed in appropriate reputation-building drivers and constantly administered via social media works to build and enhance admiration for the brand. A classic set of admiration drivers could be the Kantar–Millward Brown framework. These parameters help you curate interesting content that is sustainable and engages well with online target groups. The content strategy should also include the cadence for the content, depending on the personality of your brand. The strategy should cover a repurposing philosophy so that one narrative or theme can be used across multiple platforms.

❖ **Identify the right platforms for building a positive digital safety net:** The most important part of an ORM strategy is the universe of media that needs to be tracked/ addressed and ensuring your brand is at the top on these platforms and in search. Enough has been written about social media handles, platforms, hybrid media, online portals, etc. All we wish to say is: choose the right platform on the basis of your target audience, their data consumption patterns, your markets and your own ability to service these markets in an in-depth manner. Consistency in engagement is key, and one-off interventions do not work. Having an appropriate SEO strategy in place is useful.

❖ **Activate your owned media properties:** One of the key elements of an ORM strategy is the use of owned media platforms. Blogs, online newsletters, company websites or video channels, for instance, are very effective in pushing out content to build a digital safety net. It's an owned platform, so your authentic content reaches audiences in an unfiltered manner. If engagement rates are higher, it's one of the best investments a brand could make.

❖ **Invest in a good listening tool**: Social listening is undoubtedly the biggest part of ORM strategy. Simply put, it is the monitoring of your brand's social media presence on various channels. The monitoring could be for customer feedback, rants, kudos or any banter that can build or break your brand's credibility. This is done by tracking or crawling the digital space on the basis of keywords around the brand, its personality, unique selling propositions (USPs), etc. The process is rounded off with an analysis that offers insights on the appropriate action to take based on the situation. Done vis-à-vis the identified competition peer set, it can help build brands in an informed manner. Social listening can help identify the root causes behind conversations and aid managers in taking appropriate stands. Using social listening to package content can also help you provide the kind of content your TG wants.

As brands grow in repute and size, there is a tendency to start getting unidirectional in communications. But now, we firmly believe that this is the time to shut the microphone off and put on the headphones. Listening to your consumers has become more imperative than ever before. Consumers have become vocal about their opinions and more active as well, for instance, the 'Add Yours' feature started by Instagram is aimed at followers co-creating content with brands.

To sum up the importance of listening, here are the top five reasons why social listening has garnered so much of significance.

❖ Consumer engagement
❖ Competition tracking

* ❖ Knowing your advocates
* ❖ Understanding customer sentiments
* ❖ Managing online crises with agility

The bottom line? Proactive online reputation building and management adds to your bottom line by reinforcing the credibility of your brand. Neglecting it can nullify a great reputation built over a long period of time in mere seconds. The choice is yours.

~

Narratives on social media—how important are they in building reputation?

As recent as fifteen or twenty years ago, for most of us, a high quantum of social interactions involved only simple moments of drafting elaborate letters, shooting off holiday postcards, calling someone, exchanging emails and, of course, laughs, hugs, kisses and tears. After all, humans have always been social animals who seek out the warmth of familiar companionship. But when the internet technology boom happened, it became exponentially feasible for interactions to transcend beyond existing small circles.

Of course, the fundamentals of communication haven't changed. In fact, their effect has been enhanced. Take the case of the famous 1-9-90 principle which states that 90 per cent of the participants of any community only consume content, 9 per cent of the participants change or update content and just 1 per cent of the participants create content. This was evident even in the good old days when we had only a few storytellers sharing their anecdotes within their communities, and the cap of the narrator kept rotating. The dawn of internet technology boom gave birth to hundreds of social channels, which exponentially increased the number of the communities we can feasibly be a part of. When communities increase, it is inevitable that the absolute number of storytellers (1 per cent) and consumers (90 per cent) also increases. This has led to us consuming more as well as reacting and shaping opinions across varied communities. It has reached a point where today most of us discover, build, assess, manage and maintain our decisions through narratives consumed on social media channels. In a world where social structure is everything, the channels that host such potent narratives hold immense power.

Three things that are crucial for listening and responding

Any iteration of communication involves the basic principles of context, content and corruption. If a message has to be relayed, it is mandatory that it stems from an inferred notion, has the most appropriate permutation of words and is comprehended by the participants. When the scope of such communication scales up, it becomes paramount to emphasise these principles, especially on social media channels where chatter can be boundless.

* ❖ **Context:** We listen to obtain information. We listen to understand. We listen for enjoyment. We listen to learn. And we respond accordingly. It is imperative to understand the objective behind a given message and then marry it to our objective of listening and responding. A mismatch in expectations or contextual relevance is detrimental to a message's comprehension. We need to understand the sentiment and the topicality of its origin. A simple way to observe this at scale is to pay attention to the symbols (emojis, hashtags or graphics), the stories (point of view) and the rituals (customs or habits). Solving for context is the necessary head start and, in the modern age, we can rely on monitoring tools and tactics that compartmentalise these symbols, stories and rituals.
* ❖ **Content:** As we go through monitoring and inferring notions within chatter for context, we subconsciously

start formulating our next reaction and response. The rule of thumb here is to empathise before you communicate, especially nowadays when we consume content like relentless scrolling machines. The response has to be crisp, adapted for the medium and adequately timed to ensure maximum comprehension.

❖ **Corruption:** Motive drives what one communicates; in this era of overflow of data, analytics, AI and false stories gain traction because people don't validate before responding or amplifying. It is important to avoid corruption of communication by making efforts to validate what we listen to before we respond.

Ritesh Singh is a Co-founder and
Managing Director at #ARM Worldwide

~

Inclusion of digital media for everything

Digital media is now a part of everything, including reputation management. Today, it is a more holistic combination of platforms across national and regional centres, with digital and social media seeping in extensively across age groups.

People in their sixties are shopping on Facebook, while kids in their teens are being shaped by leaders and influencers on Instagram. One can't leave any platform untouched, or leave reputation management to chance. It has to be a carefully considered proactive process.

Three things to keep in mind when building an organisation's reputation online

- ❖ Be honest when you have messed up. Acknowledge the mistake, share the corrective measures and implement them. Hiding facts can severely damage reputation since, one way or another, they will come out someday.
- ❖ Be empathetic to customers and employees in service and communication.
- ❖ ESG policies are gaining pace in India and will influence customer loyalty going forward.

Chaavi Leekha is AVP, Corporate Communications and Brand Reputation at IndiGo

~

How your organisation can gain by integrating social listening across departments

Social listening may a relatively new term, but it is here to stay. Monitoring media and keeping your ear to the ground is an old and important PR skill. However, in the digital age, traditional PR skills have been recast. Monitoring social networks for conversations around your brand, organisation, employees, competition and industry developments has become an essential practice. It allows organisations to pick up on early signals in conversations that impact business. Companies can then devise proactive responses for the issues that could affect them. The outcome of social listening could mean improvements in products, brand relevance, marketing or customer service. It could uncover trends leading to new products and pricing strategies and point to upcoming challenges being posed by competition. Or it could simply validate existing strategies and tactics. Businesses understand and appreciate the importance of social listening. However, the most innovative organisations are learning to integrate social listening across departments. They are making it part of everything, from marketing and sales to product development, customer service, HR and PR. Social listening is becoming everyone's responsibility, not just of the social media management team.

It is easy to see why social listening as a skill must permeate every function. Using social listening tools and skills, every team in the business can proactively design initiatives, conduct deeper research, tap into emerging opportunities, surprise customers and avoid crises. This contrasts with the prevailing practice of establishing a social media team that has focused but limited mandates which might not cover employee morale, competitive vectors, industry developments, evolving customer needs and so on.

There are several advantages of integrating social listening across departments. Here are the top five:

❖ Departments such as research and development (R&D), marketing, quality, customer service or PR take ownership of a product or service-related issues they are responsible for and do not need not be told by their social media team about emerging issues.

❖ Departments can respond faster to issues without depending on a social media team to update them.

❖ Departments are better equipped to interpret the social inputs and analysis, prioritising issues based on their experience and expertise.

❖ Social listening brings every team member closer to the customer.

❖ Key performance indicators related to social listening can be created that are specific to each department's goals.

Varghese Thomas is the Chief Communications Officer at Greaves Cotton Limited

~

The Big Rejig!

With the rise of social media, we've seen one trend manifest across several spheres of life: the decentralisation of the ability to create and distribute narratives. I call it the Big Rejig.

For the longest time, the ability to create a narrative and then widely distribute it was restricted to a few, such as governments, dictators, large media houses, etc. We've seen many cases of governments changing, dictators being overthrown and media houses being made irrelevant in the last fifteen years, simply because of how social media granted regular people access to such an ability as well.

Without naming names, I can share a few examples which I'm sure will resonate. In a large democratic country, an upstart political party used social media to rapidly (within two years of formation) grow a large support base and form a government! In a country which had been under the rule of a dictator for forty years, people were able to mass coordinate and overthrow him. A group of bloggers and video producers hit back at established media houses and, in less than a decade, reached and influenced a larger number of people than the establishment media does today.

Incredible—and this all happened right in front of our eyes!

When I listed who all could create and distribute narratives, I left out one group: brands. Using paid media and advertising agencies, brands could communicate (in a one-way manner) the best things they had to offer and make sure this communication was seen by millions.

But if all the other groups I mentioned felt the impact of social media, why wouldn't brands?

To recount an early example, one must remember the *United Breaks Guitars* song. This is something that happened close to fifteen years back but is indicative of how the Big Rejig would go on to fundamentally change the relationship between brands and consumers.

Dave Carroll, a musician, was travelling on a United Airlines flight and his guitar was broken in transit. The experience he had after that while dealing with airline authorities was less than stellar. As a musician, he did what he was best at and wrote a song called *United Breaks Guitars*. In the then new world of social media, this song spread like wildfire—a small musician taking on a large airline was something that could never have been done so easily before. The music video earned millions of views, but the impact on the brand was far more severe. It was widely reported that the United Airlines stock fell by 10 per cent in the aftermath of this incident—a loss of $180 million for shareholders!

No amount of money spent on great advertising can undo the impact created by one disgruntled customer. Over the years, one has seen scores of such cases. If anything, the frequency and magnitude has only increased in the ensuing years.

What then can brands and brand custodians do in such scenarios?

Firstly, equip yourself mentally by accepting that this can happen to any brand, including yours, and also practically by selecting the right tools and setting up the right teams and processes that can rise to this challenge.

Secondly, listen. Keep your ear to the ground by tracking conversations about your brand, your industry, as well as of competitors. Be on the alert for potential online reputation bombs (ORBs) and prepared to handle them when they happen (which they will).

Further, empathise in your response to consumers (whether they are your customers or not), both in public and private. Empathy is good for business.

Lastly, use the Big Rejig to your own advantage. Build a community of advocates around your product, service or experience. Involve this community in evolving your service and they will be your biggest defence against any ORB.

Make the Big Rejig your jig!

Mihir Karkare is the Co-founder and
Executive Vice President of Mirum India

6

THE RISE OF REGIONAL INFLUENCE

We were at a communications conclave following the second COVID-19 wave and the topic of conversation was regional media. And rightfully so, as six out of the ten CCOs at the table represented large international brands with a significant footprint in the regional hinterlands. Their products were consumed in rural villages and generated more revenue than some of the large cities. The discussion of rural markets and the importance of having a good top-of-the-mind recall there was getting established. However, we could sense that there was a yawning gap in the minds of these CCOs when it came to their focus on mainline publications vis-à-vis regional publications. It was unanimously felt that most were proud of their connections with *The Economic Times* or *The Hindustan Times*, but possibly had no clue on what was happening in regional media.

Historically, our audience has been one of the most outward-focused—we have been keen about national and international events and news. However, as coronavirus gripped the world, people started consuming enormous amounts of mass media during periods of isolation. Consumption patterns evolved as home-bound global audiences started looking at regional content. Urban and suburban residents, originally belonging to smaller towns and rural areas, began relying on regional online platforms for information on happenings back home.

It is patently obvious that one needs to enhance outreach in regional media in local languages, with a focus on micro-markets, micro-influencers and small publications. In fact, this is exactly what many progressive brands have started doing. From the selection of media to the influencers, brands are focusing on conquering micro-markets through earned efforts. Micro-influencers native to a region are turning out to be more impactful than one large, popular figure. Regional influence has gone up and regional media seems to be shining. India is a land of immense cultural and linguistic diversity. Each region has its idiosyncrasies when it comes to understanding and consuming data and information, even if the modes of communication are similar. With a majority of the population living in rural and semi-urban areas, use of local language becomes important in setting narratives through media. Yet it is still surprising that a majority of brands rely on major media houses that mostly cover urban Indian cities using English. The role of regional public relations is more intrinsic to integrated communications and marketing strategies for brands that are vying for an in-depth national presence.

Rise of regional media

Regional media, as the name indicates, focuses primarily on news and events that are pertinent to the area. Some may call them Tier II or Tier III markets. Regional language media is different from standard, urban, English-speaking media. There is a huge diversity in terms of region-specific public needs, especially in India which is a country that has multiple states, villages, languages and dialects. Opportunities cannot be ignored.

Regional media growth sparked by the internet boom

A study by KPMG in India and Google brings to the fore some very interesting facts: the Indian language internet user base of about 234 million in 2016 reached 536 million by 2021, at a CAGR of 18 per cent.[*] This is compared to the English internet user base that grew by 3 per cent to reach 199 million. Indian language internet users accounted for nearly 75 per cent of India's internet user base as of 2021. This growth, the report claims, will be complemented by the increasing penetration of internet-enabled devices, availability of affordable high-speed internet, India's rising digital literacy and Indian language enablement of the ecosystem, bringing more Indian language users online.

What is even more interesting in the report is that the Hindi internet user base outgrew the English user base by 2021 and, along with Marathi and Bengali users, drove volume growth. Tamil, Kannada and Telugu users were among the most digitally engaged through 2016 to 2021. Internet-enabled mobile devices are seen to be the clear choice of an Indian language user for consuming digital

---

[*] 'Online Education in India 2021: A Study by KPGM in India and Google', KPGM, May 2017, https://assets.kpmg.com/content/dam/kpmg/in/pdf/2017/05/Online-Education-in-India-2021.pdf

content. Local language digital content will witness greater acceptance from Indian language users, as they find it more reliable than English content.

A Federation of Indian Chambers of Commerce and Industry and Ernst & Young (FICCI and E&Y) report says that regional languages will make up 60 per cent of television consumption in 2025 from around 55 per cent in 2020 and around 50 per cent of streaming video consumption from 30 per cent in 2019.[*] The lockdown saw foreign streaming video operators such as Netflix and Amazon Prime Video ramp up libraries across Indian languages. That itself is an indication of the rise of Indian language media.

Linguistic affiliation enhances effectiveness

It is no secret that communication in one's mother tongue with a dash of semantic nuance can enhance the effectiveness of the narrative being presented. It is only human to seek comfort and to feel connected. Linguistic affiliation, we feel, can attract audiences and that is one of the reasons why regional language media across newspapers, social media, digital, voice and practically all modes of communication are on the rise. Technology is also enabling this. Many studies have shown that audiences respond more effectively when a brand connects with them in their local language. The effectiveness rises when plots in stories have a cultural

---

[*] 'Tuning into Consumer: Indian M&E Rebounds with a Customer-Centric Approach', FICCI–EY, March 2022, https://assets.ey.com/content/dam/ey-sites/ey-com/en_in/topics/media-and-entertainment/2022/ey-ficci-m-and-e-report-tuning-into-consumer_v3.pdf.

significance in the regions these audiences belong to. In short, it's important for brands speak the language of their consumers.

Even regional traditional media (print) growth, circulation and reach is higher than that of their English language counterparts.

❖ As per Indian Readership Survey (IRS) figures, nine out of ten top online newspapers are in regional languages. *The Times of India* was the only English language publication on the top ten list and was placed ninth.[*]

❖ English language newspapers were hit harder and struggled to get back their circulation post the pandemic, particularly in major metro cities, while regional language newspapers recovered a larger portion of their lost circulation.

❖ Large news networks will focus on increasing the collection of regional news to create very strong regional products (print and digital) of extremely high relevance to audiences—news that national and large digital news aggregators may not be able to provide.

❖ *Malayala Manorama, Daily Thanthi, Mathrubhumi* and *Lokmat* are newspapers which cater to readers in only one regional language, unlike Hindi (which has a Hindi belt support)—and yet, their readership is far ahead.

It is no surprise that media operating at regional levels has a larger impact on a citizen's participation in democracy. The relationship between regional publications and audiences

---

[*] 'Indian Readership Survey 2019 Q4' Nielsen, 8 May 2020, https://mruc.net/uploads/posts/cd072cdc13d2fe48ac660374d0c22a5d.pdf.

from the respective province tends to be stronger and closer than the same with national publications. That linguistic affiliation and proximity often leads to loyalty towards overall regional media.

Earned media strategy in regional markets or, simply put, local PR focus by brands has been on the rise. Driven by the digital revolution, there is a clear dominance of digital publications that cater to local audiences. In fact, to make a narrative more effective, a regional twist is necessary and naturally, we see the growing significance of local or hyperlocal targeting for better results.

Regional media can deliver a robust consumer connection

Multiple reports have clearly shown that Tier II and III markets are booming and brands are vying for their share in such rural markets. With the penetration of the internet, these markets are becoming the driving force behind e-commerce growth in the country. Brands and public relations professionals now need to reflect on how they are connecting with these audiences. Are brands moulding their narratives specifically to the regions and their cultural nuances, and customising them according to local languages? One size does not fit all in this case. Does regional PR figure in the overall marketing mix as a strategic tool? Do we make efforts to understand these micro-markets and connect with the audiences through content and platforms that they find easy to access and believe?

This is the time to build that connection.

In fact, in the advertising world, although English advertisements were being dubbed into regional languages, we now see a trend of original, regional, customised content being produced. Can PR folks tailor their press notes to each specific region?

It is high time they did.

The FICCI–E&Y report also mentions that internet growth is fuelled by regional subscribers, and that the share of language advertising will only grow. Although their claim that ultimately half of the ads will be made in regional languages followed by Hindi (47 per cent) and 3–4 per cent in English needs to be tested, the fact remains that language is a great connector and consuming content in one's own mother tongue is always preferred. In its 'Year in Search 2020' report, Google said that more than 90 per cent of YouTube users preferred watching content in Indic languages.[*]

Rise of regional influence

Based on anecdotal evidence, reaching Tier II and III markets has always been a challenge for national brands. Today, however, regional influencers have become a highly sought-after set of people. They have astounding reach and engagement with their audiences and their followers look to them for new trends and information. Regional influencers create content that is relatable, culturally closer and seemingly more authentic than someone not from the same region. Such influencers have a ready-made set of customers, which makes it possible for brands to reach out through the influencer to the consumer instead of

---

[*] 'Year in Search 2020 India—India's Determined Progress', Google, 2020, https://services.google.com/fh/files/events/yis_india_2020.pdf.

trying to create their own platforms. Of course, owned media platforms are going to be the future. However, reaching audiences quickly in an reliable manner through credible influencers is a smart way too. Our research has clearly shown that more and more brands are depending on regional influencers, more than big celebrity brand advocates, to reach their potential customers. The most significant advantage of regional influencers is that they help brands engage with their audience in local languages, making it more colloquial. Of course, cost benefits are the icing on the cake!

In 2023, we have certainly stepped into a new era that is based on sharper targeting, frugality, focus on authenticity, empathy and an even bigger focus on effectiveness. Some of the emerging trends are certainly propelling regional PR in India to realms of higher affinity with brands and a need to re-examine the way brands have engaged with regional audiences through traditional and digital PR.

Regional storytelling is becoming a serious business. Crafting stories that have relevance to regional nuances has never been more important. Cultural references and habits change from region to region and Indian language users generally prefer to consume regional news. Of course, data and facts are important, but the trick is to appropriately package the narrative in a way that it connects with audiences instantly. Companies curating regional news in Indian languages are seen to be reaping significant benefits over the ones telling their stories only to English-speaking city-dwelling audiences.

Regional online platforms are booming and online platforms of regional newspapers are seemingly grabbing more eyeballs, especially from young, tech-savvy audiences. Enhanced penetration of the internet and ever-improving digital literacy is ensuring more stickiness to online platforms and the level of online news consumption has gone up. Easy availability of smartphones with regional language enablement also has led to this growth. Furthermore, significant advancement in technologies enabling voice recognition and translation abilities will lead to a language-agnostic internet and drive more Indian language consumers online. With the advent of AI and CommsTech, it is possible to get language-specific data analytical capabilities which ought to encourage brand owners to invest further in online platforms. This has the potential to become a cycle of consumers coming for content, brands creating more and more language content, leading to an increase in readership and effectiveness. Although Indian languages currently have different internet adoption levels, Marathi, Bengali, Tamilian and Telugu internet users are expected to form 30 per cent of the Indian language internet user base. The writing is on the wall.

Cracking the code

Based on our practical experience on manoeuvring through the diverse maze of the Indian PR landscape, we are sharing our thoughts on how to crack the regional media code. Here are some observations and strategies that have worked well for us.

❖ **One size does not fit all:** With the kind of diversity and complexity in terms of languages, cultures and news consumption patterns across multiple segments of audiences, it is a herculean task to reach out to all groups in India using one language. Public relations professionals need to think local and adopt strategies to conquer micro-markets. A news dissemination strategy going forward needs to have a robust mapping of regional publications along with regular English publications. A story conceptualised in English may not work in a Marathi or Tamil region unless cultural nuances of the respective regions are embedded in the story.

❖ **Localise content, making it more relevant:** Original language press notes carrying the narrative with links to the region would be more effective. Localisation of a story with the brand USP and narrative can create in-depth connections. A campaign must be able to spark local impact if the right CTA is desired.

❖ **Provide data:** PR for regional media, like any other media, relies on data. Whether for storytelling, crisis mitigation or influencer engagement—without data, you are fumbling in the dark. Stories you share with audiences must be factual, data-based and inclusive. One way to do this is to use research-driven narratives to tell your stories. The truth is that in times of shrinking editorial spaces and rising fake news, regional media trust has also been skewed towards data-driven stories.

❖ **Increase RBMs, build spokespeople:** Relationship building meetings (RBM) are key to regional media success. We have seen that city-based media rounds by PR professionals are quite calendarised. However, given the rise in the number of effective regional journalists and micro-influencers who are subject matter experts, reaching out to them formally or informally in their domains is seen as a good gesture that helps build deeper connections. In fact, our experiences says that regional media reporters look forward to meeting spokespersons in person and putting a face to the name that they cite in their stories. Senior leadership or spokespersons generally travel to regions to evaluate markets, for store openings or just to meet and motivate local staff. These opportunities could be utilised to meet key journalists informally. This, in our experience, has never gone waste. Having a spokesperson who can speak the local language is very helpful.

❖ **Localised media buying:** We have also witnessed that, in many cases, the local reporters are also the agents for collecting advertisements. They do have a target and their operations are generally commission-based. We are not going into the realm of paid media, but sometimes, it helps brands to advertise with these regional publications which generally are not recommended by media buying agencies.

❖ **Owned media platforms in regional languages:** A very important and under-explored means of effectively engaging regional audiences is to build owned media platforms in those languages. We are fully conscious that practically, it is not possible to have multiple language renditions of a website or blog. However, considering a cost-to-benefit ratio might not be such an audacious idea. Technology enables measurement and tracking of language-based communications. Readers in rural areas where English has not penetrated well can benefit from the use of owned media properties like blogs, sites, interactive games and original content in the local language.

❖ **Have focus on media and media alone, don't mix up events:** Treat local/regional media with respect and give them the desired recognition. Engage with them when you are doing a launch in rural areas. Make them partners in co-creating content. It helps. The local pride of a regional media house is immense and the influence they have is significant. Sometimes, working with them to co-host events just for media works better than only making them a part of an event as spectators. Co-creation of stories with regional media is effective and we have seen great results when ownership is shared.

❖ **Invest in a good local PR partner:** As regional PR garners more significance, consultancies with deep knowledge of the regional media landscape will as well. Regional PR partners can help brands understand the needs of local audiences, current trending situations and relevant media and can be very good for enhancing the effectiveness of communication. These partners should be able to create hyperlocal connections, counsel on realistic ground situations, know the mood of the audience and provide critical insights for developing the local outreach strategy. If not a full-fledged consultancy, a network of stringers or freelance journalists, videographers or photographers should be developed. Local publications have stringers in surrounding small towns, whereas major news organisations may have stringers in dozens of regions. Quite often, the contributions of stringers go unnoticed as they may not get the byline, but this network is indispensable when it comes to a brand's outreach in far-flung areas.

In summing up, it is indisputable that regional influence has risen exponentially. Regional media will naturally assume a large part of our communications mix. There are also powerful tools available to assist those seeking to tap into these exciting pools of opportunity spread out across the country, such as the technology to track and translate languages in real time. National brands eager to get ahead are already aware that not all customers are sitting in metropolitan cities. It is up to you to innovate in this space and raise the bar of regional media outreach endeavours.

∼

A regional twist to the existing national story is overdue

Still an unorganised segment within an organised ecosystem, regional PR in India has grown rapidly over the last two decades, with a budget allocation rising six-fold during this time frame. Regional cities and media both are ever evolving, highly dynamic and have socio-cultural nuances that are unique to their identities, making them rife with exciting new opportunities. Despite this, the current size of the regional PR pie in a country where a majority of the population lives beyond metropolitan cities is miniscule.

But why is that the case? I clearly see three reasons for it.

❖ **Indian PR business is concentrated around global brands:** In an overall Rs 2,000-crore Indian PR business, a significant part of the pie still comes from globally controlled brands. Because of strategic decisions being made outside the country and the lack of effort being put in by Indian corporate communicators on educating their global counterparts, we remain limited to English-based media and narrow geographical range. However, with the advent of the start-up and entrepreneurship culture, the scenario is changing. In the last decade, with consumers residing beyond major cities having better purchasing power and exposure, brands have had no option but to concentrate on regional India, although cracking how best to synergise their communication with regional media has remained a skill that only a few have developed.

❖ **Diverse, vast, humongous:** All three words combined can't map the ocean that regional media is. India is a land where dialect changes every few miles and thousands of media houses function in hundreds of local regional languages (more than twenty being highly prominent), where rural households still take pride in subscribing to a newspaper and tune in to their local cable TV to gather what is happening around them. It is impossible to understand the importance, stature, responsibility and power of regional media. We have started waking up to the remarkable potential that regional areas have to offer and the role regional media plays in shaping perceptions here, but there is still a long road ahead. We need to start investing in understanding how a consumer residing in a Tier II/III/IV town or a village thinks, understand their culture and belief systems and then carve out the stories relevant to them for the brands we work with. Mere replication of communication strategies drafted for major cities has ceased to work across the country and the sooner we realise this the better. Every zone of our country is a completely different matrix in itself and has to be dealt with accordingly. The last twelve years of my career have only been about understanding regional media and trying to shape impactful strategies for brands I work with, but it still amazes and surprises me every single day and that's the beauty of its diversity. You need to be connected to the roots to effectively find solutions for cracking regional media for your brand.

❖ **The problem of focus and talent:** We end up concentrating on major cities and a national PR strategy because of the two reasons mentioned above. Because we do so, in my opinion, most of the PR workforce in India remains oblivious to how regional media functions and we run into a lack of focus and a lack of talent. Unless corporates and consultancies place focus on developing professionals who understand the functioning of regional India and regional media, change will be hard to foster.

The dominance of platforms which cater to regional and local readerships is imminent. PR, as a business, is nearing a saturation point in major cities and future growth has to stem from smaller ones. I expect to see tremendous growth in the area of regional PR in coming years.

Mukesh Kharbanda is the Managing Director of
Fuzion PR

~

Regional media has always been strong. Why the sudden increase in importance?

Regional markets are accelerating digital growth

Over the last decade, digital brands have witnessed an overwhelming response from India's Tier II, III, IV and V markets. Marketers strive to influence, connect and engage with these disparate markets spread across the length and breadth of our country. With the smartphone and digital explosion, online news consumption has grown at an accelerated pace.

Emerging New India

India's economy is developing rapidly and micro, small and medium enterprises (MSMEs) are contributing to the country's growth since they span the metro cities as well as the non-metro ones. New India is not just helping build new job opportunities but also contributing to the growth of professional education, engineering, medical colleges, management education and B-Schools emerging in non-metro cities. Such activities are reflected in various city indices, including the growth of regional media.

Pandemic and reverse migration

During the COVID-19 humanitarian crisis, millions of people across sections decided to return to their hometowns and villages. The reverse migration was either for wanting to be closer to the families during a crisis or for having lost jobs. In either situation, folks embraced regional and rural lifestyles for good. This reverse migration has significantly contributed to regional media's growth.

Top three tools in dealing with regional media

Knowledge of tactical strategies

While dealing with local press, the key to success is becoming one of them. Local media tends to reject foreign treatment or lack local market knowledge while pitching for stories. Staff from top metro cities often fail to comprehend the subtle nuances of dealing with local media. Hiring a local firm or a stringer who can be an excellent asset for your campaign is recommended.

Preference of local spokesperson

Invariably, the spokesperson promoted in mainstream or national media may need to gel better in the story pitches to the regional press. It is recommended to create a local city-centric PR activity by involving the local media and a provincial spokesperson who can connect and communicate facts and findings of the local flavour.

Factual, localised information

While national media content tends to include data points or references of global or international stature, the information contained in regional press must be cross-validated to reflect local district data points only. Any disparities in such data points can be resolved by taking the help of local media and authorities.

Rachana Chowdhary is the Founder and CEO of
Media Value Works

~

Regional language media is most certainly dominating in terms of numbers

Even though the last IRS (Q4 2019) showed a steady decline of readership in regional language newspapers, the fact is that they continue to dominate the newspaper segment within media in India.

The scene is not very different when it comes to satellite TV. Broadcast Audience Research Council's (BARC) data suggests that among the top ten most-watched TV channels in India, there's not even a single English one.[*]

That's also the case with the top ten websites or mobile apps in India. Even as people use Google or WhatsApp, they continue to speak in their own languages, either by searching in Hindi or sending messages in Tamil or Telugu since every mobile phone now has Indian language keyboards.

Every way one sees it, regional language media—better framed as Indian language media—is most certainly dominating in terms of numbers. But it is also true that despite being far smaller vis-à-vis readers, viewers or users, English language media in all forms has a disproportionate share of setting the agenda in terms of conversations generated at a national level.

This is not to say that the impact of Indian language media is negligible. A better way to articulate the impact would be that there seems to be a mistaken perception that unless something makes it to the English language media, it is not relevant enough. So, the opportunity is for stakeholders to look beyond English language media consciously to create impact and craft language-specific narratives to reach those audiences.

Unfortunately, a large part of the Indian language media seems to be operating on less stringent ethical standards. So, from a PR point of view, it is almost universally understood that anything to do with Indian language media, particularly print, is via sponsored content.

But quite a few inventive PR practitioners have found ways to engage with Indian language media on behalf of clients using the oldest method in public relations:

---

[*] BARC: What India Watches, https://www.barcindia.co.in/data-insights.

understanding the target audience in those media outlets and speaking to them in a way they appreciate!

In a way, it's also the story of advertising in India. When national brands communicate through a pan-Indian campaign, there is a tendency to assume 'Hindi chalega' for all of India. Similarly, PR is presumed to be English-first in India. And this is where the opportunity lies. Just as how most PR consultancies have sector specialists (healthcare, technology, entertainment and so on), it helps to have language specialists if the consultancies or their clients want to make a notable impact in Indian language media. These language specialists would be sector-agnostic, be able to understand the crux of client communication, have the ability to creatively and intelligently translate or rephrase the content and engage meaningfully with the relevant players.

Looking beyond consultancies, from a client's perspective, Indian language-centric communication is getting hugely creative. Consider the example of a national brand like Parachute's coconut oil. The company recently launched a new product pack with Tamil text to appeal to Tamilians. Bisleri's packaging for its water bottles is in nine Indian languages for different states. Coca-Cola has product packs with the brand name written in Bangla. And Titan takes the cake—it actually has a unique watch range with the text on the dial written in Tamil!

In the entertainment industry, language barriers are being chipped away at gradually as streaming services have made dubbed and subtitled content popular, making spoken language kind of irrelevant—we have movies from all corners of the world capturing the imagination of the audiences across India. However, in entertainment, the content is the ultimate destination and product—the content's consumption is the very point and the call to action. But in corporate communications and PR, the content (whether spoken, written or any other format) is only a vehicle towards getting the target audience to perform an intended call to action.

Within that context, every client organisation, its CEO and PR practitioners could seek inspiration from an advertising veteran. David Ogilvy famously said, 'I don't know the rules of grammar. If you're trying to persuade people to do something, or buy something, it seems to me you should use their language, the language they use every day, the language in which they think.'

Karthik Srinivasan is a
communications strategy consultant

~

Regional media—a defining factor in future of communications

Communication is effective when it is personal, emotional and, most importantly, localised. Thanks to technological advancement and the digital media, the market has become hyperlocal and dynamic. The internet has bridged geographical boundaries, giving unlimited access to information and making brands, services and products universal, but a brand's success depends on speaking the local dialect. For a communications professional, this blurring of boundaries has created both opportunities and challenges, since gaining the trust of the local community is the key for any brand to enhance its national and global reputation.

It was Nelson Mandela who said: 'If you talk to a man in a language he understands, that goes to his head. If you talk to him in his language, that goes to his heart.' To be successful and accepted, whether new or established, a global brand will need to engage with the stakeholders in not just a local language but also in their local dialect. But what if you work in India, where, as the saying goes, '*Kos-kos par badle paani, chaar kos par baani*'? (The language spoken in India changes every few kilometres, just like the taste of the water).

With more than 120 major languages and 1,599 other languages, every region of India has a different culture, making it one of the most diversified nations. While Hindi and English continue to be the most commonly used languages in urban cities, the vast majority of the Indian population still lives in semi-urban and rural areas, each with its multitude of languages and regional nuances. The task of communicating to this mass population often poses interesting challenges that are typical of certain regions.

Naturally, people love attention, but what makes it more effective is personalised attention which leaves a longer imprint on them. People engage more with content in their local, regional dialect and relate with the brand campaign as it makes them feel inclusive. They tend to trust the brand more if it makes them feel that the communication is tailored just for them. This helps the brand build an active and engaged community, which, besides being their customers, will act like local brand advocates.

To maximise reach with these audiences it's important to have deep region-wise insights. The content and the entire messaging have to consider local cultural nuances and linguistic preferences and segmentation of the targeted audience. Based on these, you can craft thoughtful, localised content, which connects to folks on a more personal level, and then, through strategic integrations and dissemination, develop a closer relationship with the community.

Regional media can be used as an effective tool for communication outreach by providing localised content tailored specifically for audiences in each region or state within India. The traction on vernacular content outpaces English as these people prefer to read, listen to or watch content in their local language. It is unquestionable that there is a surge of interest in hyperlocal vernacular content. This helps organisations ensure that their message resonates with local communities and drives engagement from potential customers who may not have been exposed to such information before due to language barriers or lack of access to national news channels or publications. It also allows organisations targeting specific regions with campaigns tailored solely towards those areas, avoiding national outreach while still reaching out effectively where it matters most. These also help in strengthening the bond, generating credibility and leading to trust for the organisation.

With the growing demand for local, vernacular content, the regional content ecosystem will continue to mature and provide interesting opportunities for communication professionals. The future is full of promise and prosperity. It is critical for communicators to engage and re-engage with customised relevant content to broaden the market base for organisations.

Anup Sharma is an independent communications strategy consultant

7

QUIRK AND CREATIVITY IN PR

We were meeting a bunch of PR consultancy heads and CCOs for a brainstorming session over coffee on a subject that needed their collective attention. One of the consultancy heads had just returned from a pitch delivered to a leading brand for their PR requirements. He was smiling broadly, perhaps in the anticipation that he would most probably win the account. His bullishness over winning the pitch was due to the compliment the client had given him about how his presentation and ideas were full of 'creativity'.

Jumping into this conversation, the CCO of a large multinational in the group validated the fact that clients today are primarily looking for creativity and agility, assuming the rest is hygiene for any large PR consultancy of repute. He went on to offer an example of how an advertising agency won a pitch for one of his FMCG products on the basis of how uniquely the pitch was presented. Unlike the other participants who presented the idea for a jingle through a PowerPoint presentation with never-ending slides, they did something different. They brought out a guitar, wore T-shirts with the brand message and sang the jingle together, evoking the essence of the brand, the tune and the concept and ended by saying they were convinced that this would work wonders. They were signed up!

Despite another underwhelming year at Cannes, the 2022 'Creativity in PR' study by PRovoke Media reveals that client expectations of the creativity of PR consultancies rose during the COVID-19 era—60 per cent report higher client expectations when it began, with a weighted score of 6.59 out of 10 reflecting the higher premium placed on creative ability.[*]

Creativity, we feel, is a commonly used word but remains one that is difficult to define. Most people think they are either highly creative or hardly creative. Very few are in between. Yet, everyone wants creative people to work on projects. Creativity is subjective. Creativity is thinking on one's feet. Creativity is hitting the ground running and making an impact. Creativity is about disruption and innovation. Creativity is about standing out and making a difference. And creativity is an integral aspect of public relations.

We are personally quite intrigued with what goes into being creative and making things happen in a way that ensures a campaign stays in people's minds. One must remember that the word 'campaign' was originally used to denote ancient warfare. Today, the word has been adapted for areas such as business, marketing, advertising, communications and public relations. Everyone who pays

---

[*] 'Creativity in PR', PRovoke Media, 2022, https://www.provokemedia.com/ranking-and-data/creativity-in-pr.

for the campaign expects it to be creative. Brands want people to like a campaign, remember it and, through the process, like and recall the brand.

So, creativity can stem from a detailed brief or even be just a random idea that someone has come up with. The real test is in the execution of it. And an idea is only as good as when it is executed well.

For some reason, most of the CCOs we spoke with did not think that PR professionals are truly creative. We do not wish to generalise, but it seems true in many cases. Of course, we truly believe that a bit of enhanced creativity in PR will do a lot of good. Clients or management teams expect PR consultancies and in-house teams to suggest fresh concepts, hold innovative campaigns and demonstrate agile execution for longer-lasting impact and recall.

The PRovoke Media is a great thought leadership piece. According to the study, across the world, 68 per cent of PR consultancy respondents claim their clients are more likely to approach the PR team for 'big creative ideas' now than in the past. There has been a significant increase in consultancies who have the position of a creative director, from 37 per cent to 56 per cent. However, a barrier to PR teams showing out-of-the-box creative ideas happens to be their clients' aversion to plans untested by risk. So, the onus is on both the clients and consultancies to embrace creativity. It is, after all, storytelling, and stories can be told in many ways. PR is not a channel or a medium or a vehicle, it's a process. There is no reason why PR professionals should not be just as comfortable suggesting a flash mob as they are recommending a press conference. We firmly believe that creativity is a strong problem-solving tool to help professionals achieve their communication objectives.

Some of the current trends we've already discussed, such as social listening, tapping into micro-influencers and regional media and focusing on authentic, inclusive narratives based on data, require creative and dynamic ways of looking at how PR is done with agility.

Creativity and PR

In a nutshell, creativity embodies the ability to be fluid, inventive and come up with new ideas that can solve problems.

If we extrapolate this definition to PR, it could mean an idea, concept, design or copy that can capture audience attention and communicate the message more effectively— something that can be manifested across all modes of communications for all audiences.

The PRovoke Media study also identified that 54 per cent of clients said that creativity ranked nine out of ten for importance while considering whether to hire a specific PR consultancy. The same study also revealed that 71 per cent of PR professionals or consultancies believed that client feedback or risk aversion was the biggest barrier to creativity. This clearly demonstrates a gap between expectation and delivery.

Having said that, for a successful PR strategy, creativity is a core element among many others.

Creativity, we believe, is infinite. In PR, it can allow brands and businesses to nurture deeper engagement with their stakeholders in ways never thought of before.

For consultancies, creativity can win pitches. After all, nowadays, with the general experience across PR consultancies being almost uniform, what could be the deciding factor for a client to consider? What is that winning ingredient? We feel it is creativity across all levels—be it in approach, processes or communication. Being creative in public relations involves thinking outside the box to stand out from a crowd. Doing the same thing as everyone else tends to become mundane. The current media landscape, fuelled by digital technologies and platforms, provides multiple possibilities for introducing creativity to PR.

From a journalist's angle too, anything that is original, different or has a creative twang is likely to be picked up earlier since it is more likely to spark conversations, enhance shareability and even tap audiences at an emotional level.

Being creative in public relations also implies an ability to add multiple layers of perspective to the narrative, allowing one to tell stories with innovative hooks.

In times of diminishing attention spans, keeping your audiences captivated is critical. In fact, come to think of it, creativity plays a role in all facets of public relations— writing a press note, campaign planning, social media content, research-driven narratives, design thinking and more.

Gone are the days when just a fancy tagline, a few press notes and a story in the news could generate attention and ensure brand recall. The purpose of a brand must come alive in all aspects. The good part is that consistent messaging through different means and modes of communication is what builds brands. Creativity is crucial, irrespective of the industry. Your campaign has to be able to grab attention, leave a lasting impression and enhance consumer affinity. How do you imaginatively cut through the clutter and get picked up by the media and stay in people's minds? We spoke to many CCOs and PR professionals from various consultancies in India. The unanimous verdict: creativity is the answer. The conversations were even more exciting, with great examples of how each one of them has experimented and achieved better results with a dash of ingenuity when executing campaigns. Here's how you can do the same.

Launch formats integrated with neutral key opinion leaders

While it is amazing to talk about your own brand or service, most of the time, letting someone else do the talking is much more valuable and impressive. Third-party acknowledgement or advocacy is one of the best ways to bring out your brand's essence. Brands today follow a unique format of having a round table discussion with industry experts, key opinion leaders, influencers and even customers to bring out the 'need, solution, proof' of a brand. This format works better than just a brand head or a CEO making a presentation to the media during the launch. The narrative is generally a larger issue that the brand is trying to solve. These sorts of conversations not only help highlight the unique selling points (USPs) of the brand but also elevate it to the realms of thought leadership. The narrative is deemed authentic since it has been set by third parties. This format works best for leading brands that are trying to solve a larger issue which is generally known by the masses but needs a nudge from external credible opinion leaders like doctors, technology experts, social scientists, etc.

Piggybacking on a social cause to drive brand PR

We have seen a lot of brands effectively taking up causes that plague society. These causes may not be directly related to the purpose of the brands, but do raise the stature of the brand associating with the cause just because of the gravitas of the situation. Of course, some of the brands whose purpose is to help a particular cause can sustain their efforts and are able to showcase long-term impact. These causes could be around LGBTQ+ issues, protecting masses from diseases of various kinds, alleviating the pain of the homeless, conservation of natural resources, busting myths around cultural issues, diversity, etc. Brands seen in the correct light (attempting to solve a problem and/or supporting a cause) are considered more favourably than those that just advertise their USPs and features.

Digital PR and social press releases

Social media is an integral part of PR. Embrace it and take advantage. Digital PR, which we have defined as 'earned social media', opens a plethora of opportunities to amplify your message. We have seen the use of a digital press release where the headline is a hashtag, the boilerplate is a link to the website, the copy is a set of key messages that are shareable and the images are embedded with clickable links to various social media handles. In times to come, we reckon there would also be a rise in the use of video press releases since they would make the life of a digital influencer simpler, along with a creatively crafted digital press note that would have all that needs to said via easily shareable graphics.

Hybrid media-driven campaigns

The thin lines between paid, owned and earned media have blurred. Hybrid media campaigns have shown a lot of promise. These platforms, with millions of followers, have their own reporters who craft creative content for you. These stories strike a chord with their followers and the traction is high. Creativity also means going beyond the realms of your own bastions and experimenting with different formats. Customers are interested in authentic content and if that caveat is fulfilled, you are on a roll with hybrid media.

Conquering micro-markets

Creativity can also be demonstrated in the way one reaches out to consumers. In a diverse country like India, cultural nuances play an important role in defining the effectiveness of communications. If one must conquer micro-markets, one needs to have a strong regional media focus. In a technology-enabled world, measurement and tracking is possible in most of the languages. Creativity in packaging the content or narratives in multiple languages, laced with local cultural sensitivities, can be effective and we do see a rise in original native content being created lately.

Data and insights to build conversations

In-depth research can produce strong findings which can be woven into press releases, media interviews and sales collateral. It's just about choosing the right topics and headline-creating questions. The best part of researched data-driven campaigns is long-tailing. The data can be repurposed authentically for multiple publications and can be referred to multiple times in different stories and narratives in easy-to-understand formats.

PR professionals need to (and can) raise their creative quotient

As public relations professionals, a key to success is being one step ahead of the client and the competition. This means reinventing and reimagining their PR arsenal on the fly. Regardless of the industry, clients are expecting more. In these times, it has become vital to bring out fresh ideas and be agile in execution. For that to happen, there need to be mechanisms that constantly ignite creative thinking in the minds of public relations professionals.

So, what goes into the creative process? There is no straight answer, as creativity and the road to being creative is subjective. But there are also many factors that play a role in being creative. Let's start with the simplest ones. Creativity is all around us. It is how we tap into it and apply it to our daily adventures is what matters.

❖ **Thinking:** When we think, we get creative! Thinking is the most common reflex when being asked to get creative. We think of past events, of things we have seen and heard, our many life experiences and other factors which inform the creative process.

❖ **Being curious and observant:** Having a good nose (for news) and sharp ears (for listening to customers) is key. Be curious about understanding the product, the business landscape and your competition. A burning desire to constantly evolve in thinking, having the mindset for experimentation and being inquisitive about business levers helps.

❖ **Dreaming:** Dreaming allows us to let our imagination run wild and come up with things that may never have been done before. A lot of our creative juices flow when we dream about things that we want to see.

❖ **Reading:** When we read books and other literature, we are exposed to the thoughts of others that can inspire us in a certain direction and helps us get inventive. Reading is a great habit—it helps us store a wealth of knowledge that we can retrieve at a later stage.

❖ **Writing:** Penning our thoughts down has many benefits. It can be therapeutic and help nurture clarity in our thinking. Very often, writing ends up producing a creative flow that can enhance an idea to the next level.

❖ **Travelling:** While travel can be expensive, it is one of the best gifts one can give oneself now and then. Travel allows us to see the world through a unique lens and helps us unleash creativity.

❖ **Meeting people:** This is different from the work meetings we have. Meeting people is about exchanging notes, especially with people outside our comfort zone. Very often, a first meeting with someone triggers an idea.

❖ **Thinking like a child:** Years of conditioning and life experiences have limited the thinking capabilities of adults. A child's ability to look at things objectively and without prejudice offers unique perspectives.

❖ **Visiting stores and markets:** This is especially helpful for brands that sell via retail. A lot of FMCG brands can gain insights for creative campaigns from what goes on in the store and in the marketplace.

❖ **Watching audio-visual content:** The movies, documentaries and shows we watch are all inspired by real life. Many of these give us clues that we can include in our plans. Creativity can come from the most unlikely places.

❖ **Brainstorming:** When teams huddle together for a brainstorming session, several interesting ideas often overflow. However, brainstorming has its own limitations as ideas from the same team can become stale if tapped into again and again. We have experienced wonderful results when outsiders or non-PR professionals are brought into ideating sessions. Multiple perspectives most often help crack ideas for which PR professionals may have developed a blind spot.

❖ **Challenge every hypothesis:** The does not mean breaking norms, it means asking more questions. Speak up. Challenge the correct amount of risk a brand can take and question everything.

❖ **Current affairs:** Moment marketing is when brands pull off a campaign without too much lead time based on real-time events, be it politics, sport or business.

❖ **Cross-pollination:** Using an idea that has worked in one sector in another one can generate a fresh perspective for the latter.

Most importantly, creating a fun and a positive work ambience with no fear of failure really boosts creativity. Creativity, we firmly believe, is the X factor that boosts the outcomes of a PR campaign.

∾

Serious fun—the brief wins, always!

The first thing to always remember about PR is that it is the full of variables. It involves navigating through a rapidly changing environment with only one constant: the client's interest.

Quirkiness, however, need not necessarily be at odds with this. In fact, 'cool' communication campaigns can often lead to meaningful outcomes. Being quirky or innovative will resonate with many a target audience. I believe, however, that one can push this envelope only so far. Undoubtedly, imaginatively communicating your message may provide endless opportunities and more exciting and revolutionary ways to tell stories and engage audiences but at the same time, the campaign must not hurt the brand and strain the larger social fabric.

Some examples of 'quirky' communication campaigns that backfired include the FabIndia *Jashn-e-Riwaaz* film, the Manyavar Kanyadaan campaign, the Brooke Bond elder abandonment social campaign and the Fem bleach Karwa Chauth campaign. Many of these created huge blowbacks for the brands and mired the organisations in morasses of their own making. On the other hand, successful quirky campaigns range from the Surf COVID-19 Holi campaign, Godrej's consumer messages, advertisements by various food delivery apps—all of which have been quite successful.

The quirkiness quotient in a communications campaign must be indexed, by my reckoning, on three variables: the sector or subject you are dealing with, the audience you are talking to and the occasion. Subjects such as consumer goods, celebrity associations, leisure and other light-hearted topics eminently deserve innovative treatment and can benefit from sharp, pointed quirkiness, especially when one is addressing an audience that would appreciate a small laugh. Serious subjects such as health, policy, finance or topics with a backdrop of extreme situations involving human tragedy are best kept that way—sombre and grounded. The talisman here is insight. By using research-based insights and calculating a campaign's possible impact, negative fallouts can be anticipated and avoided.

Unlike advertising, where it is possible to exercise control over the message and the medium, a PR campaign needs more care as to how it can encompass light-hearted originality and solemnity without being too heavy-handed on either end. This is particularly true in today's hyper-sensitive environment where a campaign meant for one target audience can easily transcend and overshoot its boundaries to affect other audience groups because of social and electronic media.

As far as the issue of pepping up PR campaigns goes, here are my pointers. Firstly, be clear and remain connected with the key objective always. Use relevant humour, do not ridicule. Be bold, precise and confident. Secondly, understand all possible impact dimensions (cultural, social, historical) before mounting a campaign to avoid coming across as tone-deaf. Third, develop feedback controls early on—tune and course-correct along the campaign trail. In summary: Quirk should not irk, but work!

Dilip Yadav is Co-founder of First Partners

Cutting through the clutter

Both the message and the way of delivering it (and here we can mean the method, the channels, the time and context of delivery) are equally important for any communication, especially so in PR, an area which manages one of the most important assets anyone has: reputation. Crafting the most perfect message and then delivering it in the wrong way, to the wrong people, or at the wrong moment is like building a fantastic spaceship and then sending it to the wrong planet—a complete waste of resources. And, of course, preparing the most effective mix of channels and timing everything perfectly but then delivering an incorrect message can also do a lot more harm than good. Spending an equal amount of effort on both the message and the method of delivery is recommended.

Top three ways in which you can craft a campaign so that it stands out

❖ Make sure the whole campaign has ONE big idea—a single umbrella concept that ties all the other elements of the campaign together in a beautiful, clear, exciting narrative that communicates your message. The biggest mistake is not to have a clear umbrella concept for your campaign. The second biggest mistake is to have too many concepts in the same campaign for the same audience. It's like throwing someone many balls at the same time and expecting that person to catch them all—that's never going to happen. Keep it simple.

❖ Make sure your concept is genuinely creative. You have to embrace what's never been done before. I believe there's unfortunately little emphasis on originality in PR—professionals tend to favour the old, tried-and-tested methods versus new ones. Of course, new ideas are risky—you cannot know for sure if they're going to work. But if you want a campaign to stand out, you need a good amount of creativity or your work will get lost in the crowd and have very little impact.

❖ Make sure you actually craft the campaign. Having a great creative idea is important, but so is the way you bring that idea to life. Every element of the campaign needs love and attention.

Gabriela Lungu is the Founder of
Wings Creative Leadership Lab

~

Making the unconventional conventional

We tend to approach anything unconventional apprehensively, even though it is the first to catch our attention. The multi-channel, digital ecosystems of today have democratised reach, but commanding consumer attention is more challenging than ever. To hold the ear of the audience has become paramount to a successful narrative delivery.

We communicate to build a reputation. The goal is to let our audiences know, accept and champion the brand's DNA. Doing this well creates tight-knit tribes of brand loyalists. Doing this well *repeatedly* can help us form a self-sustaining reputation.

The story of Lady Godiva from the eleventh century is

symbolic of the unconventional. She opposed an oppressive tax imposed by her husband, the Earl of Grey, enough to take up his challenge to ride a horse across town in the nude. She rode around town with no clothes on, after issuing only a simple plea to all residents not to open their doors or windows. The incident built a memorable legacy of trust, humility and dedication to society. Lady Godiva is still synonymous with elegance and modesty.

Being different for the sake of difference achieves little. The challenge is to ensure that creativity also carries the core message of the brand, otherwise riding nude without purpose would merely come across as sensational, which is not effective.

Adding quirk to communication can help build substantial traction in attaining the reputation we desire. A memorable statement can help increase the velocity of understanding, acceptance and advocacy. As humans, we are drawn to what's different. Unconventional storytelling is magnetic and helps inspire behavioural, belief and purpose realignment within communities.

Too often, creativity is mistaken for being unusual, wacky and even outlandish. It may be, but an effective campaign cannot rely solely on what's bizarre. Here are three points to keep in mind:

* Ideas need to be massaged, sharpened and spliced to understand their effectiveness. Identifying your big, hairy, audacious goal (BHAG) can help evaluate if a unique idea has the legs to reach your vision.
* The idea must possess multi-tenancy, enabling the concept to have many manifestations across several channels.

❖ As our society continues to grow sensitive to communication, recognising your brand's Overton window (mainstream understanding and acceptance of an idea) becomes essential towards building impactful communication.

Getting this right is complex and tiresome. But the reward in building tribes that become reputation evangelists is worth the effort. Reputation is not built in a day—it is built every day. And every opportunity to communicate is a chance to take a position that far outlives the campaign. The right balance of quirk and creativity can move our narratives from 'selling' to 'connecting' with the tribes we serve.

Aniruddha Bhagwat is the CEO and Co-founder of Ideosphere

~

Offering diverse content helps retain consumers

Over two decades ago, in January 1996, Bill Gates authored an article titled 'Content is King'. He stated that content is where much of the 'real money' will be invested in on the internet. He highlighted the potential of the internet to redefine the delivery and consumption of content. And he was right. In the present day, we are being overwhelmed with content at every waking moment. We are always online, constantly connected and being fed a never-ending stream of content.

While we say that content is king, it must be agreed that it is king only when relevant. Without context and effectiveness, content is like a king without a kingdom. An overabundance of it has led consumers to seek out only what that appeals to them, thus making it imperative to curate that what is succinct, attention-grabbing and bite-sized.

Consistently creating new content is both challenging and time-consuming. However, in order to compete in today's media marketing landscape, it is a necessity. From self-employed freelancers to multinational corporations, everyone is looking to maintain a constant stream of engaging and relevant content to keep their target consumers interested.

Listed below are three tips to ensure how to curate your content the right way:

❖ **Use data:** According to the Sprout Social Index, Edition XVI: Above and Beyond, 56 per cent of social marketers use social data to gain a better understanding of their target audience and 49 per cent of them are already using it to form their creative content.[*] Similarly, one needs to use data to understand one's audience, their likes and what resonates with them.

❖ **Identify correct content before sharing:** The challenge with content curation is two-fold. Along with it, one must ensure that the content resonates and stands out, winning the audience's attention. Beyond just facilitating millions of hours of it, it is necessary to choose the correct content to be shared to ensure brand relevance.

---

[*] 'Sprout Social Index, Edition XVI: Above and Beyond', Sprout Social, https://sproutsocial.com/insights/data/2020-index/.

❖ **Offer unique content to match brand standards:** Building and retaining the audience is key to any content curation strategy. Audiences are consuming content from a plethora of mediums available today and new platforms are constantly being added. With an increasing appetite for high-quality content, and to attract potential consumers, one must offer material that is fresh, unique and diverse, which is what retains consumers.

Content curation might look like an easy job, but can take quite some time to master. The challenges of finding relevant material combined with value addition can be tough. It has to be curated for a specific target group, delivered and promoted through appropriate mediums and analysed to ensure it succeeds. And when done right, it can offer clear purpose and add tremendous value.

Faiza Kapoor is the Founder and CEO of
Mondial Kommunications

8

REIMAGINING INTERNAL COMMUNICATIONS

Imagine a large joint family staying under the same roof. Assume each member brings to the table a few unique competencies that complement and supplement what the others have to offer. Now imagine, if some day, the head of the family decides to stop communicating with the others and there are no interdependencies anymore. What happens next could be detrimental. Everybody stops sharing responsibilities or does their own bit but with no shared sense of purpose. In either scenario, can the house function normally?

Isn't that the same with businesses? With no shared sense of purpose and direction, no collaboration within and across functions, what would happen? Teams would stop interacting, engagement would suffer and it could lead to poor outcomes, unsatisfied employees, disgruntled customers, a fall in profits and so on.

At a very basic level, internal communication is the glue that holds families or companies together—now more than ever.

Simply put, in an organisational context, internal communications is nothing but the dissemination of information about the organisation for employees so that they can perform their jobs well with a shared sense of purpose. The purpose is to provide an effective two-way flow of information between an organisation's management and its employees. It is also useful for employees who are interacting with each other in the company. Solid internal communication helps create better company culture and enhances employee engagement.

Before we get into the latest trends that we are witnessing and what practices managers should focus on, let's examine and establish the importance of internal communications in current organisational context without jargon.

Keeps people informed

Keeping people informed about upcoming events, policy changes, engagement initiatives, headcount changes and updates on the overall health of the business helps create a sense of transparency and openness that people respect. People don't like to be kept in the dark. They crave information about the company they're working for, the projects they're working on and the overarching goals of both. Good internal communication is all about getting the word out to everyone, preferably in a way that gets them involved in the bigger picture.

Gives people a more holistic view of the organisation

While internal communications is often thought of as top-down messaging written by leaders for the consumption of employees, it really is a two-way street. An organisation can craft its messaging to attract people's attention, but eventually, their attention will wane, especially if they feel voiceless. In other words, it's not about captivating a passive audience with the right messaging; rather, it's about promoting two-way communication around what's happening at the organisation. People want to feel like their input matters, and creating an avenue for them to do so does wonders for building engagement. This works especially well if messaging, news and announcements are delegated not only to the public relations or human resources department but also to representatives of the different departments within the organisation. Every team should have the opportunity to explain what they're working on, which helps in cultivating an interdisciplinary approach. Appointing news reporters and event coordinators from multiple departments to publish their own updates gives people a more holistic view of the things that matter at the organisation. So, use internal communications to give people a voice.

Helps build the organisation's culture

In many ways, the primary role of internal communications is to help the company's culture manifest. If done well, the strategy will bring the workplace culture to life. After all, each announcement, update or blog post plays a role in how people interpret the cultural landscape of the organisation: what it stands for, who it values, why its mission matters. The culture of the organisation is the sum of its parts and good internal communications takes this into account. Organisational culture should guide internal communications and vice versa.

Keeps people engaged

Creating a two-way conversation should be one of the main goals with an internal communications strategy. It is the difference between boring top-down messaging (like mass emails that no one reads) and pertinent, interactive conversations that promote engagement. Engagement can mean several things: asking thoughtful questions at a town hall event, commenting on an important news update posted on the company's intranet or sharing what your team is working on with the rest of the company. Good internal communication creates space for small yet meaningful acts. Again, it's not just about communicating ideas as much as it is encouraging communication among people. Employees who feel that their voice matters, that their ideas are worth listening to, are more likely to go above and beyond when the organisation needs them. And the value of that can't be underestimated.

Helps keep people calm in times of crisis

Things don't always go seamlessly. Business sometimes suffers, teams are sometimes forced to restructure and mergers and acquisitions happen. This is when people need internal communications the most. Announcements of impending structural changes need to be treated with extra care because the morale of the organisation and the continuity of its existence are at stake. Being open about what went wrong, who was affected, how they were taken care of and what this means for the organisation requires a delicate tone and complete transparency, especially in the case of layoffs. People will have questions, and the way the leadership answers those questions will remain in people's minds for a long time. Use internal communications to create a considerate setting for these difficult-to-have conversations and you'll earn the respect of your people. Being transparent and mindful when delivering bad news creates an atmosphere of openness and caring that can help sustain the organisation through tough times.

Besides that, employees will have more respect for telling it like it is. This is one of the most crucial aspects of good internal communications and demonstrates why underutilising it can quickly turn people against their organisation.

Adds another dimension to the workplace

A lot of people find their jobs dull. They go to work, talk to a colleague or two, attend meetings, get their work done and then leave for the day as soon as possible. That's perfectly fine for most. But for those who crave more involvement in their workplace and want to play a more direct role in the development of its culture, such a work style isn't satisfying. This is where good internal communication steps in. It promotes learning at speaking events and leadership training programmes, shares customer feedback and media coverage and provides opportunities for people to get more involved if they want to. For some people, this isn't important—and that's okay! But there will be some who want to get more out of the workplace, whether that's in the form of education, training, finding meaning in company values and goals or just being included in creating fun activities.

Creates a channel for feedback, debate and discussion

To promote open communication in the organisation, you need to create a space for the debate of issues and ideas. This is how collaboration and trust improve. Internal communications can be harnessed to create a channel for tough discussions. This can happen in several ways: polls, a link to an discussion forum, an event announcement to encourage feedback and criticism or even an organisation-wide invitation to debate a particular goal or project. Remember: good communication is a two-way street. By actively inviting and listening to feedback, one can learn how to avoid making mistakes in the future. Good internal communications is always about finding a way to better serve the people of the organisation.

The most important power of good internal communications is converting ordinary employees into extraordinary ambassadors. Creating an internal communications programme is an ongoing exercise in collaboration. It requires prioritisation and buy-in from leadership as well as frequent check-ins with managers across the business. Before we discuss a few strategies on how to kick off an internal communications programme, let us visit the trends currently prevailing around this subject.

Trends governing internal communications

The COVID-19 crisis made it clear how critical internal communications is to a company's success. We reckon that the coming years will demonstrate this enhanced acceptance of internal communications as a vertical. It has become clear that, moving forward, the way employee communications are carried out will change dramatically.

Already the days of gate meetings, emails, instant messaging and impersonal bulletin boards for keeping employees informed are gone. It was quite difficult to measure success or establish outcomes.

The need is for instant communication with an empathetic tone repurposed to reach employees on channels they prefer consuming data from. The good news is that technology has enabled a robust measurement of success.

We see a few key trends that will govern internal communications in the years to come.

A shift from employee communications to employee experiences

Ask a set of employees what employee experience is and you will get a range of answers. Each segment of employees has a different need. We feel employee experience can improve if we start treating them as customers. Engagement, we feel, is directly proportional to the kind of experiences an individual has from the day of joining to the day of exit. It is a known fact that close to 25 per cent new employees quit within the first ninety days, predominantly due to a mismatch in expectations. Hence, an intervention in communications that shapes an employee's perception of the company and their place within the company needs to be well planned.

Just like checking the customer's pulse, one of the foundations for internal communications should be monitoring the pulse of employee experiences—it could be through surveys, chats, town hall or any other technology-enabled platforms.

To make employee experience a reality, we need to start looking at the world through the lens of one. This will help a company be more empathetic towards employees' needs of being updated, counselled, recognised and developed. One may ask, what value would this add to an organisation? Well, the answer is 'immense' for the following reasons:

❖ Boosts an individual's sense of belonging
❖ Eliminates the ambiguity of roles
❖ Enhances employee productivity
❖ Builds a strong employer brand
❖ Creates strong internal advocates
❖ Curbs attrition
❖ Adds to the bottom line

Our combined experience says that employee experience is largely a subset of three things: the workplace culture, workplace enablers (technology and infrastructure) and, most importantly, authentic internal communication. Progressive companies have been taking steps towards creating a holistic and happy experience for their employees.

Enhanced focus on employee well-being and related communications

A new consciousness about mental health issues is one of the main trends in internal communications. The recent pandemic drew attention to employee well-being like never before. A McKinsey report showed that 62 per cent of employees globally consider mental health issues to be a top challenge.[*] The same report also says that 96 per cent of companies globally provided mental health resources to employees, but that only one in six employees reported feeling supported. Could poor internal communications be at fault? Perhaps, to an extent, as many might not be aware of the support available.

To ensure a resilient workforce, employers should prioritise well-being, which, we feel, is all about employees being healthy, motivated and engaged. Internal communications plays a major role in establishing this.

We are particularly intrigued by what Gallup refers to as 'thriving well-being', that is, employees who are engaged but not thriving and may be suffering from high levels of stress, anger and sadness despite their positive experiences at work.

Good internal communications processes on this front— steps such as opening feedback channels for employees to talk freely and share concerns while ensuring the availability of (and easy access to) counsellors—have never been more important. There are multiple ways in which an organisational pulse can be gauged, such as through confidential surveys, call centre monitoring and one-on-one conversations.

Going forward, we believe that organisations that communicate and support each aspect of staff well-being, from physical and mental to social and financial, will enjoy higher engagement rates and a good corporate culture.

---

* 'Diverse employees are struggling the most during COVID-19—here's how companies can respond', McKinsey & Company, 17 November 2020, https://www.mckinsey.com/featured-insights/diversity-and-inclusion/diverse-employees-are-struggling-the-most-during-covid-19-heres-how-companies-can-respond.

Rise in authentic, instant and personal communication

Have you thought about whether a TikTok video and good communication could share similarities? Well, in a way, both espouse shortform storytelling. Short, snackable content works best in a world where attention spans have limits. The fact is that a short video, an infographic or a quick voice note can explain a complex topic in a more appealing and interesting manner rather than a long email on the subject. With Gen Z beginning to enter the workforce, capturing the attention of young employees in unconventional ways will be useful. Another insight that we have garnered is that employees want to be included in conversations. With more social platforms available, the ability to have a voice and be heard is also high. Employees want to tell stories, share achievements, appreciate peers and colleagues and be seen at the forefront. Making communication instant through platforms will give employees an opportunity to be heard in an authentic manner. Platforms like Facebook at Work are helping employees create communities within organisations. They are becoming platforms for recognition and for sharing news in a personalised way. Of course, authenticity is most important for building stronger connections with the staff. Only then will they be truly invested in a leader's vision. Leadership communication, hence, must be real and not staged. Employees switch off the moment they find it superficial and insincere.

Building authenticity by embracing real-life storytelling and being empathetic works wonders. Telling employee stories celebrating achievements and demonstrating alignment with organisational values works even better.

Multi-channel communication approach to reach preferred points of consumption

In our forty-odd years of combined experience, we have not seen one single channel being solely effective in reaching out to all employees in an organisation. With increased diversity in employee demography, choices and priorities, it is even more difficult today. To be effective, communication has to reach employees where they consume it. This means a communicator needs to use multiple channels, such as an employee app for frontline workers, newsletters for print lovers, intranet for office employees, notice boards for factory workers, theatre for communities, etc. Polls on consumption preferences can help you understand which mode works for whom.

With the advent of technology, most employees are digitally savvy. A multi-channel intranet can be a platform where communicators can curate messages and campaigns, repurpose content and then send them out to different groups in channels where they would be seen. Analytics, measurement of efficacy and efficiency then become easy, as the reach, impressions and other key performance indicators can be recorded.

Data-driven internal communication

We are confident that just like external communications, internal communications will also become more data-driven. Effectiveness of the various tools of internal communications can go up only if there are baseline surveys done to understand ground realities. Gone are the days of having frivolous events and get-togethers or generalised mails based on anecdotal evidence of employee issues. Technology enables us to capture the sentiments of employees across segments, departments and locations. Of course, reaching out to dispersed and remote workforces is much simpler today, but then what is more important is the analysis of this data and rolling out interventions that can help alleviate the pains of employees. Going forward, we'll see a rise in such surveys with robust and focused interventions based on data.

Rise in employee communications apps and mobile platforms

As hybrid working becomes the norm and more and more organisations adopt it, it is inevitable that some employees will be based out of the head office, some will prefer working from home and others, such as the sales team, will be on the road. This will mean that traditional internal communications methods, such as newsletters in print form, large town hall meetings and employee events, may become unviable. In that case, how does one keep employees connected? The need would be to have good internal communication channels that can connect employees instantly at their respective locations. Going digital is the answer, and this trend will only gather pace. Of course, video meets, chat platforms and organisational social media handles are one thing, but we'll also see a prevalence of special apps that will ensure instant two-way communication, feedback, videos from leadership, event calendars, recognition boards and all that's possible to keep employees engaged.

Direct leadership communications will rise

Edelman's Trust Barometer shows that 86 per cent of people believe CEOs should speak out publicly on societal issues, and 68 per cent believe they should step in on issues where governments fail.[*] Leadership communication also plays an important role in addressing employee concerns. In fact, the disruption seen during the pandemic has forced leaders to be more visible than ever.

Business updates, clarity on the future of the organisation, key policy changes and mergers and acquisitions (M&A) outcomes are some themes that employees prefer to hear about from company leadership rather than through the grapevine during watercooler chats. Going forward, internal communications strategies will place strong emphasis on leadership dialogues, offering employees direct visibility of leadership.

Direct leadership communication should encompass themes like purpose, vision and employee well-being clearly in their engagements. Demonstrating the courage to be upfront and, at the same time, empathetic towards employee concerns as well as having a call to action can build a culture of listening and appreciation. While in-person meets may be a challenge at times, use of videos and voice recordings works well.

Rise in communication with frontline employees

You may call 2021 a year of resilience, emergence or going back to the drawing board, but it was certainly the year

---

[*] 'Edelman Trust Barometer 2021', Edelman, 2021, https://www.edelman.com/sites/g/files/aatuss191/files/2021-03/2021%20Edelman%20Trust%20Barometer.pdf.

of frontline workers. Companies around the world realised the importance of communicating with last-mile employees who may not have had the luxury of reporting to an air-conditioned office every day but were the ones who kept the fires burning for the organisation. Operational challenges, uncertainty, fear-mongering and the Great Resignation shifted serious focus onto communicating with frontline employees and good leaders made a point to connect with them via digital tools and apps. Although an evolving market, mobile channels can link frontline workers more effectively. We see a rise in app-based modes used to share data with frontline staff, which makes it both easy and effective to send out important information required to carry out their work effectively. They also make it easier to distribute important messages around training, mental health or organisational announcements using videos or any other contemporary tool.

The points discussed above make one thing very clear: authenticity, empathy, technology, relevance, leadership involvement and the right channels carry immense importance in the crafting of an internal communications strategy which needs to align organisational growth policy with measurable goals and objectives.

Before you get into the formulation of your internal communications strategy, consider the following.

❖ **Assess your current strategy:** You probably have some internal communication processes already in place, so it's always best to start with research. It's time to assess what's working and what isn't. Revamping an internal communications strategy includes asking the following questions: What is your current performance and how effective is the current strategy? What are the organisation's biggest strengths and weaknesses? Who is currently involved in shaping and executing the plan and who can be added to improve it? What are your goals for your internal communications programme? Who is your audience? Is it the entire organisation or a select business unit? How does one plan to get there—what is it going to take to achieve objectives in terms of resources, budget or tools? What type of content will resonate the most with the staff? What's the difference between how long it should take versus a realistic timeline for your team? Who's involved—is the current team too small? Are there too many cooks in the kitchen? Where can you add to or streamline your internal communications team? Answering (or at least introspecting on) the answers to these questions will be your lodestar as you design your strategy and also map out your larger vision before you dive into tactical details.

- ❖ **Set realistic goals and timelines:** A new internal communications strategy won't magically transform employee experiences overnight. These things take time, so it's important to keep goals realistic. One way to set intelligent goals is by looking at internal benchmarks and noting where one can make an immediate impact. One may also want to send out a survey to gauge a better understanding of what employees want from your programme.

Setting S.M.A.R.T. goals is useful.

- ■ *Specific:* Define what you want to accomplish in clear, simple terms that your entire team can understand.

- *Measurable:* Create milestones and targets that can help you see your progress in each aspect of your goal.
- *Attainable:* It's good to have lofty ambitions, but you need to know if they're manageable and realistic.
- *Relevant:* Create goals that are linked to developing your team and connected seamlessly with your business model.
- *Time-based:* Create a specific time frame for reaching your goals to maintain accountability and create an opportunity to reflect on your performance.

❖ **Identify the key metrics to track for success:** Just like most other facets of business, an internal communications strategy can and should be measurable. To do this, one needs to choose the core metrics that will demonstrate whether the strategy is working or not. This data will also help determine if employees are using the resources that are being provided. This means one can dissect strategy and learn about what areas need more attention and what can be skipped. For example, one may find that the team overwhelmingly prefers one channel over another, or that certain departments pay more attention to communication from executive leadership rather than peers or team managers. Some things, like anecdotal feedback, can't be measured. Still, it's important to build on the understanding of employees' experiences with data.

❖ **Segment and map out the audience:** Once there is an idea of what could bolster an internal communications strategy, it's time to determine who to target. The content should always target a specific audience, even when it's internal. It's important to figure out what messages and formats will resonate with different employees in the business. Another major misconception is that to have a successful internal communications strategy, one has to include everyone in all messages for transparency—that's just not true. While employees want to be in the loop on news and company information, overwhelming them with too much detail could cause them to ignore updates as they come through. Strategically mapping out their exposure to updates can minimise information overload. Partner with leaders and internal subject matter experts to discuss what type of content would be necessary or helpful for their teams. Rather than sending the same information to everyone (regardless of role, location or department), the strategy should focus on delivering relevant information to the right people at the right time.

❖ **Build an approval process:** A key part of planning out the internal communications strategy is creating an approval process for content. This will prevent any unnecessary errors, like confidential news being accidentally published to the wrong segments of the team. First, one needs to determine who or what team owns the internal communications process. If there is no dedicated internal communications resource, nobody who will read, write or approve the messages that are sent out, then someone needs to be put in charge. Next, one needs to know what stakeholders from each department can contribute to the content approval process. In most cases, this responsibility falls on the communication teams—and for good reason. These are the team members who are most confident in their ability to convey company voice, brand and overall behaviour. The public relations team should ideally be part of crafting almost every company update and campaign, so that they can easily curate the most current content and point co-workers to industry-specific resources that speak of relevant trends. All these capabilities are critical to have when leading employee advocacy efforts. Another important ability—and one that often comes naturally to public relations professionals—is crafting social media messaging that's concise, impactful and relevant to the platform it's being shared on.

❖ **Identify internal communications tools:** Certain messages are best suited for specific channels. Internal process changes might be better suited to an email update, whereas a quick announcement might get more traction on an internal messaging platform. Internal communications is more than updates and announcements. It's how information flows through a company, whether that information is from the C-suite, a department manager or a project manager. If one doesn't have technology or infrastructure in place to support internal communications initiatives, it needs attention. The technology used may hold the key to creating more equitable experiences for remote and in-office employees. If one wants to help maintain employee satisfaction, one will need to make the investment.

❖ **Evaluate progress and optimise:** Key performance indicators shouldn't be used just for tracking progress. Learn from them and continually optimise what is being done for the best results possible. Conduct quarterly or even monthly evaluations of the communications strategy and build these into the workflow. Sending out routine surveys can help track how employees are feeling about the content and cadence of your messages. Be sure to leave a few questions for open feedback, so employees have an opportunity to candidly share their thoughts. Some questions one could ask include:

- How well do you think we are communicating internally?
- Are we doing everything we can to keep the company vision transparent?
- What setbacks limit you from working with others on projects?
- Do you believe we could increase our communication across departments?
- What barriers prevent you from communicating internally each day?
- Where can we improve the most?

As one continually reevaluates the internal communications strategy, let people know that they are being heard.

Today, more companies are beginning to recognise that one-way communication is a thing of the past. Employees who feel as though they're being listened to are more likely to stay with their employers and contribute meaningfully to the team. An engagement strategy that's rooted in communication should leave every employee feeling educated, informed and motivated.

❖ **Give managers a heads-up:** If you have a question about a company decision or initiative, whom do you ask? Chances are that the manager is the go-to person.

Managers are the first in line to field questions from direct reports, making them key players in distributed workforces. When making a companywide announcement or rolling out a new programme, always be sure to provide managers with talking points ahead of time. This will help them prepare for any potential questions their direct reports may have, which in turn cuts down additional work for the leadership team. This also helps in ensuring that a single, unified message is shared at every level of the company.

❖ **Try a new approach to building company culture:** Attitudes toward company culture have shifted. The allure of ping pong tables and free drinks has lost its shine. Now, what people want is a work culture that values respect, balance and accountability. While these new culture requirements may seem like table stakes, they're all much easier said than done. Luckily, strong internal communications practices can foster a culture of accountability. By sending clear, consistent updates that clarify internal processes like performance reviews and promotions, one creates the top-down transparency needed to ensure that everyone is respected and informed.

In conclusion, it's time to renew the focus on an often-overlooked audience. A powerful internal communications strategy drives higher employee engagement, which in turn leads to stronger productivity, profitability and reduced turnover—all things that can help the business thrive.

~

Building a corporate narrative using strong internal communications

What is a corporate narrative? A simple story, articulated well and truthfully, about the company's purpose and the value it has created for its customers, people, partners and shareholders. The company's growth story is driven by its vision and delivered by its people and its reputation is built on the experiences the company offers.

The company's success hinges on the quality of talent, their passion and alignment with the corporate purpose and their commitment towards organisational success. Research suggests that employees who are engaged, connected and dedicated are most suited to play the role of brand advocates.

The role of internal communications naturally assumes great importance in encouraging employees to be brand advocates.

Effective internal communication provides employees with a sense of shared purpose. This requires more than the exchange of information; it needs a culture which is inclusive and encourages open dialogues between employees, their managers, peers and the leadership on a frequent basis.

Authentic internal communication fosters greater understanding and creates an environment of mutual respect. It forges connections between people, strengthens relationships and leads to improved teamwork and better performance both individually and collectively. Having an engaged workforce is imperative not only for building a strong corporate narrative for brand reputation but for also improving overall business performance.

When the environment inside the company is motivating and empowering, giving employees opportunities to thrive and grow, it starts to permeate to the external world, leading to better customer service and higher customer satisfaction, thus building long-term trust for the brand.

Today, a large part of the workforce comprises millennials and Gen Z and it is very important to keep them engaged and motivated for organisational success. Their experiences at the organisation are built largely by their managers and peers. Hence, effective employee engagement must work at three levels.

Organisational

At the organisational level, development of a culture where employee engagement is valued, prioritised and invested in is extremely critical. Recognition and appreciation of employees across all levels are key aspects of effective engagement.

Leadership

The management needs to invest in resources to increase employee engagement and the leadership team needs to be seen as engaging with people on diverse topics.

At the same time, leaders and people managers must engage authentically with employees: listening to them, paying close attention to their concerns and expectations and mentoring them to build on their strengths and overcome their weaknesses.

Individual

At an individual level, every employee must participate in various engagement initiatives for them to be fruitful.

Employees need to have a positive mindset and should focus on channelising their energy in the right direction while making space for fun work activities. Ownership of one's own work and contributions to the organisational goals are sacrosanct.

Seema Ahuja is the Global Head of Communications and Corporate Brand at Biocon Group

~

Re-thinking internal communications

Public relations has always meant different things at different companies. For some, it's a highly strategic function and part of the management group and for others, it's just an extension of marketing largely understood as media relations. But when it comes to internal communications, even the savviest of the lot underinvested in its potential. Many companies realised this during the pandemic when remote working became a reality overnight. Everyone found themselves in unfamiliar territory with no playbook to rely on. Teams meant only for producing and delivering top-down news and building messages on behalf of management had to roll up their sleeves and join the task force to find the best ways to help the company and its employees navigate and settle into the new normal.

In the process, many have discovered that they don't have enough channels to communicate and drive company-wide dialogue with employees and if they did, they had not invested enough to measure their effectiveness. The concepts of keeping employees engaged, motivated and maintaining the company culture are dominating discussions as companies contemplate the future of work. But there is definitely a new-found appreciation for internal communications and investing in it as a strategic function.

Today, in many companies where remote working continues to be an option, internal communications is playing a crucial role in partnering with human resources and management to reimagine recruitment and onboarding processes. How a new employee experiences the company and its culture is still a real challenge. Concerns around employee well-being are actively being discussed.

While our reliance on digital tools and collaborative tools has increased, there is no replacement for authentic human connection. Internal communications professionals are partnering with managers to invest in building trust in teams working remotely, helping them develop a more mindful approach to maintaining transparency and doubling down on inclusion. The role of internal communications in helping employees understand the external news environment and striking the right balance between external and internal, especially in remote or hybrid workforce set-ups, has become even more crucial.

Every company is going through this process of change and digital transformation; where they will settle or continue to evolve will vary from place to place. The steps companies take today by focusing on employee experience will give them the competitive edge in employer branding and attracting new talent.

This is a critical time for companies to relook and rethink their internal communications plan and pay much closer attention to the role they have played so far. Even with the best leaders, great business strategy and vision, you will need a plan to include employees who are as engaged, passionate and committed to executing the plan. It's critical to partner with your internal communications team to not just set and communicate the rules for playing but actively work with them to manage how the game is played. Win or lose, your reputation will be built by how you play the game.

Gaurav Bhaskar is the Director of Corporate Communications and Public Affairs at Google India

~

Beautiful, inside out

The reputation of a company is no façade. The reach and impact of an organisation's reputation emanates from the core—its people. Much like 'true beauty' is perceived as the glow that results from good health, good deeds and a good character, a strong employer brand must be evocative amongst employees for it to also resonate externally.

Employer branding contributes to the overall company reputation. It is the outcome of strategies designed to build credibility from the inside out by being authentic (seeing is believing), distinctive (standing out in a crowd) and renewable (every day is a new day).

Strategy 1: Seeing is believing

As employees: Your employees must be the believers as well as implementers of your organisation's culture, values and ways of working. Regular discussions for sharing news and recognising team contributions empowers employees, gives them perspective and helps them understand their role better. Be innovative, be consistent and customise content to co-create an organisation the employees are all proud of. Also, listen to and act upon the input and feedback of a diverse cross-section based on employees' tenure, gender, experience levels, locations, etc.

As potential employees and other external stakeholders: Interactions with HR and other external functions, like procurement, communications or public affairs, should reflect the passion and enthusiasm of engaged employees creating an organisation they believe in. For example, drop terms like 'vendors', and start conversations with them as business enablers or partners. Share your vision for the future and invite them to work with you to deliver the organisation's promise to your customers and the community.

Strategy 2: Standing out in a crowd

It is common practice amongst many companies to project their purpose and values as identity markers. These inadvertently end up being common denominators rather than differentiators across companies. So, what could you do to create a unique persona for your organisation? The first step would be to recognise your organisation's USP, then building a vocabulary around it, as well as imagery and proof-points. Share such brand tools with all employees and train your spokespersons to communicate consistently.

To maintain freshness while consistently reinforcing key messages, you could convey these USPs across all your corporate brand channels using different voices, such as employee narratives, stakeholder testimonials, descriptions of key initiatives, corporate social responsibility (CSR) engagements and awards received for HR practices and business excellence.

Strategy 3: Every day is a new day

Start today. Trigger the process of defining your brand identity and once you're done, create rituals and channels to reinforce them with stakeholders.

Sustain every day. Allocate resources for your leadership team and ambassadors (across hierarchies/roles) to amplify messages. Routinely anticipate issues and crisis scenarios and create processes to prevent or mitigate them. Finally, leverage reputation enhancers to complement the brand and have long-lasting impact, such as simple, meaningful and courteous actions towards fellow employees and recruitment candidates.

The world over, top employers practise these strategies to create distinctive brands that are a joy to work for and have a strong reputation that can be counted upon, through good times and otherwise.

Aparna Thomas is the Senior Director, Communications and CSR, India and South Asia, at Sanofi

~

Making advocates of staff—why employee branding delivers better results than employer branding

What makes some organisations stand out from the rest? How do firms get staff to advocate for the brand in a highly competitive marketplace? In what ways can companies become valued employers by tapping the power of their employees?

Often, when leaders look for answers to such questions, they focus on elements like workplace facilities, salaries, benefits, policies, products and services. Or they invite external validation to bolster their image. Or (worse) they only invest in branding. Unfortunately, they miss out on the biggest asset—their own staff as brand advocates who can drive connection and engagement at unprecedented levels.

To help clarify the differences and the interlinkages, it helps to understand how terms such as employer branding, employee branding and employee advocacy are defined and understood.

❖ Employer branding is the management of stakeholder perceptions leading to reputation-building. Defining and articulating a strong employee value proposition is crucial for employer branding.

❖ Employee branding, on the other hand, is defined as the image presented to the organisation's stakeholders through the eyes of the staff, which is more credible and trustworthy. When employees are in the know, they are more equipped to promote the brand.

❖ Employee advocacy takes the association to the next level, that is, the voluntary actions that staff carry out because they feel psychologically safe, find purpose at work, are highly engaged and want to do more for the brand.

Only when employees can internalise the company's purpose, believe in what the organisation does, are equipped to be their best selves through training and guidance and are willing to promote the brand can there be optimal results.

However, here is where it gets tricky.

❖ Employees are considering employers and choosing organisations on the basis of which company can help fulfill their ambitions and aspirations. There is a significant gap between what leaders believe and what is experienced by managers and frontline workers.

❖ Research studies have indicated an erosion of trust and rising clout of employees as influencers, activists, promoters and much more.

❖ Employees, who are people like us, are more credible than CEOs and it only means that organisations and communicators need to revisit how they engage staff.

❖ Organisations are struggling because they haven't defined their employee value proposition well enough. Those who do can decrease turnover, improve productivity and more.

❖ Employees are largely dissatisfied with their experiences and don't feel like going over and beyond. Those organisations that shape experiences can increase discretionary efforts significantly

❖ Employees are sharing more than before, driving more job views and more job applications. Not just that, the Pareto principal also applies here, with less than 20 per cent of employees creating over 80 per cent of engagement on social media.

Therefore, for companies to fully appreciate and tap the power of their biggest assets, they need to start from within and at the top.

First, they need to re-imagine their structures and approach to dealing with employees in order to make it more flexible and more accommodating.

Second, they need to hire people who have an open mindset, enabling conversations with employees as brands.

Third, the culture within needs to change to be more inclusive and enabling. Organisations and communicators need to let go of control and focus on partnering and influencing.

Fourth, finding employees who are keen to work in an environment where they can be themselves and also contribute to the collective wisdom within organisations is important.

Lastly, the role of communicators has changed—from 'owning' communication to 'enabling' employees to be their best selves. That means revisiting channels and modes of engagement, truly listening to employees and involving and empowering employees to partner, co-create, advocate and communicate on behalf of the organisation. The skills that most communicators have today need to change to suit new expectations at the workplace.

It works to the organisation's advantage when they focus on developing and honing employees' talents and strengths. Facing the realities of today can help shape the organisations of tomorrow.

Dr Aniisu Verghese is the Director of
Corporate Communications at Sabre Poland

9

THE WEB OF RESPONSIBLE COMMUNICATIONS

The responsibility of a business starts with a promoter creating an enterprise by keeping public interest a priority. Responsible communications ensures that the promise of the business offering and adherence to the stated objectives is fulfilled.

Currently, many terms are used to depict the philosophy of fulfilment of the promises made by an organisation in a sustainable and ethical manner. The more common word used currently is 'purpose'. While the objective of any business is to make profit, there is always an intent to do good for society, offer employment as well as to provide a superior product or service at fair value.

In a larger organisational context, it is common to hear the terms CR (community relations or corporate responsibility) and CSR. These days, there is also a term called 'social impact', referred to at a higher level as sustainability. In some cases, we also hear of corporate philanthropy. These terms are different but have a lot in common.

In order to deliberate on the subject of responsible communications, we convened a meeting with senior professionals.

The banter soon got heated as multiple views were being floated on the basis of the non-uniform understanding of the subject or, to put it another way, non-alignment of the definitions. Of course, that was to be expected, as multiple departments from large corporates were represented in the august gathering. There were a few veteran CSR professionals, a few chief sustainability and communications officers, investor relations representatives and public relations professionals. We were discussing the newest kid on the block: ESG.

We posed a question to the participants to gauge their understanding of ESG and asked them to define what they thought 'responsible communications' was. The objective was to arrive at a common understanding, making it conducive to create a framework of ESG communications strategy and define responsible communications in a way that could be referred to across the industry.

Some of the responses were:

'It's a long way to go from CSR focus to ESG focus.'

'We have begun, but we're grappling. We do communicate responsibly, though.'

'We have been reporting it but in silos.'

'We understand it but do not have a framework.'

'It is unclear—we are a WIP.'

It was also evident that many PR professionals understand the principles of ESG but are yet to create clear frameworks for the business and communications function.

There was a time when demonstration of CSR was the

only option for companies looking to do good. It was also what customers, investors and other stakeholders sought from socially conscious enterprises and brands. Over the years, due to visible impacts of global warming, diversity issues and other complexities, sustainability as a concept took prominence. Now, the latest buzz is around the overall intentions behind CSR and sustainability initiatives regarding ESG. The aim is to provide a framework for better measures doing greater good with greater transparency.

Over the next few paragraphs, we will briefly explain six concepts and bring out how they are an inherent part of the public relations DNA.

Sustainability immediately conjures up thoughts about the environment. However, it is much more. In simple terms, it is about what can be done to ensure the areas which need support are sustained. As per Investopedia, 'In the broadest possible sense, sustainability refers to the ability of something to maintain or "sustain" itself over time. In business and policy contexts, limits to sustainability are determined by physical and natural factors, environmental degradation, and social resources. Accordingly, sustainable policies place some emphasis on the future effect of any given policy or business practice on humans, the economy and ecology. The concept often corresponds to the belief that without major changes to the way the planet is run, it will suffer irreparable degradation.'[*]

Purpose is about having a clear-cut goal that goes beyond profit. We hear this word from various sources and very

---

[*] Daniel Thomas Mollenkamp, 'What is Sustainability?', Investopedia, https://www.investopedia.com/terms/s/sustainability.asp.

often, it is used without too much thought put into it. However, purpose is the reason for existence. It is the gap you are promising to bridge between various stakeholders.

Corporate philanthropy is when a company dips into its budget—either after making a profit, or during the year based on either the previous year's profit or anticipated profit—and sets aside cash to be given away to a cause or non-profit or a foundation that has been created by the organisation. In essence, giving back to society what has come from society.

Social impact, as the term denotes, is about impact made on society. There are social impact funds, and those are different. Here, the context is about how organisations volunteer their time or how employees are involved in causes which can go a long way in making a difference to the beneficiary.

CSR is a traditional method of making time to volunteer for causes, writing cheques periodically to preferred charities or creating a department that focuses on giving back to communities.

ESG has been around for a while but has gained traction in the last couple of years. Environmental, social and corporate governance is an evaluation of a firm's collective conscientiousness for social and environmental factors. It is typically a score that is compiled using data collected around specific metrics related to intangible assets within the enterprise. It could be considered a kind of corporate social credit score.

All of the above have overlaps. Very often, organisations look at doing one or more of the above to get mileage from the same. Mileage accrues in different ways: reports in the media talking about what an organisation does, employees sharing details with their connections, management being able to talk about it at various forums.

It is here that a brand needs to take an ethical stance and answer a simple question: are these activities undertaken to contribute to others, get a pat on the back ... or both?

Our take is simple. All these activities are certainly public relations. However, self-praise or showing off any work done is purely branding, not public relations. Real public relations happens when beneficiaries talk about it of their own accord and when word gets out without any prompting from the management or its partners.

Public relations executives play the role of harmony officers. Their key job in the realm of communicating larger sustainability initiatives is to inform and update the impacted stakeholders in an authentic and ethical manner, bringing everyone together harmoniously.

To arrive at a definition for responsible communications, let's delve deeper into the concept of CSR and ESG. We feel that even though the two are not interchangeable, without CSR, there would be no ESG. The basic issue, we feel, is that one tends to look at ESG through the lens of CSR activities. In fact, CSR probably fits only into a subsection of the ESG.

CSR, we feel, makes a business accountable but ESG sets a criterion to make it measurable. Even for a lot of serious businesses, unfortunately, CSR never graduated beyond being the arm to do good publicly, reporting on activities like opening schools, volunteering, beneficiary visits, etc. It has become a marketing tool with anecdotal outcomes. We know it is hard for many to accept this. Many of our professional acquaintances running CSR mandates agree that, most of the time, it is an activity trap rather than having an actual impact—the reason being lack of measurement. ESG policies, however, need to be embedded in the core of a business' strategy, rather than operating on the side like CSR. ESG scores have numbers and ratings on how enterprises treat their staff, address climate change issues, manage supply chains, work on diversity and inclusion and many more parameters. The best part is that the momentum to embed ESG as an integrated part of business is driven by investors and aware employees and consumers.

Investors (more so the younger generations) have, in recent years, shown increased affinity to invest in and work with companies that share their values across the various dimensions of ESG. ESG criteria are a set of standards that socially conscious investors use to screen potential investments in a business.

To make it simple, as you are aware, there are three key parts to ESG investing—environmental, social and governance.

- ❖ **Environmental:** The environmental criteria include energy usage, waste management, resource conservation, etc. The criteria also help evaluate environmental risks and mitigation processes. Examples could be management of effluents, toxic emissions, compliance with norms, etc.
- ❖ **Social:** Social criteria focus on human relationships such as the working conditions of employees, community

engagement, vendor management, employee volunteering, etc.

❖ **Governance:** Governance criteria deal with disclosures, audit, accounting standards, transparency in dealings, managing conflict of interest, political contributions, board structures, etc.

A recent report from Vuelio found that there's growing emphasis on ESG among leaders, managers and communicators. Nearly a third (31 per cent) of organisations said they have a policy in place to manage ESG and 41 per cent said that it was a work in progress. The report also found that 63 per cent of PR professionals can confidently define ESG and the impact it has on their clients or company. According to Vuelio, 'ESG is one of the most radical developments in business within the last 50 years. It's likely to shape the way both organisations and the communications sector evolve and operate for years to come.'[*]

As a very progressive move in India, the top 1,000 listed companies in India (by market capitalisation) will need to prepare a business responsibility and sustainability report (BRSR), containing detailed ESG disclosures effective from Financial Year 2022-2023.

The BRSR will be part of the annual report which gets notified to the stock exchanges, published on official company websites and provided to shareholders.

---

[*] Stephen Waddington and Dr Jon White, 'The Environment, Social and Corporate Governance (ESG) Opportunity for Public Relations', Vuelio, https://www.vuelio.com/uk/resources/white-papers/environment-social-corporate-governance-opportunity-public-relations.

There is empirical proof that there is strong linkage between ESG and the financial performance of an enterprise. A lower ESG score (meaning lack of focus on ESG dimensions) can lead to issues on multiple fronts. Investors may avoid investing, raising the enterprise cost of capital. Employees may be hard to find and attrition could be higher, leading to increased costs of hiring and retaining talent. Regulatory costs may go up due to environmental issues, reducing the support needed to operate. Customers may boycott products. Practically the entire stakeholder network could be affected in some way or the other.

In a recent survey by Allianz, it was found that only 15 per cent of Americans recognise the term 'ESG'. While this is low, the majority (79 per cent) like the idea of investing in a company that cares about issues. This could be almost the same in India too. While the young generation leads the push to ESG (64 per cent are more likely to make investment decisions on issues they care about), even the older generation (boomers at 42 per cent) are getting on board.[*] The younger generation, research has shown, is more likely to associate with companies that care about social issues as they have better long-term success.

With this background and commentary, it is evident that public relations and corporate communication professionals have a massive role to play on the ESG communications front beyond just educating and communicating ESG dimensions and updates to external and internal stakeholders.

---

[*] 'Allianz Group: Sustainability Report 2022', Allianz, 2022, https://www. allianz.com/content/dam/onemarketing/azcom/Allianz_com/sustainability/ documents/Allianz_Group_Sustainability_Report_2022-web.pdf.

Responsible communications

With the context set, explaining the concept of responsible communications in the parlance of ESG becomes easy.

We would define it as, 'Managing communication processes, content and impact in an accountable, ethical and transparent manner and recognising stakeholder interests and human rights with no harm to the environment in order to contribute to the growth of an enterprise.'

More than just a definition, it can be a strong paradigm in the field of public relations and corporate communications. Responsible communications can strengthen the PR arsenal of an enterprise. It would be the best tool to attract consumers who are increasingly passionate about environmental and social aspects. The impact of consistent responsible communications can lead to loyal, long-term customers. These very customers can play the role of advocates in the eventuality of an adverse incident since they understand the ethos of the company, support that one cannot expect from customers who may see your messaging as 'greenwashing'. Excessive claims and promises made for short-term gains get called out and are more damaging. Customers today are aware and shift loyalty the moment they sense anything that is untruthful and unethical.

Corporate scrutiny has gone up significantly. Businesses are expected to be transparent and aligned to their purpose. The vulnerability of getting called out for even small slips in corporate behaviour is high. With social media, the potential of an incident becoming a crisis also skyrockets. We feel that the only trustworthy solution is to have a responsible communications strategy.

The benefits of embracing responsible communication

❖ **Alleviating risk:** Risk reduction is a major outcome if one embeds the concept of responsible communication in the overall organisational communications strategy. It is akin to embedding ESG into your company culture. Of course, being oblivious and neglecting it has its own perils at multiple levels across various stakeholders. The impact on finances, employee morale, right to operate, defecting customers and legal settlements can take a toll on overall corporate reputation. Having the right responsible communications strategy and ESG embedded in the business also means having a good crisis mitigation and management plan with regular rehearsals and drills. The positive digital safety net that responsible communication creates also helps alleviate the impact of any negatives on the social media front. Techniques in issues management include monitoring the organisation's environment and consistently listening to the concerns of stakeholder groups to identify and understand issues at the earliest possible point in their development. A good listening tool naturally becomes an important cog in the wheel of your responsible communications strategy.

❖ **Boosting investors' affinity:** Companies that can successfully communicate their ESG commitments and report authentic indicators attract more investors. HSBC's 2021 corporate risk management survey validates this. According to the survey, investors are increasingly considering ESG criteria in their decision-making frameworks. An average of 80 per cent of chief financial officers (CFOs) across global regions believe ESG criteria are important across both financial investments and supply chains.[*] Sustainable investment is big, and only set to grow further. With a tremendous amount of awareness and consciousness of the environment, it is but obvious that businesses that are able to project a sustainable image will thrive. Deloitte's 2021 Global Millennial and Gen Z Survey, which asked people about their attitude to the values of their business partners, found that a third of respondents said they had 'lessened business relationships' with companies they thought were doing harm to the environment.[†]

❖ **Lowering employee attrition:** The pandemic has redefined the tenets of human resource management. The focus on employee well-being, effective internal communications, empathy and retention has never been higher. When it comes to human rights, diversity and inclusion angles, organisations have become serious like never before. Young employees prefer working for organisations that have similar values. Deloitte's report says that millennials and Gen Z considered the issue of climate change at the top of their list of concerns. Having ESG dimensions and a responsible communications strategy in place will mean that you have taken appropriate care of all the above insights and are proactively prepared. This

---

[*] 'Corporate Treasury Risk Management Survey', HSBC, 2021, https://www.gbm.hsbc.com/en-gb/campaigns/rethinking-treasury-survey-2021.

[†] 'The Deloitte 2021 Global Millennial and Gen Z Survey', Deloitte, 2021, https://www2.deloitte.com/content/dam/Deloitte/mk/Documents/about-deloitte/2021-deloitte-global-millennial-survey-report.pdf.

gives you an edge over the competition. Well-engaged employees are the best advocates and ambassadors of your business and that does come in handy most of the time.

❖ **No rocket science:** It is undisputable that an embedded and robustly implemented ESG strategy has an extremely positive impact on business performance. Responsible communication based on ESG will continue to play an important role in the evolution of public relations in times to come.

An ability to communicate a company's ESG goals authentically and effectively, along with the appropriate actions it is taking to achieve them, will be critical. Teams that can master this will emerge stronger. By setting and communicating commitments internally and externally, organisations allow their employees and the public to hold them accountable. This accountability helps garner trust and create more supporters.

There is tremendous opportunity for public relations to help shape and inform a response to ESG, helping enterprises map relevant stakeholders and influence behaviour.

Understanding the audience and their data consumption patterns is a vital step in strengthening your responsible communications strategy. Yet another insight that surveys can provide is on the key elements of ESG which are most important to your target audience. This helps build a robust plan and messaging that can then be manifested via the platform best suited for the respective demographic. For example, consistent use of social media to communicate and amplify your responsible achievements can be a good way to engage younger consumers. Or having a corporate blog on your website for those audiences that like to consume information from the company online.

Outlining the purpose of your organisation and defining goals to pursue it relentlessly is intricately linked to ESG performance. Communicating these to relevant stakeholders is also crucial. Most importantly, the cadence in communicating the success stories, beneficiary testimonials, videos of impact and ESG outcomes will play a huge role in making your responsible communications strategy successful. Infographics to simplify ESG data are a great way to communicate on multiple platforms.

ESG investors are always on the lookout for authentic and dependable information before choosing how to allocate capital and where to invest. This translates into a higher impetus on ESG disclosure and reporting, not just by investors and lenders but by governments and regulators as well. Responsible communication enables this aspect and can make or break a deal.

Remember, ESG investing, in simple terms, means investing based on not just traditional financial factors but also on non-financial ESG factors. This momentum is further supported by increasing evidence of a positive correlation between rates of return and higher ESG scores of organisations. Consistent and honest communication helps build this positioning and gives a reason to believe that the organisation is worth investing in, and it goes without saying that public relations will play a role in making this a reality.

Learning from India's most trusted brand

The hallmark of a great brand is its ability to earn the trust of its stakeholders and sustain its leadership through periods of great challenge. Tata is one such brand, one that continues to be rated the most valuable Indian corporate brand (according to third-party studies by Interbrand and Brand Finance). The brand has powered the Tata group into the big-league tables of the top ten Indian corporates for every decade through the past 120 years.

At its core, the brand proposition is inspired by founder Jamsetji Tata's vision of the role of business in the community. He believed that in a free enterprise, the community is not just another stakeholder in business but is, in fact, the very purpose of its existence. If the community is not successful, if the customers, suppliers, lenders and investors in that community are not successful, it is hardly likely that the corporate which serves that community will survive.

This focus on community was further reinforced by the culture of philanthropy institutionalised by the founder and his sons. They created the charities that today are the major shareholders of the Tata Group's holding company, Tata Sons. As the longest serving Tata Chairman (1938–1991) JRD Tata put it, 'The wealth gathered by Jamsetji Tata and his sons ... is held in trust for the people and used exclusively for their benefit. The cycle is thus complete. What came from the people has gone back to the people many times over.'

The present-day Tata mission ('To improve the quality of life of the communities we serve globally through long-term stakeholder value creation based on leadership with trust') harnesses this rich legacy. One of my proudest accomplishments as the first brand custodian of the Tata Group was to enhance the connection of Tata's people with this mission through a focus on employee volunteering. We found that in addition to the obvious social benefits of volunteering, this allowed volunteers to expand their skill sets, increased their job satisfaction and morale and supported team-building, while reducing attrition in the organisation, building brand awareness and creating loyalty among consumers and shareholders.

Tata leaders have sensibly invoked the ideals that appeal not just to their employees but also to other stakeholders and the community, and this has played a vital part in winning their trust. Be it the courage demonstrated in taking on powerful governments on issues of policy (the Tatas' tryst with civil aviation being a case in point) or the willingness to take media criticism on the chin when explaining and defending its actions (during the infamous Tata finance scandal, for example), the Tata Group has done well to pinpoint these and other stories of its commitment to ethical conduct in an otherwise difficult and often corrupt Indian business environment, and to build a sense of pride within and outside the organisation.

Three key factors, then, have played an influential role in the brand's sustainability:

* Leadership and the tone at the top
* Authenticity by walking the talk
* Unceasing, open and transparent communication

These factors have reinforced the sense of purpose with which many employees approach their duties at the workplace and, ultimately, it is what will permit the perpetuation of the organisation's legacy.

Dr Mukund Rajan is Chairman at
ECube Investment Advisors Private Limited

~

The basis of trust, credibility and reputation is ethics

It was very early in my career in a start-up public relations firm that I realised that every PR practitioner is responsible for a) her client's credibility b) the credibility of the firm she represents and c) her own credibility. It was important to masterfully juggle the three, as dropping even one could cast a shadow on the others.

Deeply rooted in words like trust, credibility, reputation (words that define public relations) is ethics. In my early days as a student and practitioner, I often heard the comparison of public relations professionals to medical and legal practitioners who have a strong ethical obligation to their profession. Clauses in client contracts, precepts in engaging with the media, saying no to competing businesses and the importance of confidentiality—not merely of client information but between colleagues and other stakeholders—formed some of the early learnings in my career.

Today, the role of ethics is even more critical. There is enough going on today that reveals the incompatibility between personal, professional, societal and environmental values. In such times, bandying around 'purpose' without an effort to acknowledge, deepen and imbibe values and ethics that are less self-serving threatens to dent the credibility of public relations. Ethics must, therefore, return to the front and centre of the public relations discourse.

Responsible communication, in today's chaotic world, may seem like an oxymoron. The upside is that today, public relations capabilities are being sought by all. The downside is that the motives are diverse and often opaque.

❖ Persuasion is the wheat; propaganda, the chaff. Separate the two. This requires a sense of integrity, objectivity and honesty. Stakeholder engagement sits at the heart of persuasion and it requires space for debate and discourse that brings to light all points of view. Propaganda, on the other hand, drowns debate and discourse in the din of catchy captions, terms and hashtags that capture the imagination of the unaware and often creates an illusion of reality because of the frenzy and followership it can garner.

❖ As storytelling dominates communications, fact-based narratives are important. PR is about facts, not whitewashing. Fact-based narratives require verification and accurate representation, as well as the ability to communicate complex issues.

❖ Are we merely adding to the noise or are we truly adding value? Are we communicating to confuse, to drown sanity or are we communicating to clarify and truly help people make decisions and choose what matters to them?

Nandita Lakshmanan is the Founder and
Chairperson of The PRactice

Knowing the difference between what you have a right to do and what is right to do

'If you can't measure it, you can't manage it. Things you measure tend to improve.' This seems like a reasonable statement to make in the PR profession. But on the topic of ethics, how does one tangibly measure transparency, integrity and trust?

Ethics is about knowing the difference between what you have a right to do and what is right to do. This is a quote I live by and something that I reinforce in my professional life—both at work and with the life and leadership coaching I do.

In the case of PR professionals, this becomes even more important as their primary responsibility is helping organisations build trusted relationships with their key stakeholders. A great deal of work has been done in the last decade to measure these intangibles, yet when all is said and done, we may not be any closer to quantifying these matrices. One way is to measure the strength of relationships built, with a focus on the role of communications in building loyalty and trust-based relationships.

As PR professionals, what we know is what goes into building these relationships. Trust takes time to build, yet it can be destroyed in an instant; we have seen big brands lose their value due to a seemingly small oversight. The admiration, respect and support you believe you had just a moment ago from your customers may evaporate because of something someone in your company did or is alleged to have done. Protecting reputation in such a complex web may be the most difficult assignment, but today this is the work of PR professionals.

To me, the three things that impact the power of transparency in stakeholder communications which could be helpful to achieve this trust are:

* **Tell the truth:** We, as communicators, need to provide stakeholders an ethically accurate picture of the organisation's purpose, values, ideals and actions, with honesty and good intentions. Businesses prefer to keep information confidential. Often there are good reasons to do so, but sometimes, disclosure can build trust too. It's important to make these decisions with an eye on the appropriate balance between the business' proprietary interests and public interest. Excessive secrecy can be just as damaging as excessive disclosure. Trust is impossible when information is distorted, spun, altered or deliberately withheld.

* **Credible two-way communication:** Prioritising transparency makes it much easier to flatten your organisation and avoid a bureaucratic work environment. Listening to your stakeholders across multiple mediums and offering a credible face of the organisation while engaging and addressing them periodically also helps build trust.

* **Promoting a transparent culture:** The onus is also on public relations practitioners to encourage transparency in their respective organisations. The good news is that 87 per cent of people want to work for transparent companies, according to the 2018 Slack 'Future of Work' study,[*] so by building transparency into your

---

[*] 'Trust, tools and teamwork: what workers want', Slack, 2018, https://slack.com/intl/en-in/blog/transformation/trust-tools-and-teamwork-what-workers-want.

culture, you will retain your talent and attract many great candidates, which is a bonus for organisations.

The future predicts a more expansive role for public relations. Although there will always be naysayers who talk about PR practitioners practising persuasion or manipulation, the expectations from the profession have changed for the better. Today, PR is the credible voice of the organisation and of practitioners who are helping institutions be more responsible and responsive, building the cornerstones of ethics and transparency into the profession.

Varsha Chainani is the Group Head of Corporate Communications at Adani Group

~

Ethics in PR makes it more effective

Historically, PR has been often associated with all things unethical—lying, spin-doctoring, manipulating, rigging, rumour-mongering and even espionage. Many journalists, policymakers and members of the public believe that the term 'public relations ethics' is an oxymoron—either an unreal possibility, or smoke and mirrors to hide deception.

In a way, in principle, ethics and public relations are not very different from ethics and lawyers. It is a Hobson's choice, to say the least. We also have a tendency to confuse ethics with morality. Ethics is not the same as moral values. Ethics, in my humble opinion, is about discipline. Ethics in public relations should represent values such as honesty, openness, loyalty, fair-mindedness, respect, integrity and forthright communication. That is the only reason why ethics ought to be integral to public relations.

Like any young profession, the historical development of public relations shows a progression towards more self-aware and ethical models of communication. The negative status of public relations is slowly giving in to its potential for ethical communication. We can now see the maturity of the profession—from one engaged in the simple dissemination of information to one involved in the creation of ethical communication.

To start with, public relations cannot contribute to an organisation's effectiveness without presenting the views of strategic stakeholders to the executive management of clients. Nor can it refrain from advising on the ethical issues and dilemmas that stand to damage an organisation's credibility.

Counselling senior management on ethical decisions is happening in practice, and perhaps more widely than one might guess. Management is realising the value of incorporating a strategic communications perspective in their decisions. Many progressive organisations are already implementing this policy. PR professionals are increasingly paying attention to ethics and how to analyse ethical dilemmas.

We also need to realise that brands have traditionally been studied only as an economic construct. Brands, as a social construct, are still in the process of evolving. A corporate brand is a vital part of corporate reputation management. On the one hand, an ethical brand enhances the firm's reputation; such a reputation in turn reinforces the brand. On the other, any unethical behaviour will severely damage or even destroy intangible assets, as evidenced by high-profile corporate scandals. Ethical branding could provide the company with a differential advantage as a growing number of consumers become more ethically conscious.

Communications professionals must pay attention to ethics before they reach a point where they desperately need it. Once a crisis of conflicting ethics or high media interest befalls the organisation, it is too late to begin searching for ethical guidance. Professional communicators must be conversant with the value systems of their organisations before these values are publicly called into question.

Failing to identify an ethical issue before it is acted upon can result in expensive consequences, in terms of operational costs in the resulting loss of reputation as an ethical organisation. Being hyper-vigilant about the early identification of ethical issues allows more time for analysis, research, discussion and resolution. Early identification also allows the organisation to take a proactive stance in specifying and managing the issue rather than a defensive stance when it is delineated by others.

The time has come now to identify the approach in ethics closest to existing organisational values. The public relations profession needs to include deontological philosophy in its mandate. Deontology is the study of duty which should translate into justice, fairness and responsibility as a more widely ethical organisational culture. The public relations function can encourage ethical debate and consideration through the organisation by using internal communications to focus on these issues.

Therefore, attention to astute and rigorous ethical analysis is essential not only for individual practitioners or the public relations profession but also for organisational effectiveness in achieving long-term success in business outcomes. To integrate ethics into our profession, we need to believe and act accordingly so that public relations is perceived as the corporate conscience of India.

Sunil Gautam is the Founder and Partner of Pitchfork Partners Strategic Consulting LLP

~

Mind the gap

'Why do you exist beyond making money and why should anyone care?' It's the fundamental question all brands must answer if they want to connect authentically with stakeholders beyond shareholders.

India's economy is growing faster than most. The way in which India chooses to grow in the next decade will decide whether we are addressing inequality or growing the gap between the haves and have-nots. While the government's role in shaping policies will have the biggest impact, brands are expected to take a stand for what they believe in to attract a more loyal customer base that aligns with its value systems. More than clever marketing campaigns, we're looking towards brands as role models which can bring people together around shared beliefs and give us something bigger to believe in.

Here are five mistakes CEOs can avoid to mind the gap with responsible communications:

❖ **Hiring a PR consultancy to decide your purpose:** Purpose is an inside-out thing. We either have it or we don't. It starts with answering the questions of why do you exist beyond making money and why should anyone care? A consultancy can help articulate it, shape it and design a framework that puts it at the centre, but it cannot define purpose that doesn't exist in the first place.

❖ **Using purpose to greenwash:** Barack Obama once said, 'You can put lipstick on a pig. It's still a pig.' We cannot buy credibility by merely stating good intent. The purpose of the communications function must not be to 'cover' for business decisions that put profit over purpose.

❖ **Mistaking ESG for CSR for purpose:** Metrics and compliance with good governance practices don't make a brand alone. Brands are built by being consistent with value systems and minding the gap that exists in its stated intent and actions. Treat ESG and CSR as the bare minimum that must be done to be in business. Use communications to tell stories of how lives are changing as a result of them for a stronger emotional connect.

❖ **Getting communications to report to marketing:** The purpose of communications is to build an organisation's relationship with its public. It involves listening to voices that represent stakeholder interests and positioning the organisation as a problem-solver, even if the solutions might take time. It's about building communities of common interest that go beyond making a purchase. Please don't use communications simply to amplify for better marketing.

❖ **Only communicating good news:** Like all relationships, honesty and transparency go a long way in building trust. By proactively sharing tough news, we're demonstrating an ability to accept the hard times and prepare for a stronger future. Vulnerability creates empathy. Consistency will build integrity.

If I could leave you with a simple compass to guide you towards responsible communications, it is to follow the principle of 'no surprises' and to mind the gap between what an organisation says and what it does.

Girish Balachandran is the Founder of ON PURPOSE

10

POWER OF EMOTIONS
IN PR

What stays at the back of the mind after a piece of communication reaches someone? Is it the colour scheme, is it the product USP, is it the format? Or is it that ubiquitous phenomenon called 'emotion'?

Over the past few years, we have been consciously trying to build up a case for emotions in PR. We have realised that as consumers, our brains tend to encrypt emotional memories more than mere data floating around. Data is, of course, very important. It fortifies emotions. It is the RTB—reason to believe!

Every communications professional wants that their brand should be remembered in a more enduring manner so that consumers advocate it more positively than competing brands. The key to this, we believe, is 'emotion'. We say this with a significant sense of confidence. And this confidence comes from the validation of this concept through multiple conversations with business leaders, marketers, brand managers across organisations and many communications thought leaders. We also realised that most of the successful public relations campaigns that we have had the pleasure of being a part of had some emotional hook that connected well with the audiences and created a bond.

We have been advocating the idea that brands should try to create an emotional aura as a part of their everyday manifestations. This builds a deeper foundation for a positive relationship with stakeholders that matter for the brand.

Emotion is the force that helps us sustain memories. In the public relations context, emotions can help sustain the brand message and, most importantly, help create brand advocates who stand up for it in any adverse situation. We have, time and again, also noticed that a consistent subsequent tactical build-up around emotion attached to a brand strengthens this association.

For us, a brand is nothing but a mental image of a product or service created in our minds. The more the emotions attached, the more loyal we are towards it.

The foundation for a brand's emotions is in its 'narrative' or the story they must tell. If one gets the 'who', 'what' and 'why' (who it is for, what it means to the user, why the buyer should purchase it), it's a job well done. Take the example of Tata Salt as 'Desh ka Namak'. The emotion of 'pride' is so overwhelming that we would never think of any other salt brand even if it is brought from the moon (if at all)! Human beings have always loved good stories with emotions and we as communicators must use this to our advantage, albeit in a genuine and honest manner.

Most often for us as consumers, in a brand's communication, we tend to recall the emotions (pride, joy, hope, fear, excitement, anger or guilt) that it provoked in us, more than the USP (features and facts) of the product. Emotions play a significant role in decision-making. It is after this impulse that we try and rationalise. Communicators who have mastered the psychology of emotional connection end up having better outcomes and their brands enjoy top rankings.

Emotional branding can be a differentiator for brands and can help create deeper intrinsic relationships between brands and consumers. These relations, with the emotional dimension, can reduce the risk of a consumer deserting the brand vis-à-vis relations that are need- and cost-based. Of course, creating an emotional bond with stakeholders will require much more than just good communication.

Our strong belief is that emotion in communications can ensure that customers stay loyal for the long haul.

Another common observation is that customers define themselves through the brands they use—clothing brands, watch brands, choice of cars and, nowadays, even the university they went to! Connections happen on an emotional level even in relationships between brands and people.

Consumers like to connect with brands which they feel are reflections of their actual or aspired identity, and when these emotional links to a brand are strong, passions can run high. Take the example of Pepsi and Coke—the legendary wars.

There are so many other examples. Take Nike; the brand has used the idea of feeling heroic to inspire customers across the globe.

A classic example that comes to mind is Dabur Vatika's touching and inspirational 'Brave and Beautiful' campaign that shows a woman who goes bald due to cancer and how her husband and colleagues show faith in her and bring a smile on her face.

Another interesting example is Cinthol's campaign aimed at women: '#ReadyForAwesome'. The narrative uses sports as a metaphor to depict today's women who are poised to own the world against all odds. It is supported by a narrative that captures the bold spirit of women rejecting all societal constructs. It is an ode to those who want to achieve their dreams under any circumstances. The video immediately strikes an emotional chord with viewers as it urges them to overcome every obstacle and face the world.

Many of our advertising friends opine that it is better to sell positive anticipation than anxiety. While we mostly agree, sometimes negative emotions (fear, anger, anxiety) also work if done right. After all, certain categories definitely need it—insurance, for instance, relies on reminding us of the possibility of sudden calamity.

Narratives with emotions that can evoke fear or anxiety have been used with significant success. For example, Saffola's message aims to raise the anxiety of a wife over a husband's stressful life which can cause lifestyle diseases at a young age. The brand's ad, which shows a husband being taken into an operation theatre while there is an ambulance siren in the background, is memorable.

Another classic example of using negative emotions is Hit, an anti-mosquito spray. The brand has used the emotion of fear (of disease such as malaria, dengue, etc.) and anger (due to disturbed sleep by mosquitoes) to come out with effective campaigns that have made it such a huge brand today.

Every communicator knows that branding is incredibly

important—it enables customers familiar with your brand to distinguish it from a sea of competitors. The success of all these brands is about much more than the logo, it is about forming an emotional connection with their customers.

India is a country where emotions run high; watch an Indian Premier League (IPL) cricket match and you will agree. Emotion truly is a catalyst for a purchase decision. However, emotional communication or messaging for a brand is not a cakewalk. It is not as simple as identifying an emotion, creating the message and expecting sales to roll in.

If PR practitioners figure out an emotional angle in their campaigns, we feel it can work wonders. After all, PR is mostly about making an emotional appeal rather than just addressing the reason.

To validate this point, just ask yourself—has anyone brought a fully-loaded variant of Mercedes Benz just to go from point A to B, or do you know many people who would splurge a couple of lakhs to buy a Rolex just to see the time? Any good brand can ensure buyers good quality but in the battle for attention, a brand that truly appeals to the customer's emotion the most wins.

You have done your job as a PR professional if you have enlightened your audiences at an emotional level about how your product or brand would benefit them or those they care about. Each product or service, at its core, is a solution that helps people work, live or play better. So, selling benefits over features is the key.

As such, you might notice (as we have) over the past few years that travel agents don't sell trips, they sell exploration, relaxation, adventure. Lifestyle brands in cars, properties and fashion spaces sell power and status. Hybrid and electric car manufacturers are selling care for the environment. Movie theatres sell romance, time out with family, excitement. Jewellery manufacturers do not sell gold or diamonds—they sell self-esteem. The list can go on and on.

At a very hypothetical level, we have tried to make a framework to generate or infuse emotion in PR messaging. These could help your customers to understand on an emotional level the various benefits your brands can deliver. We base it on the assumption that customers generally respond to an appeal that addresses their multiple needs as mentioned below. You can relate to and remember the brands that have possibly used this thinking process.

- ❖ **Competitiveness/goals/leadership:** Can your product or service help them achieve their goals, make them better than their peers, get a promotion or make them heroes?
- ❖ **Self-esteem/social lifestyle/status:** Does it make lives more comfortable, enjoyable or healthier, or make their friends, co-workers or peers envious of the user of your brand? Do you relate to the customers' aspiration to find love or be seen as a trendsetter?
- ❖ **Dreams/aspirations:** Does your brand connect them with their fantasies, take them away from routine and make them feel like a maharaja or maharani?
- ❖ **Egalitarianism/altruism:** Does your brand give the users an opportunity to feel better and more privileged than most people or give them a sense of purpose?

We can go on and on about how if one can address a few needs at an emotional level, the chances of customers responding favourably to a brand will be high.

Emotions can lead to actions, and as PR practitioners,

it is in our hands to make customers take the actions that we want them to take. That is the outcome we can deliver for our bands or clients.

So, if we agree that emotions are valuable in PR, then it is obvious that we need to figure out the triggers that can actually help us make our messaging stronger. Some brands have mastered it, some are still trying to figure it out and some are oblivious to the fact that authentic emotions generated in the minds of a customer can increase business prospects.

It is no secret that customers bond with brands that understand and connect with their motivations and whose messages touch a chord in their hearts. It is all about putting the customers at the forefront.

We would like to present a three-step thinking process in our PR planning, which can help demonstrate this customer-first focus:

- ❖ Pick an emotion that can create a bond between your product and the customer. It should be sharp and connect with your audience's core emotional needs. This should then be manifested across all your communication modes.
- ❖ Your messaging should then inspire the audiences to emotionally bond with the product. Consumer insights based on needs, aspirations and current trends can help sharpen the messaging further.
- ❖ Reinforce this messaging at every touch point, especially through experiential engagements.

If done correctly, this will take your consumer engagement scores through the roof.

Let us now try and get a bit tactical and list the various emotional triggers that have been used over the past so many years. These are triggers that affect the way consumers feel about your brand, the element that really makes or breaks a decision to buy!

Triggers:

* Sense of belonging (to a community, a cause, family, etc.)
* Freedom and independence
* Fear of missing out, not being ready, or not able to fit in a trend
* Trust as a value
* Competitive spirit: 'Bhala uski kameez meri kameez se safed kaise?' Remember?
* Guilt of not doing the right things, not taking care of self, parents, etc.
* Security and safety as in peace of mind, protection
* Leadership
* Accomplishment or achievement
* Being with the times
* Instant gratification, satisfaction
* Care
* Sadness
* Joy/happiness

And every other emotion that comes to your mind!

PR professionals have a great role to play in figuring out the exact emotions to tap into through their messaging and modes of communication. One wrong step and a lifelong association with an incorrect emotion and the brand is finished.

Research in PR is still in its early stages. We have not seen many brands doing it. They simply latch onto whatever messaging is available and push it through the media. At the moment, researched and data-driven narratives to craft the right emotions around brands and services are essential.

~

Emotional maturity is indispensable and integral to any communications campaign

The success of any PR campaign greatly depends on the ability of the executioner to empathise with the stakeholders and engage them through content and tonality that they understand. This makes emotional maturity integral to the conceptualisation and execution of any communications campaign.

Emotional integration of the thought process into a campaign entails many significant aspects—some deliberate and some subconscious. Since we have limited control over the latter, it may be worth detailing three of the most important aspects of deliberate emotional investment while designing a campaign.

First, the narrative should be driven by our empathy and understanding of the target audience rather than our own perception of the situation. It is significant to point out that this is where the subconscious is most entrenched into our emotional quotient. Take, for example, how we feel about education as a domain. Our own upbringing, academic performance and consumption of what we read and see in mass media, married with our own internalisation of these external factors, can decide our emotional reaction while designing a communications plan. At that moment, it is important to step back, understand the client's business and branding limitations and design campaigns that address the target audience rather than let our inherent biases creep in.

Next, it is paramount to be sensitive towards political, religious, social, geographical or any other divisive emotion while designing a communications campaign. It is also important to be aware that your target audiences will be carrying biases and to interpret communications programmes against the backdrop of those biases. Taking education as an example again—if a brand announces scholarships for students of a university which is in a stand-off with the government, the context and reception of the narrative by the target audience would be hugely different than on other days. In this context, it is very important that the professional makes a deliberate effort to shut out contextual emotions while empathising with the public and advise the brand accordingly.

Lastly, in an ever-dynamic and fast-paced world, it is also important to nurture a good DEQ or Digital Emotional Quotient. One must try to keep pace with the various forms of content consumption and the evolution of their relationship with audiences. Whether it is GIFs, doodles, cartoon strips or animated infographics, the modes of communication are transforming at a frantic pace. Along with these modes, the matrix of evaluation is also changing rapidly. If, around a year ago, it was about page views and engagement numbers, today it is about clickthrough rate campaigns and time spent on a landing page. This might well have evolved further by the time this book goes to print! Along with this, social commentary also presents the hazard of falsely creating an image based on few comments, positive or negative. Understanding such digital nuances will help develop and exhibit social prowess emotionally. Take the example of education again. When developing a crisis management programme for an institution facing regulatory action, while engaging all stakeholders positively is the ultimate intent, it is important to know that when it comes to making choices, 'the influential' is more important than 'the influencer' and 'the customer' is more critical to your narrative than 'the commentator'.

Pranshu Sikka is the CEO of The Pivotals

~

The role of emotions in effectiveness of a campaign

Books. A weekend drive with family. The plaster for that bruise on the playground. Sliced bread. Rice. Poha. Shoes that don't skid. Catching up on my favourite OTT shows. The shortest route. The longest one. The morning alarm. Reading by the night light. Fresh food on the table. The warmth of home. Love. Health. Holidays. Moving house. The job I didn't get. Sadness. Loss. Hope. Dreams. My family. Prayers.

These are some of the things that mark my days. These are just some of the things that have a strong emotional hold for me.

Sometimes, even the simplest of acts come with deep-rooted memories or experiences and, therefore, feelings.

What is life without emotion?

Is the question, therefore, on whether emotion plays a role in any campaign or narrative? Or is it about the kind of emotion or the depth and relevance of it that creates an impact and evokes an action? To me, it is the latter. The former is table stakes. Without it, we have indifference—the last place any brand should land in. Because indifference leads to total lack of relevance and meaning.

What makes it matter?

How do we arrive at the kind of emotion that will make that vital difference?

I have grown up in the world of advertising when digital data at scale was nowhere close to what we have today. We did it in a very simple way. We met people, visited home after home. Spoke to the consumer, her family, her doctor, school teacher and just about everyone who could give us an insight into her life.

I remember spending a full day with a family in south India for research on packaged food. It was 2008, the year of recession and constrained income. The woman of the house showed me how she made ends meet by cutting down on the staple lentils and innovating on interesting curries, as vegetables were cheaper. I felt her pain and her pride in equal measure. Her love for her family and her finding innovative solutions so that mealtimes were not a compromise. Her role as nurturer was clear. She enriched me with learnings at multiple levels. Each learning was an emotion—a story worth telling.

So many of us have grown up walking into stores where the manager greeted our parents warmly by their first names, enquired about our school and health and fished out the exact pair of black school shoes, but only after a pleasant chat. Year after year.

Finally, what makes a narrative rich and relevant is the depth of the insight. The rigour that goes behind understanding the pulse of the consumer. It results in weaving a narrative that never fails to connect with an emotion, making us respond, react, participate.

Emotions in the data-driven world

I have read about and seen debates on whether the data-driven world today is eroding powerful storytelling. Is logic overpowering magic? Does the head matter more or the heart?

In my experience, people-centric, human insight-driven data has led to new business models, opportunities and the power to connect, engage and drive growth. But this can happen only when data is analysed and interpreted to cause a deep human connection based on emotion.

I worked in an area that is largely perceived as transactional. On the back of some strong consumer data-led bedrock, the brand we partnered with made a bold pivot on a proposition that was disruptive to the category. It was on the commitment of trust and care, like only a family can make. The results were significant, with clear shifts favouring the outcome the business had set out to achieve.

Emotions go beyond a good film script or copy. They rest on what the narrative is based on.

In conclusion, emotions help us differentiate, connect and spark off engagement, passion and action. With the right emotion, the potential of effectiveness of a campaign or narrative is very high.

It's down to how we feel about things that make us act.

Babita Baruah is the Executive Director,
VMLYR and Regional Client Lead at WPP

PR campaigns driven by an emotional insight offer unique advantages

Ideas are no longer the domain of the advertising agency. They come from anywhere and when the idea has relatability and relevance, it can become part of a cultural narrative or conversation. We have delivered some iconic campaigns like 'Daag Acche Hain' for Surf, 'Help a Child Reach 5' for Lifebuoy, 'Jaago Re' for Tata Tea and so many more; the common thread being that they all have had emotion at the core and formed a connection with their audience, but they were also primarily television commercials. PR campaigns today have all these ingredients and more. They have the additional ability to get ideas shared on social media, be covered by journalists and bloggers and then have the message amplified by influencers. Powerful ideas need to live in a digital ecosystem, which is where even small ideas can achieve traction. For instance, during the pandemic, a simple idea for the Indian police called 'Main Bhi India Police', an emotional message urging citizens to self-police (delivered through a film that was shot from home), gained enormous traction through earned media, likes and shares, and many top celebrities and influencers spread the message to millions of their followers.

It's wonderful to see the evolution of PR and I have been blessed to be a part of this journey for the better part of three decades. Much of that tenure has been spent in Lintas, an institution that I have called my professional home now for over twenty-five years. My decision to belong to a consultancy group that was multi-disciplinary was an engrained belief that brand communications was not siloed and one has to have a wider understanding. Today, clients expect consultancies to deliver results, and don't particularly care whether the idea and its manifestation into content comes from their PR consultancy partner or their advertising agency. Brands and companies need to build relationships with their audiences, and this is possible only if they communicate meaningfully and authentically. When the communication strikes an emotional chord, the impact of what you say (and do) is significantly higher.

The need for an emotional connection with the audience is even more imperative. Today, a consumer will only be interested in what a brand has to say if there is an emotional core or purpose attached, and this is where the PR professional's storytelling skills come in. There was a study done by researchers at Wharton School of Business in 2011 where articles published by *The New York Times* were analysed to find out which ones got the most social shares. They found that the more the content evoked emotions, such as anger, anxiety, fear, sadness, humour or wonder, the better its chances of being shared repeatedly.[*] Studies also have shown that advertising campaigns with purely emotional content perform almost twice as well as those with just rational content.

My advice to CCOs and other PR professionals would be to make emotions an integral part of the brand strategy. Pick insights and topics that your audience cares about and the response will likely far outweigh a functional piece of

---

[*] Jonah Berger and Katherine L. MilkMan, 'What Makes Online Content Viral?', *Journal of Marketing Research*, 2011, https://faculty.wharton. upenn.edu/wp-content/uploads/2011/11/Virality.pdf.

communication. Today, opinions get formed dynamically and in real time, and it's important to prioritise ideas that strike an emotional chord with consumers and fans, in addition to journalists and influencers. Lastly, measure everything and quantify success on the shareability and social currency of the idea over just PR value.

Ameer Ismail is the President of Lintas Live
and MullenLowe Lintas Group

~

The case for emotional authenticity

In today's times, it is imperative for every brand, business or service to promote their image through emotions. It is no longer enough for brands to engage a popular actor or sportsperson to endorse their product or service and consider the job done. Brands are increasingly feeling the need to engage directly with the consumer and that cannot happen without an emotional connection. This is where the authenticity of the brand, its values and mission become central. Along with the excellence of the end product reaching the consumer, almost every aspect of the brand and the entire journey of the product is scrutinised, and rightly so. Sustainability, carbon footprints, good governance, equal representation or employee welfare are just some of the aspects that have become the mainstay of a brand's reputation now and can only be conveyed with a certain sincerity of emotion and transparency of information.

Three things to keep in mind when using emotions in public relations and advocacy

- ❖ **Authenticity:** This is perhaps the most important aspect to keep in mind while using emotions. If you aren't authentic, you won't connect with people. It is important for brands to build an image that is true to their story and be honest in their day-to-day communications. Even during crisis situations, remember: to err is human and to own up to it is divine. If mistakes have been made, denying and hiding facts is a sure-shot way to pull a brand down. Be it a CEO or a personality endorsing a brand, showing a humane side goes a long way in mitigating the damage.

- ❖ **Sensitivity and timing:** It is important for brands to remember that their communications are intricately intertwined with the fabric of the society we live in. Therefore, it is important to be sensitive to the emotions of the audience they are engaging with, as well to the timing of our efforts. A misplaced press release or communication that doesn't take into account the subtle nuances of public discourse will do more harm than good. The messaging needs to adapt to relevant social topics affecting the audience at that particular point in time, and being sensitive to current issues will enhance the quality of interaction manifold.

- ❖ **Patience:** With a tsunami of advertisements and the downloading of information happening on a minute-to-minute basis, the audience is unable to form an image of the brand immediately. This is especially true for smaller brands that are competing for our short attention spans.

Despite extensive market surveys, hits and misses are common; hence, consistency along with patience must be factored in while communicating in our times. It is important that brands value consistency above all else, appropriately allocate adequate resources to be able to connect with the audience and eventually strike that emotional chord.

Sunanda Rao-Erdem is the Founder and CEO of Seraphim Communications LLP

11

RESEARCH AND DATA-DRIVEN NARRATIVES

It's time to play your CARDS well: Communication Actioned through Research, Design and Strategy.

It was one of the editions of PRAXIS a few years ago. During a general catch-up over drinks with some of the biggest names in the Indian PR business, the conversation took a turn towards a pertinent common issue: how the earned media space has become so cluttered, and the space for good stories has shrunk.

In another setting, a leading PR consultancy CEO highlighted the strenuous efforts his team had to put in just to get a small press note out. It was even more complex when it came to multiple clients vying for the same space. A leading journalist snapped, 'Well, let's swap positions and see whose job is more complicated. With a deluge of press releases, calls, requests on SMS and a constant follow-up by PR types, it becomes a nightmare.'

Such an exchange highlights the inherent overload of information and the challenge for media outlets to create relevant stories to keep readers engaged.

After all, it's no longer about one-sided boastful narratives and expecting the media to pick up stories that only smell of your product USP! Some veteran PR practitioners, even in this day and age, are under the misconception that public relations alone can persuade the public to think in a particular way. Stories you share with audiences must be factual, data-driven and even more inclusive. Our experience also suggests that journalists love these type of stories, as they hold human interest, are backed by evidence and larger consensus and are believable.

In our many years of working in public relations, we have realised one thing: the impact or outcome of a campaign is high if we play our CARDS well, i.e., Communication Actioned through Research, Design and Strategy (another original by us!).

But even if CARDS is just a spontaneously created acronym, it carries a lot of weight.

In the current PR landscape where social media plays such a significant role, public relations is arguably an applied social science. Going forward, it will be more about looking at the stakeholders through a psychological (emotional) lens, deriving insights based on research through conversations with them and then designing campaigns that are more authentic. This, we feel, helps influence public opinion and builds deeper connections between an organisation and its stakeholders.

As we brainstormed more on this topic and remembered some of the successful campaigns that we have had the good fortune to be a part of or lead, one thing is certain: research is the master key to unlock the most robust outcomes from any PR and communications strategy!

Unfortunately, research as a stream of business has always been seen as 'confidential', 'proprietary' and all such terms that create a sinister aura around it.

'Do not share the results in public.'

'It is internal, not for public consumption.'

These are common statements that we have always heard. This has resulted in positioning research as 'stodgy', 'secretive' and 'bland'. Sometimes, 'humbug'.

Research for public relations can set authentic narratives for reputation-building. It can totally flip perception about it, and can be fun, inclusive and creative with outcomes that touch and resonate with the public at large.

Simple narratives can be created with collective wisdom, accrued from audiences segmented appropriately as per demographic and psychographic profiles. Interesting results can be generated, leading to authentic headlines that can attract attention.

After all, credibility is what we want, right?

However, it is sometimes quite disheartening to hear from senior PR professionals who have often found themselves trying to convince their chief executives to provide budgets for conducting research. We pity leaders who do not understand the fact that research is such a fundamental part of communications planning.

Our firm belief is that research is vital at all stages of a campaign—before a campaign commences, during the campaign and at the end of it. Here is why:

❖ Research provides an opportunity to engage with the respective stakeholders. It helps us understand their beliefs and needs and gain insights that can aid appropriate messaging.

❖ Research eliminates the errors that can creep in when the outreach is based on instinct or past experiences. It ensures that the communication is relevant to the stakeholders who need and care for the information. It makes communications strategic, rather than random and aimless.

❖ Research can demonstrate results, help measure impact, check for behaviour change or generally gauge the pulse of the stakeholders. It helps course-correct the strategy, in case the communication is not working out, and ensures better bang for your buck.

A public relations (PR) function without research can never qualify as a true management function which can be tasked to recognise issues and provide solutions. One of the key roles of a strategic communications function is to make the organisation agile in engaging with its stakeholders, be seen as a good corporate citizen and be empathetic to the needs of its customers and employees. Only research enables this.

Competency in analysing data and applying research in our PR operations can certainly give us a significant voice to back our decisions and demonstrate the value of strategic PR initiatives.

This marks the entry of research-driven PR.

If your PR process relies on statistical evidence to generate awareness and uses insights to drive brand narratives, it is data- or research-driven PR.

Although it sounds simple, it can be one hell of an operation. But results are guaranteed. We can vouch for the fact that brands or organisations that use a data-driven PR approach have the upper hand. They do not have to rely on events, announcements or launches to create news. This approach helps in all seasons, especially during a period of lull.

What makes us so bullish about it?

Simply put, results from research can be convincing, authoritative and, most importantly, influential.

Here are four reasons why it works:

* All media houses want exclusive data and findings in a pitch. Original research has the most appeal, as questions are structured in a way that generate fascinating insights to catch reader attention. Journalists love data. Opinions are easily available, but it is quite rare to find someone who has the data to validate them. Original research capabilities make you a credible source for media outlets.

* Research findings are for public consumption. It positions the brand as a thought leader in a topic or industry. For example, a housing finance company that does research on the pains or concerns of an individual seeking a home loan and then provides tips to alleviate these challenges.

* White papers based on research around customer demographics can be used non-intrusively as a hook to generate leads for your sales teams to follow up.

* Research findings packaged well and published online can generate multiple backlinks from just one study. Also known as 'inbound links', they are links from one website to a page on another website. Search engines consider them votes for a specific page. Pages with more backlinks tend to get higher search engine rankings. This helps SEO and site traffic.

Based on our own research, personal experience and conversations with leading PR professionals, we are presenting a simple process and approach to establishing effective, research-driven narratives as a powerful tool in your overall PR arsenal.

Construct a hypothesis that helps validate the brand USP, purpose or narrative that you want to set

Of course, data garnered through research is the true star. But if you do not present the data as a story, the impact may not be as desired. It is imperative that as a PR professional, one must be able to craft a narrative around the data. As we all agree, a story backed with data will only make it more compelling for the media to pick it up.

A smart way to plan a data-driven campaign could be to anticipate the kind of headlines or narratives you want to set for the brand. This hypothesis is based on the problem your brand is trying to solve. For instance, we spoke to a young communications leader who had this to share: 'We used research-driven narratives as a tool to launch a new liquid vaporiser machine. We needed a story hook to grab media and public attention. Our research indicated that about 92 per cent of people were unaware that the dengue mosquito bites in the morning. That became the headline of a story on the importance and effectiveness of using liquid vaporisers against mosquitoes. This was in line with our recommendation that repellents should also be used during the daytime if necessary.'

Segment the target group in a way that multiple cuts of data can be generated from the insights

Segmentation is very important, as research must yield multiple cuts of data. Mass inputs from unplanned samples leads to blunt outcomes. Diversity of the sample could be on the basis of the regular aspects of demography and psychography. The sample may differ from research to research and should be aligned to the respective target groups.

We have observed that an increase in number of responses leads to a reduction in the margin of error and gives a more credible outcome. So, a sample size of about 2,500 across regions can yield enough data to frame an authentic narrative. Of course, the more the responses, the higher the chances of getting picked up by media outlets.

Do a study to validate data

The most effective way to maximise the use of research is to design the questionnaire with the aim of accruing authentic headlines. The process should involve brainstorming ideas and possibilities. This creative process should not be rushed. Research in public relations can be rolled out effectively in a short period of time. Insights can be framed qualitatively and then fortified quantitatively. If the hypothesis in the earlier case was that not many consumers knew that the dengue mosquito bites in the morning, the research could quantify the number so we could understand the gravitas of the situation. It was found that 92 per cent did not know. This became the headline and a call to action.

Analyse the results to pick newsworthy elements

Developing story angles and narratives based on numbers and insights becomes very important. In the above case, if it was now known that the dengue mosquito bites in the morning, the susceptibility of kids getting bitten was high as they are in school during daytime and none of the schools have repellents. It again qualified as an authentic public interest concern and paved the path for popularising outdoor repellent formats like roll-ons or patches. This is the power of research-driven narratives. If smartly rolled out, multiple insights with connected, believable and influential stories and narratives can be generated.

The best part of a well-defined and segmented survey is that data cuts related to specific geographies, age and other demography and psychography parameters can be derived to form hyperlocal narratives.

Work with media outlets

When the insights, data and narratives are robust, authentic and relevant, the media is more than happy to pick them up. The fact is that the humble press release is never going to die. Original research findings through detailed press notes also help journalists to add their own views and recommendations. Dissemination through the wire can lead to voluminous coverage. Online coverage and digital PR possibilities leading to backlinks can position your host site as more credible for Google in terms of SEO and improve rankings.

Repackaging research narratives

The best thing we like about research-driven narratives is the possibility of long tailing. It covers all the content that generates traffic for multiple days. This increases brand thought leadership, helps in backlinking and helps in raising and maintaining search engine rankings for years from when first published. These narratives, if packaged well, can be long-term dividend-paying investments and be packaged into multiple social assets.

Much beyond the essential manifestation of these narratives through earned media and news coverage, a lot of creative options are available to fuel your PR outcomes.

Listed below are some of the formats in which the narratives can be repurposed.

❖ **Infographics:** Infographics are truly in vogue. Visually appealing, to-the-point and fresh, they are the best solution to present complex data to an audience whose attention spans are constantly challenged. Charts, bar graphs and line diagrams are dead. Infographics are shareable and if designed well, people will spread them online, making them go viral.

❖ **Blogs:** Blogs are great in terms of shareability, easy to navigate and perfect for short, crisp reading experiences. When you have great data, it can be creatively presented in a blog. The best part is that one research study can lead to multiple blogs, increasing the chances of backlinking. They can be customised for different audiences. A good blog will not only showcase the research findings but can also incorporate recommendations from experts.

❖ **White papers:** White papers can be very effectively used to share data and insights. A simple compilation of all the data into valuable insights, hypothesis, a solution to the issues and a potential way to implement it with a call to action can be a super downloadable asset on your website, not to mention that people who download the white papers are potential leads.

❖ **Webinars/podcasts:** Webinars and podcasts are more personable, and allow for listening to the views of experts on the research subject and narratives, with content that is easy to repurpose for various other platforms.

❖ **Quotes/social snackable content:** We have always been intrigued with the shortening of formats. Social snackable content is designed for social media. They could just be quotes, images or 'did you know' highlights of research data points. For example, 'Did you know the dengue mosquito bites in the morning?' with an image. Multiple data points manifested like this, with a link to the page where the original research is hosted, is a great way of mobilising traffic. They can be thumbnail formats and promoted on social media platforms for mass consumption.

The simple point that we are trying to make is use research, invest in it and generate narratives that are backed by it. The level of research could be directly proportionate to the type of product, the brand or industry. It is amazing to see what authentic data can to your campaigns.

Research and PR

In the foreword to his seminal book on public relations *Crystallizing Public Opinion*, written in 1923, Edward Bernays, considered to be the founding father of the practice of public relations, notes:

'In writing this book I have tried to set down the broad principles that govern the new profession of public relations counsel. These principles I have on one hand substantiated by the findings of psychologists, sociologists ...'

He ends it by writing: 'If I shall, by this survey of the field, stimulate a scientific attitude towards the study of public relations, I feel that this book has fulfilled my purpose in writing it.'

Further, whilst lamenting the labelling of the public relations counsel as a 'propagandist', he articulates the scope and the function of a public relations counsel as 'one who directs and supervises activities of his clients wherever they impinge upon the daily life of the public. He interprets the client to the public, which he is enabled to do in part because he interprets the public to the client'.

Bernays clearly suggests that the practice of public relations was 'rooted in the study of public opinion' and the work of the professional counsel was based on 'interpreting that opinion to the client'—this is what we at Astrum call the 'science of reputation'.

He wrote this almost a century ago. Unfortunately, as the wheel of time turned, science-based public relations did not progress; instead, creativity in being an effective propagandist for clients came to be recognised as PR's most valuable stock-in-trade, and PR professionals, for the most part of the twentieth century, were recognised as 'masters of spin'.

Even in the twenty-first century, the profession continues to be largely associated with either mitigating bad press or generating good press, now popularly known as 'earned media', whether online or otherwise. The work involved in generating insights to understand public opinion in the domain of public relations continues to remain largely elusive, though we do see some islands of excellence.

Mark Penn, the founder of Stagwell Group and my mentor in research-based consulting, would be one such island of excellence and a global leader in the application of the study of public opinion. And in the intersection of academia and business, I am a student of Professor Robert Cialdini's science of persuasion.

Why don't we see more of it?

Millions are invested in the study of consumer behaviour. So why does study of other stakeholders not attract the same level of investment? In my experience of over two decades in public relations, and over a decade in science-based reputation management, I can attribute the lack of mainstream investment in understanding stakeholders to two factors. One, public relations is a victim of its own image of a 'publicist par excellence' and valued more for the creative expertise and access to editorial decision-makers and other opinion-makers. Thus, basing the work on the structured understanding of public opinion is a tenuous connection. Second, the continued inability of public relations majors to walk their talk in making a stakeholder insights-led public relations programmes the foundation of their work. Barring a few firms which make serious investment in developing research-based consulting capabilities, most make very little use of science to study and interpret public opinion as the basis of public relations campaigns.

However, it is encouraging that today, almost all juries at awards for the public relations profession seek 'stakeholder insights' as an essential criterion. As an increasing number of science-based programmes win accolades, it will encourage clients and consultancies to invest more in generating relevant insights.

To conclude, if the purpose of all public relations is to create a preference in the minds of the stakeholders, then understanding their minds and hearts is the natural beginning and end of the process of preference creation—the end being measuring 'shifts in preference' as the metric of success. Using 'Net Promoter Score' is a good beginning.

I have learnt that reputation research is unlike consumer research because of the complexity of factors that influence it, as well as the hard-to-reach respondents to generate authentic insights.

In the end, I would say that research is not the end, but a beginning to generate the insights that are most pertinent to inform your reputation strategy. Focus on the relevance and authenticity of insights to inform both actions and communication, as good communication cannot be a substitute for bad actions.

Ashwani Singla is the Founding Managing Partner
at Astrum

Why brands should invest in research-driven narratives

Social media has disrupted not merely the way we communicate but *what* we communicate about. Brands may be reluctant to admit it, but they are rarely the protagonist of people's social media feeds. Most people's favourite subject is, in fact, themselves.

From a consumer perspective, personalisation is not just a value addition but an absolute; consumers will simply ignore generic, impersonal content. And indifference has become a brand's public enemy number one. As such, brands that are perceived as irrelevant and that don't generate engagement have to systematically invest more in marketing, advertising and communications to generate a response.

The effects can also be found within the workplace: nine out of ten millennials today claim that they would take a pay cut to work for a company that supported their personal values.* Again, the financial implications are equally valid—employer brands which don't connect to employees on their terms tend to have to pay more to recruit and retain the best talent than brands that do.

This is where research-based narratives can prove indispensable. Given the above logic, brands that speak directly to and about their audience are more likely to enjoy a competitive advantage on all fronts, from sales and marketing to recruitment and retention.

---

* Zameena Mejia, 'Nearly 9 Out of 10 Millennials Would Consider Taking a Pay Cut to Get This', CNBC, 28 June 2018, https://www.cnbc.com/2018/06/27/nearly-9-out-of-10-millennials-would-consider-a-pay-cut-to-get-this.html.

A narrative that is compelling and repeatable, with a long shelf life that people can relate to and find interesting, is useful. If suitably constructed, it represents a bridge from the product to the wider, common ground of daily discussion and conversation—the connection between the brand and its potential audience.

I emphasise the term 'potential audience' since one of the advantages of a well-constructed narrative is that it can enable a brand to relate to a consumer (or employee, or investor, or regulator) who may otherwise remain indifferent. The trick, of course, is that the individual must believe that the brand is talking about them (that is, the starting point of the narrative). In reality, this is just a means to an end; the resulting engagement will be used to 'imperceptibly' introduce the brand and its proposition, all on the individual's terms and from their perspective.

The research aspect is also critical; the best narratives are based on genuine insights about the audience. Your brand or product may not necessarily figure in the same narrative. Not yet, anyway. The opportunity is to make the two synonymous.

There are countless examples of established narratives connecting brands with their potential audiences. In each case, it's not the product that is the protagonist but the audience. Once the connection is established, the product can then be introduced.

My favourite one dates back over sixty years; in the 1950s, the then managing director of Guinness Brewery attended a shooting party (yes, those were the days; think PG Wodehouse!) in County Wexford, Ireland. There, he and his hosts argued about the fastest game bird in Europe and failed to agree on the answer.

Inspired by this incident, in 1954—the idea of a definitive compendium of verified records—the *Guinness Book of Records* was born. Today, it remains the singular authoritative source of human and animal achievement. I love this story because it perfectly demonstrates the process and power of audience-based programming. The campaign was based on a human insight (life before 'big data', remember?), the latter was based entirely on the audience (drinkers who found themselves in bars arguing over the fastest, longest, heaviest, oldest). And, most of all, it is this insight—rather than the nature and characteristics of the product—that connects the brand of stout to the audience. It's pure association.

Many others are also notable for their longevity. Michelin's little red guidebook was originally conceived simply to encourage more motorists to take to the road. At a time when there were fewer than 3,000 cars in France, a guide listing reputable and safe guest houses and restaurants along France's less frequented highways would become an essential glove compartment accessory. Today, it rates over 30,000 establishments across three continents; more than thirty million Michelin guides have been sold worldwide to date.

Keep in mind that Michelin is a tyre and rubber manufacturer. Yet, in the guidebook, there are no references to tyre treads or pressures in sight! Once again, it all started with the audience; in this case, current and potential car drivers.

Starbucks' 'third place' story has been running for nearly fifty years; again, it's all about the audience (there's no mention of coffee). The third place wasn't even a Starbucks concept. It was first elucidated in a book by sociologist Ray Oldenburg, *The Great Good Place*: '... One's "first place" [is] the home and those that one lives with. The "second place" is the workplace—where people may actually spend most of their time. Third places, then, are "anchors" of community life and facilitate and foster broader, more creative interaction. All societies already have informal meeting places; what is new in modern times is the intentionality of seeking them out as vital to current societal needs ...' Starbucks seeks to be that such a space for its consumers, who similarly recognise the value in that and visit their stores for the sense of sense of community the company strives to provide, making their value proposition something intangible, yet desirable, beyond just coffee.

In essence, if your audience believes that they are the protagonists of your story, they'll willingly connect to your brand. And that makes business sense—whether you are selling products, recruiting staff, raising funds or all three.

Roger Darashah is the Founding Partner at
LatAm Intersect PR

USPs or consumer research to build narratives?

A while ago, I came across a very simple idea which, like most simple things, can often evade us. Helene Deutsch, the Polish-American psychoanalyst, wrote, 'After all, the ultimate goal of research is not objectivity, but truth.' This has left an indelible mark on my mind. As we would all have experienced often enough in our profession, objectivity is a lens applied when evaluating established information. That, however, is not the purpose of research. So, what is?

Research, as I see it, is not about looking at existing knowledge, but about opening up a clean slate to note down facts—new or otherwise.

The golden rule in communication is to address what resonates with the audience in a manner that works for them. Imagine the magic that will unfold when our messaging fits in perfectly with what our audience wants to hear. No matter what we say and how well we say it, communication only becomes effective if the audience connects with our messaging. Thus, in my experience, it is not an 'or', but an 'and' that connects the two—USPs and consumer research. One without the other is, quite frankly, redundant.

In my experience, there are two aspects to effective communication: relevant messages and a strong reason for communication. If I have to approach a client and pitch Alphabet Media, presenting a well-strategised and articulated presentation six months into them onboarding a new consultancy, the entire outreach would be a wasted exercise. In a similar vein, a detailed presentation during the multi-consultancy pitch that does not speak about my team's strengths would not serve any purpose either. Timing and depth of information have to come together to seal the deal.

When working on a new campaign, we (as a team) spend a great deal of time with the client understanding the research and its findings, what it means for the client and what it reflects about their audience. This throws up several interesting aspects about the requirements of the audience and the need that the product satisfies within them. It gives us deep insights into their ecosystem, their considerations at the time of making a choice and so on.

And this rich background helps us design the best possible solutions—both for the client and their audience.

Thus, knowing what to communicate and when and to whom are essential to business success. This research is a strong foundation for the effort to follow and increases the chances of success.

Three roles that research plays in brand building and messaging

* **Understanding the audience:** We can all safely say that research helps us to deep-dive into the psyche of our audience. And the first step towards this is to define them accurately—a step that requires us to go back to the drawing board from time to time.
* **Ear to the ground:** Market conditions are dynamic—a truth that we, as brand builders, live with every day. And it is imperative, as a good marketer, that one has a keen understanding of the on-ground rumblings that may turn the tide for the brand—in favour of or against.
* **In times of crisis:** Research may be multi-pronged. It may be deployed at the beginning of an assignment to gauge market conditions, in the midst of an ongoing campaign to understand efficacy and effectiveness and at the end to judge impact. And it comes in handy most when the brand may be going through a crisis. The impact of the crisis on the brand image, how consumers are impacted by it, the resultant effect on business and many such aspects can be gauged by deploying tools of research in a timely manner.

Tejal Daftary is the Founder of Alphabet Media

Quality matters

Financial data and numbers do add value to a news report or feature, but qualitative research could be a game changer.

Having been a magazine journalist for a large part of my career, 'research' has been the cornerstone of my storytelling. As business journalists, most of us write about the strategies of various corporations, dissect their P&Ls and do endless calculations to prove our point as to how the strategy of a company could go horribly wrong in the long run. However, more than often, the in-depth analysis we do runs the risk of sounding like a research report of a brokerage. Why would a reader read our stories if we are going to sound like a research report? Our stories need to have much wider perspectives beyond what an organisation and its competitors are doing. The focus has to be a lot more on qualitative research.

If we are writing about an FMCG company, for instance, apart from speaking to the company, competitors and a few analysts, it may be worthwhile to spend time with the distributors, retailers and consumers. Talking to wholesalers in Tier II or III markets could generate a wealth of information—whether the company's newly launched products have enough takers, whether the packaging needs to be re-looked at or whether the brand has stiff competition from local players. Nuances such as these significantly add value to the storytelling. In fact, well-rounded qualitative research could even capture trends that market research agencies and brokerages may have missed out.

During most parts of 2022, FMCG companies reported low volume growth, especially in rural markets. While most of us believed that consumer sentiments were low due to hyper-inflation, that actually wasn't the case. Consumer sentiments, on the contrary, were upbeat as the monsoons were good and they had disposable income. Yes, they were buying less of national brands and had downgraded to regional alternatives but the desire to consume was very much there. What surprised me immensely was while they had cut down on grocery spends, they were investing in farm equipment to enhance their produce. A lot of farmers were investing in electric scooters as they needed to save fuel for their tractors, with fuel prices rising sharply. What I am trying to convey through this example is the importance of qualitative research. Since I visited these markets to do research, I could bring in significant value into my storytelling.

Now, if I were to talk about the importance of data, there is no doubt that it plays a crucial role in enhancing the authenticity of the story. Getting financial data is the easiest bit. What about access to interesting qualitative data? That is what would add further value to the narrative. Qualitative data needn't necessarily be about consumption trends. Information about consumer mindsets, culture and food habits could also come in extremely handy.

Finally, my two cents for PR and corporate communication professionals would be to be thorough about the sector of the business they are representing. While pitching a story, it could be useful if they can also include a fair bit of qualitative data points, as that helps in evoking the interest of the writer to explore the topic.

Ajita Shashidhar is the Editor-at-Large of Fortune India

12

COMMSTECH, AI AND ALL THAT JAZZ

Picture the scene from the hit Hindi movie *Dilwale Dulhania Le Jayenge*. The train on which Raj is travelling has left the station. And Simran is running to catch it. Likewise, the technology and data train has left the station and the PR profession is trying to catch it. It may be immaterial to some whether or not Simran caught the train. However, it is imperative that PR professionals get on the technology one. During conversations with many senior PR professionals, it has also dawned on us that many trains carrying verticals that could be owned and nurtured by PR have already left the platform while the profession is still struggling to catch them. Just to validate the point, about a decade ago, 'digital' became a buzzword and there was an explosion of everything related to digital—resources, agencies, platforms. Did the PR community ever join the bandwagon? At the moment, it's still catching up.

Now the buzz is around AI, the metaverse, ChatGPT and virtual and augmented reality (VR, AR). At the moment, we are witnessing a huge trend of 'cognification' and we feel

AI will certainly permeate every aspect of our lives. Has PR caught this train? More on this and the impact of AI on PR in a later part of this chapter.

Technology in PR and corporate communications has been a topic of discussion at almost every conference. We have seen PR folks discussing the pros and cons, non-availability of budgets, competency issues, lack of good partners and many more impediments, although some organisations and consultancies are much ahead of the curve when it comes to adopting technology.

A quick poll we did of thirty top corporate communicators and PR consultancy heads revealed that 85 per cent agree that technology could free up a lot of time and lead to better productivity. However, only about 60 per cent said that they fully utilise technology to enable decision-making and measurement.

Mundane tasks like tracking media clips, message analysis, tracking influencers, quick desk research and more can be technology-driven, and the time saved can be used for strategising the finer aspects of public relations. There is huge scope to employ technology in measurement, tracking journalists, content analysis, understanding sentiments across multiple segments, competition analysis, consumer insights, etc. It can be an endless list. Some major parameters are listed on the next page.

Qualitative measures	Quantitative measures
• Share of voice	• Press release hit ratio
• Coverage tonality	• Journalist hit ratio
• Coverage spread by geographies	• Industry stories participation hit-ratio
• Coverage contribution by journalists	• Key message analysis
• Measuring the reach	• Thought leadership analysis
• Headlines and photograph mentions	• Correlation with viewership data
• Presence in articles	• Correlation of PR data with footfalls/sales
• Content categorisation across themes	

Technology can throw a lot of data at you. With the right tools, good technological infrastructure, a lot of common sense and the ability to connect the dots, one can really come close to being a data scientist. Of course, no one can replace a good data scientist! We need more of them in PR circles.

The marketing fraternity learnt quite early on to leverage the software and tools to roll out campaigns based on data and insights, measure them and showcase their value. The term used by some of the marketers is 'MarTech', and it has become big business.

MarTech, which could be called the evolved sibling of CommsTech, has helped marketers automate their tasks and take data-driven decisions. A simple key result area (KRA) for MarTech has been to find customers, reach out to and engage with them, personalise offerings and demonstrate effectiveness. Some classic examples are tools like programmatic platforms to target content for sharp demographics, using a content management system (CMS) to assimilate relevant content or using web analytics software that helps attract and retain customers.

Similarly, for the PR profession, CommsTech is the answer to the need for technology tools that can help better planning, execution, analysis and measurement of campaigns. Technology will keep evolving. It is the PR professionals who have to keep up by using data and technology in their operations. All we can say is that the sooner professionals adapt to these changes and jump on the CommsTech bandwagon, the better they will be able to face a VUCA world.

CommsTech offers the following possibilities:

- ❖ Daily, weekly, monthly, quarterly or yearly dashboards with insights around your brands vis-à-vis competition
- ❖ Insights related to the broader impact of political, cultural, economic and environmental issues on brands
- ❖ Alerts for tracking adverse narratives and banter, or raising flags on potential risks and opportunities
- ❖ Real-time notifications on keywords when mentioned on social media (leadership team names, brands etc.)
- ❖ Performance of messaging and product launches in segmented geographies
- ❖ Performance of content in micro-markets
- ❖ AI to monitor campaigns, bots and curb misinformation using quick responses.

We observe that the PR profession, even if it must deal with more complex data (simply because of more stakeholders), has predominantly not utilised technology the way marketing has. The PR community should look seriously at CommsTech to enhance effectiveness. The good news is that there are multiple tech tools available for PR professionals to base their campaigns and measurements on. The real challenge is how to integrate all tools together, mine the data effectively, base the PR strategy on the data and see the PR effectiveness curve moves northwards.

Let us try and delve more into CommsTech.

We have noticed an uptick in conversations around data, analytics, measurement and predictions when it comes to public relations. CommsTech, which is short for communications technology, became the new, commonly-used term for the tools and platforms that communications professionals can leverage to plan, execute and measure communications campaigns. In essence, CommsTech helps communicators do what they were doing more effectively. And since digital engagement has become the predominant way in which one measures how people interact and consume information, it is time to reimagine the public relations function. Credit goes to Page Society for advocating the need to adopt CommsTech.

Progressive PR organisations have taken steps to adopt CommsTech. They have inched forward from simply churning out press notes and focusing on corporate reporting to becoming digitally savvy and more stakeholder-focused, reputation-driving operations, all the while engaging with the right people, developing contemporary competencies and sharpening online presence.

It's time others joined them. Using CommsTech to deploy analytical PR and communications functions means gaining the ability and the data to test the effectiveness of content, map stakeholders, track and generate trends on the basis of consumer insights and set narratives with a call to action that is beneficial for business. This is useful not just for reputation-building but also for other tangible business outcomes like leads, sales, employer brand, valuations, etc. This will help the profession to be seen as a value creator rather than a cost factor.

One of the fallouts of the pandemic has been summed up by the phrase 'planning is out, agility is in'. The past two years have prepared us significantly to deal with ambiguities. The number of times campaign dates were changed or one had to hold back releases or sometimes create one overnight went up significantly. The rate at which social media crises amplified has touched the roof and without technology, tracking and responding to adverse narratives is nightmarish. It is also no longer useful to solely follow annual content calendars. Going forward, PR's turnaround time will be minimised further. An ability to quickly create or change plans, or simply listen and respond in an agile manner will differentiate good teams from others.

We believe CommsTech can significantly increase the ability of public relations professionals to deliver much more than they currently are. Progressive teams are fast acquiring contemporary skills, enhancing tech skills and boosting their digital savvy. Some of the teams that we have tracked are consciously working on building skills around analytics, data science, agile content creation, etc. These are great steps towards the adoption of CommsTech. We feel the true manifestation will be seen when PR and communications teams will also include data scientists, behavioural scientists and experts from the field of sociology or anthropology. With the adoption of these elements of CommsTech, it will be a new era for PR and communications professionals.

If you are a trend tracker, you would have probably heard the word 'metaverse' more frequently in recent times. Metaverse for PR is taking shape. A virtual world that we can access using VR and AR headsets is not a new idea but has suddenly become a frequent topic of discussion. It can allow brands to tell their stories and connect with consumers in ways unimagined. No geographical limitations, direct-to-consumers, deeper engagement—these are the phrases a PR professional loves to hear. The possibilities are immense and we see increased chatter around this subject. Be prepared.

The question is, are we willing to adopt? Where do PR professionals rate themselves on the scale of digital fluency?

Are we adept at analytics and number-crunching? Are we tech-savvy?

Contrary to popular belief, to set up your own CommsTech infrastructure, you do not need huge budgets and complex labs. One just needs to believe in the possibilities that CommsTech opens up.

PR professionals need to get out of their comfort zone and start believing in automation and enhanced use of technology. A budding young PR professional of high calibre showed us an article that projected 25 per cent redundancy in organisational positions by 2025 because of use of technologies and automation in PR processes. He saw this as a threat and was contemplating moving out of the profession. Of course, with AI and other enabling technologies, the worry is that mundane repetitive jobs which can be programmed would possibly become redundant. However, organisations would benefit in terms of strategic contribution from PR and rise in productivity and profitability. We are certain that if implemented well, CommsTech will have an excellent impact on PR and corporate communications. It will bring some sanity to data mining, which will lead to a new level of trust in insights—for instance, the ability to predict trends and public sentiment can help launch products at the appropriate time and can help proactively mitigate crisis situations.

Come to think of it, the sky is the limit!

Organisations have to foster a culture where decisions are based on data and consumer insights. Traditional data gathering processes are slow and costly. Technology can help get data faster and enhance agility in taking decisions. The culture of customer obsession will help increase the sharpness and impact of communications.

Demystifying AI in the PR context

We realised that this is such a hot yet misunderstood topic when, during one of the PR conferences, a presentation on the future of our industry mentioned AI, which sparked furious debate afterwards.

As we understand it, AI is an assortment of technologies, algorithms and tools that aspire to make machines as smart as humans. It entails use of data, detailed algorithms and processing technologies and learns from patterns in the information that's available. A popular example is ChatGPT (Chat Generative Pre-Trained Transformer), an artificial intelligence chatbot developed by OpenAI and launched in November 2022. It is built on top of OpenAI's GPT-3.5 and GPT-4 families of large language models and has been fine-tuned using both supervised and reinforcement learning techniques.

Depending on the way we adapt and look at it, the impact of AI on PR could be huge, mostly positive. Just imagine a world where machines have the competency of understanding audience sentiment in real time on the basis of immense data and can also create bespoke messages and get them to audience segments via sharp targeting, all without human mediation!

AI may sound sinister, but we believe it has the power to take things to the next level.

Organisations have experienced that enabling AI at their enterprise level has increased their operational efficiencies. Artificial intelligence will certainly be more productive than human workers when it comes to repetitive programmable tasks. However, humans will always outperform machines in jobs requiring empathy, relationships and imagination. And these are basic tenets of PR and communications. So, we are one up!

Coming to the fear of job losses across the spectrum due to AI and ChatGPT, there are multiple reports claiming different time frames and percentages. However, these are vague estimates and statements, and we would rather think about how we can use AI to our benefit. Change is constant. For example, when computers came in, professional typists (typewriter operators) went out of a job. Those who enhanced their competencies survived. So, it is all about being up-to-date on skills and using technology to our own benefit. AI in PR, we feel, is an enabler. Any professional should be happy to have these technologies to help them perform better.

We firmly believe that AI will not define us—in fact, we could define it in a way that it is beneficial and adds value. AI is not good or bad. It is the manifestation of the user, just like the internet—it can be used both for fake news and for authentic narratives. AI's true value is in augmenting the human experience.

Here's our take on where AI can be an ally for PR folks:

❖ **Data-driven decision-making:** AI is all about data, cognification of information and identifying patterns to predict the next steps. If the data is correct, decisions cannot be wrong. So, at a very base level, with AI at work, PR professionals would be able to avoid guesswork and decide when to launch a campaign, which region to pilot it, whom to engage with and maybe even narrow down on the most appropriate influencers to work with. Imagine your system's media lists giving you pop-up recommendations for journalists based on the stories they do (just like how streaming services recommend movies of similar genres). Think about the impact analysis that AI can carry out, that too with real-time updates, trends and coverage sentiment and what it could do for your decision-making. The measurements would become robust, and we feel there could be a completely new set of success metrics that will replace the anecdotal ones currently used by many.

❖ **Realistic audience sentiment analysis during crisis and brand health:** We have all personally experienced the 'need to respond' during an incident (that is not even a crisis yet). An ambiguous situation can make even the best crisis communicators overreact and make decisions that may be regrettable. Again, imagine, during a crisis, if your AI-based crisis communication system mines data globally and the algorithms, using their language processing ability, establish the region- and audience segment-wise sentiment of the narrative. How easy it would be for crisis managers to then respond without getting emotional. Let us stretch this imagination further: today, a lot of digital content, be it tweets, posts, videos, podcasts, text messages, etc., goes unmined. How cool would it be if an AI-based system could process this data and give out indicators of the brand health vis-à-vis competition in real time?

❖ **Bespoke messaging with micro-targeting:** Stories are what we absorb as humans. Imagine if they accurately target specific audience segments in a way they like and on platforms where they consume it most of the time. This could be epic. The era of bespoke messaging could be just around the corner. AI can enable micro-targeting and that too in innovative ways, maybe even using VR and AR apart from regular modes. It could even redefine how press conferences or briefings are conducted. For global organisations, AI could help better localisation of content. In essence, PR professionals should enhance their skill sets and adopt AI to underline the indispensable value that they bring to the table. In fact, contrary to the theory that AI will replace jobs, we feel that it will up the game of PR. Very soon, AI/ChatGPT is likely to generate media lists, recommend influencers, analyse sentiments or even write a press release in a hundred languages with zero error. However, can AI take stakeholders for lunch to discuss issues or story angles, empathetically explain the organisation's stance during a crisis or plan exclusives with favourite media friends? No, not yet, at least. That's what we're here for!

Cut through the hype

Technology has revolutionised the legal, finance and marketing worlds. Communications and public relations are playing catch up. The Edelman 'Future of Corporate Communications Study 2021' reports that 70 per cent of CCOs say that communications technology is a top area of investment and 56 per cent say they are increasing their use of technology.[*]

If corporate communications professionals are to succeed, they need to understand and embrace the opportunities that technology offers to transform the way they work. But then, the big challenge is to be able to identify which technologies are going to be essential and which are simply hyped. And when there are competing technologies, which are the ones that will win? In the 1980s, the VHS–Betamax war resulted in a substantial win for VHS, despite Betamax being significantly technically superior.

At a mundane level, communications should already have mastered contact relationship management systems (CRM), analytics and data. But the sad reality is that many professionals still only have a rudimentary grasp of their potential and uses.

The one technology that is already making major waves is AI. AI can impact just about every area of professional communications and corporate affairs.

The AI already exists to predict if an article or social media post will go viral. There are hundreds of start-ups

---

[*] 'The Future of Corporate Communications', Edelman, 29 September 2021, https://www.edelman.com/sites/g/files/aatuss191/files/2021-10/Future%20of%20Corporate%20Communications_FINAL_FULL_REPORT.pdf.

using the GPT-3 engine to create automated writing tools and for sentiment analysis, most of which have potential for PR and communications. AI can analyse and catalogue images and videos. It can be used to automate elements of video editing and production.

But beyond AI, there are other technologies we need to be aware of, such as how blockchain can be used to verify corporate facts and news. We need to know how deep fakes can be used against us or how we can use the same technology to create digital humans as virtual spokespeople.

Cutting through the hype is essential, as one of the big challenges is being able to justify the investment as a priority to the CEO or C-suite. Another challenge is being able to resolve internal politics and conflicts. Adopting new CommsTech often requires buy-in from other departments such as corporate IT, sales or marketing. The same technology might be used in different ways, by different people, for different purposes.

However, the biggest challenge for introducing new technology is always the cultural change it needs. Successful digital transformation requires the right leadership. It isn't just about the technology, but also about addressing workflows, processes and professional practice.

Communications teams also need to be offered the support to help them embrace the new technology and see it as a benefit, not a threat. AI writing could soon replace some PR writing jobs, but that should free up those doing the writing to do other work that AI can't.

Stuart Bruce is a PR futurist and
the Co-founder of Purposeful Relations

Future of CommsTech in India

When I imagine the future of communications in India, I see a world embedded with technology that can empower communicators with insights, not just from the past but also from the future. I imagine a world where I read a magazine and the magazine reads me and dishes out dynamic content that is not a function of my past searches but informed by my state of mind and heart. I imagine an era of humanised tech.

The possibilities of conversational AI, which leverages our voice, and better still our thoughts, can bridge the linguistic, neuro-diversity and illiteracy gaps in the true sense. I imagine real-time response methods available to communications practitioners informed by big data analytics at the fingertips, tools that read not only keywords but actual emotions and understand the spice of human discourse: humour, satire, irony and the whole nine yards.

Now, let's reflect on the current state of CommsTech in India. We are exploring the dimensions of big data analytics, making decisions informed by target audiences, competitive landscapes, dynamic geopolitical developments, weather and climate dependencies, cultural nuances and a whole lot more.

We are also witnessing the rise of the bot economy and the application of blockchain in marketing and communication in the age of self-publishing corporates and individual content creators. The new data privacy and social media laws and governance structures are taking form. Technologies like deepfake AI and its consequences are still being understood.

New practices like data journalism, fact-checking and content engines are all being deployed in spades. Measurement tools are pushing for professional benchmarking but the jury is still out.

Three challenges of implementing tech in PR

- ❖ **Domain-specific skills and knowledge:** The core of any successful technology deployment begins with design thinking with the user at the core. Technology cannot be an afterthought to domain knowledge and communication skills. If public communication is the paintbrush, technology is the canvas of the digital era. We need interdisciplinary skill sets like techies, architects, designers and filmmakers, among other experts, to design for the needs of dynamic audiences.
- ❖ **Corporate sponsorships/budgets:** Technology needs investment and a long-term view to leverage its benefits. Technology is not perfect; it learns, evolves, fails and triumphs just like any other human endeavour. And it needs budget and leadership commitment over time to assess and realise its full potential.
- ❖ **Professional standards:** We need professional bodies to dedicate time, energy and mindshare to light up the path and hone the collective intelligence to ensure that communications practitioners have the contours needed to successfully implement technologies in ever-changing regulatory frameworks.

Today's communications profession in India is seeing the early stages of tech evolution with a tremendous growth opportunity, given its complex and diverse cultural context and affordable cost of innovation. The question is whether public relations will lead or follow the tech revolution. The answer, as always, depends on the choices we make today.

Tuhina Pandey is Communications Leader at
IBM, India and South Asia

~

Technology enhances value of PR

Technological advancement and adoption across all walks of life has gained significant momentum in the last few years. It has challenged the way businesses approach their operations and competitiveness and embedded new behaviours in people across the board. PR, as a key enabler of brand building and brand reputation management, is no exception. However, the role of technology is that of an enabler—a starting point is understanding how it can contribute to PR beyond just offering great tools and platforms in search of problems to apply to. Instead, identifying areas and domains through strategic thinking and planning, where tech tools and platforms can come in and help improve processes and outcomes, ought to be the approach.

In my view, the role of technology in enhancing the way PR works with brands to achieve outcomes can be broadly classified into three buckets. First, helping automate repetitive tasks to improve efficiency and enhance responsiveness. Second, keeping up with evolving communication channels and the new ways of engagement that they spawn by becoming adequately familiar with the underlying logic and algorithms that make these possible. Third (and this is where we are in the early stages of adoption within PR), leveraging technology to deliver high-value outcomes for brands.

Several routine tasks such as media monitoring, social listening, media landscape mapping, creating information dockets, information dissemination, internal data management and many others can all benefit from automation. Setting up processes to manage the flow of information (internal and external) and speeding up decision-making during dynamic situations is increasingly becoming a routine expectation from brands. All this can help free up a lot of time within a PR organisation to spend on more strategic and creative thinking and value-adding brand-centric activities.

The explosion of consumer and business platforms and new channels of communication and influence are making demands on business practitioners across sectors and functions—especially PR and marketing—to keep pace with understanding, adopting and applying. The ability to identify and adopt appropriate tools, platforms and techniques to manage multiple channels and mixed media is essential for orchestrating effective reputation management for clients in a digitally matrixed world. This cannot be achieved without having more than a passing familiarity with how information flows within and across channels, the underlying algorithms of reach, engagement and impressions, their associated analytics and the appropriate measurement metrics to gauge success in meeting specific objectives. This is not a matter of choice or convenience anymore—almost all of this is now considered part of the core remit of a PR organisation.

Finally, using technologies under the broader umbrella of AI can drive competitive advantage for communication firms and brands. The starting point is invariably data: internal, external and third-party. While data is available in plenty, in and of itself it has no value. Knowing how to harness it is what drives value for PR practitioners and brands alike. Knowing where to look for appropriate data and information, reducing noise by discarding what's irrelevant and applying the right research and analytics techniques to the contextual information signal is critical to an enhanced understanding of the brand, its performance, its competitive landscape, its target audiences, the media landscape and other levers of influence, which will enhance the ROI on content and campaigns and offer tangible measurements of outcomes at low cost.

Evidently, technology will have an increasingly important role to play in how PR helps brands take themselves and their stories to their target audiences. However, key elements such as critical thinking, creative storytelling, crafting innovative campaigns and pitches, developing meaningful relationships with media stakeholders and influencers and appropriately defining the metrics to measure and establish the success of outcomes are still the remit of PR professionals, and I believe technology doesn't have answers to these questions yet.

Abhilasha Padhy is the Co-founder and Joint Managing Director of 80 dB Communications

Metaverse and PR

Whatever we may write about the metaverse and its impact today is likely to change rapidly. Global tech, economy and policy environment are evolving fast and this dynamism will continue to accelerate. But for now, there is enhanced focus on VR and AR and how they can augment the connection between physical and digital worlds, providing options for leisure, entertainment, gaming, work and other areas of critical use.

If you have participated in an immersive virtual experience, it is possible you've been to the metaverse as it exists today: a wide range of virtual online experiences that can extend to the physical world. While still developing, the metaverse is making inroads into several sectors, including those that can help in socio-economic development, such as health and education. The metaverse can also aid in the skilling of workforce as well as provide opportunities for greater social inclusion.

But what does the metaverse mean for brands and businesses? New Web 3.0 technology has started opening fresh avenues and opportunities for brands; for instance, VR can provide interactive shopping adventures using new currencies built using blockchain technology.

However, it's still early days and brands need to be strategic about the use of developing technologies and ascertain if these align with their business goals. When we look back at how Web 2.0 and social media redefined the media landscape, we can be certain that Web 3.0 will take that experience further. The metaverse presents new ways to create, consume and experience content.

But the metaverse, while promising opportunities for brands and users, comes with its own set of challenges.

Given how nascent it is, there are ample risks and challenges in areas such regulation and privacy that need to be addressed in order to keep it safe. Brands should take pre-emptive steps to resolve potential concerns in areas such as reputation protection, intellectual property, trademarks, data privacy, regulations, compliance and ethics. Keep in mind that the technology is still new and one must study user behaviour and early adoption. Brands should approach the metaverse with a view to test, learn, experiment, explore and innovate.

The metaverse has the potential to change industries the way social media changed the course of PR and marketing, and take brands to a new digital frontier. PR professionals have to think beyond traditional tactics and discover experiential routes within the metaverse to attract and engage consumers. For that, education for yourself as well as for your client is critical to understand the opportunities and challenges thrown up by Web 3.0. Exploring the metaverse may challenge comfort zones, but will also open up vistas for creativity and innovation.

We need to look at more holistic and multidimensional communications solutions beyond PR. With the metaverse and similar tech developments, the most important change will be the choices that audiences are presented with. Brands will need to prepare for that opportunity for audiences using new immersive tools.

It is still very early to see where the metaverse is headed. But it is clear that it can change the face of sectors such as gaming and entertainment and have far-reaching effects for health, education and other service delivery mechanisms.

Rakesh Thukral is the Managing Director of Edelman India

~

PR re-imagined in the realm of VR

The metaverse has all the potential to be a game changer for new-age PR; we just need to be mindful of the pitfalls.

Digital creativity is the mainstay of marketing, communications and public relations today. And with creators harnessing the power of sophisticated technology to build smart brand narratives, the customer engagement game is getting edgier by the minute.

The newest contributor to this game is the metaverse.

The metaverse has opened the doors to a world with infinite possibilities. A world where brands can create real-as-life digital experiences and build relationships with customers in immersive ways like never before.

Although the physical world will always remain relevant, the potential of practising public relations in this cutting-edge virtual world is mind-boggling.

'Experience' is the new black

Storytelling is one of the most impactful tools used by PR experts. The metaverse can give a whole new meaning to storytelling by moving the audience from the periphery to the centre.

It can also bring real presence into any digital space. PR professionals could help their clients build brand stories that audiences can 'experience'. Be it a fashion show, a movie launch or celebrity meet-and-greets, the metaverse can allow PR innovators to push boundaries and create new, experiential campaigns.

And imagine how media engagement can work in the metaverse. Forget press releases and media kits. Think virtual reality tours of new stores, product trials, celebrity interviews—PR on steroids!

Easy does it

Exciting as it sounds, let's not lose sight of the fact that it's still early days for the metaverse. The technology is still being fine-tuned. Moreover, like most advanced tech, it can have security and safety risks.

It is crucial for PR practitioners, therefore, to first educate themselves about the metaverse so that they can provide proper guidance to clients and even draw up best practices to use it as an engagement tool. Clients need to be made aware of the importance of respecting consumer privacy when engaging with them in the virtual world. They must be advised to invest in cybersecurity measures to keep malicious attacks, data leaks and brand manipulation at bay.

The immersive aspect of metaverse technology also means sensory exposure. PR consultants must be transparent with clients about the sensory impact of virtual experiences when designing campaigns in extended reality spaces. This is critical for the safety of the audiences and to ensure that brands do not lose customers due to badly designed, overwhelming advertisements.

'The most human thing about us is our technology,' media theorist and philosopher Marshall McLuhan once said. And that is what I believe PR futurists see when they look at opportunities to use the metaverse—the mind-boggling potential of bringing together the two main drivers of PR strategy today: people and technology. Emotions and intellect. The heart and the brain behind modern-day PR strategy.

Nitin Mantri is the Group CEO of Avian WE

Can the metaverse change the way we do public relations?

Disruptive technologies and powerful, transformative forces have been chiselling away at the face of communications and PR as we've known it. As a society, we have rapidly moved from texting to more visual and mobile content within a few short years. The next stage is nearly upon us: Web 3.0. There are going to be big new disruptions that we need to gear up for, as it promises to offer immersive experiences where users can meet, collaborate and play in online virtual spaces.

For PR and communications professionals, the metaverse presents a huge opportunity. From the perspective of the industry, some of the fundamentals we should focus on are as follows:

❖ **Opportunity to create immersive, meaningful experiences:** For instance, it will not just be about pitting physical events against virtual ones. It will be about strategies that provide a seamless hybrid opportunity to engage consumers where they want to be—a continuum of the physical world. Apps and experiences that would be interoperable between the physical and digital world will provide additional touchpoints as well as greater opportunity on virtual platforms.

❖ **Creating personalised engagement:** Crafting touchpoints irrespective of the physical challenges will be possible. For example, a 3D tour of a US-based research facility or a virtual workshop with digital avatars of key opinion leaders—such experiences will be possible, although understanding and executing them will entail a steep learning curve.

❖ **Scaling and expanding possibilities**: The metaverse will also help make initiatives global, allowing them to transcend barriers. The magnitude and reach (and consequently, the new possibilities) for a brand to reach consumers and drive differentiated engagement is immense.

❖ **New game, new rules**: Even though a playbook doesn't exist, as the space matures, we will learn and adapt. Therefore, upskilling to be able to leverage these technologies, whether it's understanding the platforms, their technical workings and the guardrails around them, will be critical to thrive in this ecosystem.

❖ **Possibility of misuse**: As it is with every technology, there is good potential and there is misuse. The pitfalls around potential brand risks will need communicators and brand custodians to assume the role of watchdogs and brand safety stewards. As new ecosystems mature, the crisis playbook will need to be modified.

What are the three things in-house communications leaders will need to bear in mind as they plan campaigns around metaverse?

❖ One must learn and adopt the right skill set to embrace new technologies and deliver pathbreaking campaigns. Today, we talk about integrated communications but the metaverse gives the opportunity to do so much more. Understanding how to do is an absolute must in order to win in this space.

❖ With the metaverse, brands will be able to record each step of the consumer's journey. Comms and marketing teams will need to be agile and responsive as they track consumer engagement, define growth channels for the brand, create personalised experiences for consumers and incentivise positive consumer behaviour.

❖ Data security and consumer privacy will continue to be major issues, as data ultimately drives the experience and enhances it. Balancing the risk and the opportunity will thus be an imperative for communicators.

Notwithstanding the risks, it is a new era for the internet. Now, more than ever, is the time to learn and adapt.

Sunayna Malik is the Managing Director, India, Senior Vice President, APAC of Archetype

≈

Metaverse is the future that we will create, not predict

The concept of a metaverse is relatively recent, still in development and not well understood, not yet. But though it is still in its infancy, it is likely to shape the future of the internet. And India has numerous reasons to be optimistic about its potential impact. As the world's most populous nation with a substantial smartphone user base and some of the lowest data prices globally, India is well-positioned to embrace and take advantage of this new technology. Additionally, India's relatively young population has a history of quickly adopting new technologies and openly expressing their thoughts and emotions, making it likely that the metaverse will have significant ramifications for the country.

Brands, not audiences, will determine the future of the metaverse, unlike Web 2.0, which was shaped by consumers.

Companies like Nike, Adidas and Starbucks, recognising the immense potential of the metaverse, have already begun investing in it, creating a vision of a new digital economy where users can generate, purchase, and exchange goods.

Greater accessibility

In the current social media landscape, while brands collaborate with third-party platforms to tell their stories, their fanbase remains inaccessible, limiting the brand's ability to build loyalty and engagement. One of the first ways brands can benefit from the metaverse is by establishing a direct relationship with their fans rather than relying on a third-party platform like LinkedIn or Instagram. Starbucks is a pioneer in this space. The Starbucks Odyssey program offers fans access to non-fungible tokens (NFTs) that they can earn by spending and buying experiences at different stores. This creates a range of possibilities for fan engagement, including the ability to trade NFTs, receive discounts and interact with fans of other brands. The metaverse provides unlimited opportunities for brands to connect with their fans in new and exciting ways.

Immersive experiences

The future of the metaverse holds immense potential for brands. By leveraging the metaverse, brands will have the opportunity to create a new level of immersive experiences for their customers. For instance, in sports, live matches are a significant experience for brands, but in the future, the metaverse will allow for a wider range of interactions, from the build-up to the aftermath of an event. Fans will have the opportunity to connect with like-minded individuals globally, share memorabilia and create lasting memories. Brands will have access to the cultural and behavioural nuances of their fans, allowing them to create even stronger relationships.

Monetisation

The metaverse also provides increased monetisation opportunities for brands. The virtual world allows for the creation of unique and engaging experiences, from live events to product releases that drive customer engagement and loyalty. Brands can monetise these experiences through various means such as ticket sales, virtual product sales and advertising. Additionally, owning a direct relationship with customers in the metaverse enables brands to gather valuable data and insights, allowing for targeted and personalised marketing campaigns. This results in higher conversion rates and increased revenue.

The future is uncertain, but I am certain that very soon, brands, entrepreneurs and influencers will be able to operate their businesses in the metaverse with endless opportunities.

Atul Sharma is the CEO of Ruder Finn India and Head–Middle East

~

Ways organisations may benefit because of the metaverse

The metaverse opens up a number of possibilities for organisations that want to benefit from this new wave of opportunities stemming from the virtual world of reality.

As the metaverse grows and adds more and more users who engage with brands and experiences in this world, organisations that adapt and adopt this as a means and form of communicating with their customers will benefit from the trend.

Speaking of engagement, from virtual events and virtual tours to curated experiences that are tailormade for brands, customers can get an array of options to learn more about the products or services on offer via concept- and theme-based engagements. Organisations can also invest in showcasing their product diversity, finding innovative ways to advertise and get an edge over competition. From a reputation and marketing standpoint, this creates newer ways of interaction with a cross-section of customer profiles that will give the brand an added advantage.

Not only will engagement change but it will also lead to new ways of transactions with virtual wallets and cryptocurrency coming into play. This also means economies of scale will kick in with leverage that can be driven in terms of optimising operations, driving better cost efficiency and having a direct impact on operational costs.

The future is all about communities and collaboration, and virtual communities are a great way to find and build connections for businesses which are not as geographically diverse in the real world, giving them access to wider networks that are spread across the world without having to physically transport people or businesses into spaces in the real world. The virtual world helps create new partnerships for brands that can link up for similar customer profiles, which subsequently leads to better brand awareness and market reach.

The future of work is now a talking point everywhere, with newer models of hybrid work and work-from-anywhere gaining traction. The metaverse offers new forms of communicating that haven't been possible before. This creates a wave of opportunities for companies to engage with internal stakeholders for collaboration and investment. This also extends to training, gamified education and awareness for employees. Imagine the possibilities of team building and team engagement that can be crafted for better retention as well as better coordination between people and teams.

While we wait for the full tilt of the possibilities to arise, it will be good for organisations to start recognising this as an area for investment of research, resources and how to leverage the space to craft a fine, niche identity for themselves.

Shreya Krishnan is the Executive Vice President and Head of Marketing and Communications at Aon India

13

EVERY COMPANY IS A MEDIA COMPANY

During a general catch-up over drinks with our friends from the PR fraternity, we were discussing the issue of the clutter prevalent in all genres of media. The topic of discussion was the 'battle for attention'. Fake news, constriction of the media space and the general perils of low coverage were being dissected.

The conversation veered towards how difficult it was getting to reach consumers.

Is earned media enough? Would reaching out to stakeholders directly through owned media be more beneficial and is paid media's effectiveness dwindling? The conversation was interesting but there was no decisive verdict as to what the best way is.

Common sense says that a judicious mix of all is the solution.

Integrated communications has been the talk of the town, but the larger question is about the trustworthiness of the content, the structuring, the size and the source.

At the moment, customer experience and brand ethos are the core of any owned media platform strategy—the aim is to bring brands, influencers and consumers together to co-create content and engage wider audiences. 'Being heard' is one of the most valued aspects that audiences seek today from brands. We believe that one should make the consumer the protagonist and not limit the engagement to transactional purposes.

Direct consumer engagement

The trend and strategy of engaging directly with audiences and influencers has grown stronger. This approach gives consumers (and potential users) the possibility of connecting with the brand, experiencing the product or service and being a part of the brand's story moving forward.

The latter point is particularly important for direct communication to be successful; in this case, the audience is the main character and needs to feel like a part of the story. Any such engagement is ultimately dependent on the participation of the audience, not only during the event or campaign itself but also (for direct engagement to achieve its true potential) long afterwards.

Direct engagement represents a complementary approach to a traditional communications strategy and is not an alternative. Consumers today prefer to have a direct channel of engagement with brands since, unfortunately, there is a shrinking trust in communications channels due to fake and paid news.

Apart from the many one-way, traditional means of communication, companies have started mastering social media technologies, enabling their customers and other stakeholders to be a part of conversations. It is no longer a one-way broadcast medium; it is an open platform where conversations develop and narratives are formed. Millions watch, participate, comment and create perceptions.

Today, one needs to master media technologies more than ever before. Companies that successfully manage to do so will be far ahead of those that sit back and wait. Content creation has been decentralised. Everyone is a publisher and smart brands have proactively begun building relations and forming ecosystems of partners for content creation as well as advocacy and testimonials via influencers, key opinion leaders or employees using WordPress, Drupal and many more tools that have made publishing content easy.

The key aspect of any communications strategy is to generate awareness and engagement amongst the existing and potential audiences of the brand. While earned, paid and social media offer this, owned media gives brands the opportunity to share stories creatively with their customers and vice versa, albeit with more control regarding content and narratives. Though it's a slow-burn process, it builds a bridge between customers and brands to engage with each other more experientially, authentically and effectively. Godrej L'Affaire, Lakme Fashion Week and Design Dekko are classic examples of owned media properties in the experiential genre. They are completely PR-driven and the outcomes have been significant.

Experiential owned media properties with a direct consumer connection are increasingly becoming a powerful tool for building communities and mobilising influencers. We firmly believe the best brand stories are the ones woven along with consumers. If your process of driving your own media experiential content strategy is right, your consumers and influencers will become your advocates.

The theory of gatekeepers in journalism is offset in owned media with the theory of RECCE (relevance, engagement, content, community and experience). Since customer experience and brand ethos are the core part of owned media platforms, it pushes brands to create relevance among its target consumers by driving engagement using interesting content which eventually leads to community-building through experience. Earned media at its best!

How does experiential PR fit in?

Engaging the millennial consumer is a different ballgame today, as the average consumer is well-informed and pandered to with multiple choices. Merely offering a high-quality product isn't enough. The right engagement is the important.

Brand owners including marketers, PR professionals and digital folk are finding creative ways to showcase narratives through innovative experiences that will help build sustained brand equity. Organisations must provide customers with personalised experiences within the overarching narrative that can help them connect with the brand.

Experiential PR can play a strong role in ensuring share of mind space and this is supported by data. A Harvard Business Review survey showed that 93 per cent of business owners say that hosting an event is integral to their marketing plan. This after 91 per cent of consumers say they look at brands more favourably after attending events and 85 per cent are more likely to buy a product or service after going to one.[*]

---

[*] 'The Event Marketing Evolution: An Era of Data, Technology and Revenue Impact', Harvard Business Review Analytical Services, https://go.splashthat.com/rs/985-MUN-268/images/HBR-Report-Event-Marketing-Evolution-Splash.pdf.

Experience it, believe it!

Through strategically designed experiential owned media platforms, brands can help foster trust and brand loyalty; they also help build a community, especially when experiences are effectively combined with influencer engagement and digital storytelling.

The One Plus Music Festival, which included a star-studded line-up of artistes such as Katy Perry, Dua Lipa and Amit Trivedi is a good example. Through this unique experience, the brand catered to its own community as well as youngsters who craved global music festivals.

Immersive storytelling

Another example of experiential marketing that is trending now (and has the potential to evolve further) is immersive storytelling. An organisation can get consumers to 'feel' the brand and forge a meaningful connection by crafting a unique and engaging sensory experience that forms the centre of its story. One brand which has successfully used an immersive platform and digital storytelling to reach out to its consumers is Bacardi.

Casa Bacardi—the brand's experience-driven consumer engagement initiative—features music, fashion, sustainability and mixology. The alcoholic beverage brand has been co-creating fresh digital content that resonates with consumer passion points to drive the message of its global '#DoWhatMovesYou' campaign.

Owned media over paid and earned media?

Well, it is not an either/or choice. A robust strategy will use a judicious mix of owned, paid and earned media to reach its ultimate objective: brand resonance and equity. Today, the lines between paid, owned and earned content have blurred. Therefore, any strategy must find a sweet spot where there exists a confluence of all four channels (paid, owned, earned and social).

Earned or organic media will never lose its relevance. Print will never die. There have been many obituaries penned for print media in the past, but it has shown tremendous resilience. In India, we have always considered printed information to be a trusted source of information, and this shall continue. In fact, India is one of the only few countries in the world where readership has been growing. Digital mediums continue to thrive as well. Therefore, we firmly believe that there is enough space for all channels to co-exist. How suited a channel will be for a particular campaign entirely depends on the stickiness one can create.

While earned, paid and social media are mediums to do this, they come at a cost but offer less control. Owned media creates a bridge between brands and its consumers that strengthens with bi-directional exchange of ideas and stories. It also offers more control and opportunities to co-create stories that are driven by experiences, which leads to more authentic engagement.

Owned media channels must be based on **authentic** content creation through influencers, a **community** of KOLs to drive thought leadership and **engaging** audience through experiences. If your owned media strategy is built on these pillars, it will create strong resonance with your target groups.

During the pandemic, the sensitivity threshold of the audience fell remarkably. Any form of vulturism or cause-washing was frowned upon. At the same time, not everything must be looked at with a myopic view and be branded as opportunistic. Some stories must be told notwithstanding the risk, but only if they truly represent the values of the brand.

Therefore, brands are trying to build a strong and direct communication channel with its audience. If a brand weaves a narrative that is built on authentic brand connect and experiential engagement, it will resonate with the audience and increase chances of shareability. In current times, engagement and experiences are the two most important currencies for brands.

Key to a successful content channel owned by a brand

How does the audience perceive a brand? What are the expectations in terms of value, narrative and experience? A robust owned media strategy fills the gaps between the brand and audience. Once you figure out the answers, each channel warrants a different content strategy and tonality. Like the four Ps of marketing, the four Ps of owned media channels are: people, platform, participation and perseverance. Understand your audience, choose the right platform, make them participate and persevere towards building a long-term connection with them.

～

Refresh, reinvent and stay relevant

The question that communicators should ask themselves is not whether one should build their own media platform, but rather how long their organisations can survive without building one. The easy accessibility of social media platforms as well as content management systems like Wordpress has made building an owned editorial platform very easy. However, the challenge lies not in starting a platform but in sustaining it; not just producing content, but also telling thoughtful stories. The demands of an owned platform are as strenuous as the ones faced by any publisher running a digital platform. This includes building a loyal audience, measuring metrics rigorously and bringing out engaging content.

In 2015, when I conceived Flipkart Stories, an initiative that *The Mint* called 'a public relations coup in the world of corporate communications', I was very clear in my mind that we would create an editorial platform that would be as good as any independent global digital publication. The first task was creating a crack team of writers, copyeditors, illustrators and designers led by an experienced editor assisted by a data and analytics expert. Their job was not just to find out interesting stories from within Flipkart but to also build readership, dominate SEO and evangelise the goodness of e-commerce.

The team came up with interesting stories like how Naxalbari, a village that gave its name to the Naxalite movement, is now embracing e-commerce with gusto or how Pokhran, the site of India's first nuclear test, is now a thriving e-commerce centre. These were all stories reported on the ground from the heartland of India that included iconic places such as Jhumri Talaiya, Mughal Sarai and Wasseypur.

When unscrupulous elements started running fraud campaigns using Flipkart's name, we came up with stories on how to differentiate fake products from real ones. Even today, if you search for 'Flipkart fraud' or 'Flipkart fake' on Google, the first set of search results will always lead to Flipkart Stories.

Any owned editorial platform is incomplete when it does not tell the stories of the employees. However, the mandate to the team was not just to tell plain, vanilla ones. The stories that the team discovered and produced included an intern who came up with the blueprint of Ekart, and the office boy who pretty much started the delivery network of Flipkart.

The biggest challenge that any owned platform faces is sustaining it after the euphoria of the first few months. How do you ensure that despite it being an owned platform, it does not become a staid mouthpiece? How do you refresh, reinvent and stay relevant? In the final analysis, it is you, the communicator, who will be the editor-in-chief, the publisher and marketing head of this platform. The buck stops firmly there itself.

Senjam Raj Shekhar is the Head of Global Communications at Mobile Premier League

~

Owned media is driving earned media for brands

Media consumption patterns have undergone a drastic shift in the past decade. A robust communications strategy can gauge the audience's needs based on their content consumption habits across media types, be it owned, earned or paid media platforms.

It is important for brands to generate customised and engaging content that forms the backbone of owned media. Owned media channels are perhaps the only vehicles that deliver the exact message brands want their audience to receive. With no filters and unmediated by any third party, they help establish brand presence by increasing awareness and building trust.

Owned media gives absolute control to the brand and is a great source of data regarding customer preferences or buying patterns. All this data, if used effectively, can become the bedrock of effective customer engagement across all platforms. When looking at owned media platforms, there is a range of mediums available, each with their own distinctive attributes. The goal here is to ensure that brand communication is crafted specific to the medium in use. If the delivery method is not suitable for the medium in question, the outreach is likely to fall flat with no effect on long-term brand recall. Even the way app notifications are crafted affects a brand's image amongst customers. Style, quality and delivery method are important aspects, regardless of the way it is being pushed.

Every platform has a place in the overall brand communication strategy and with equal weightage given to each. While a brand's website is a true reflection of its identity that allows consumers to deep-dive into its world, it ought to also use social media channels since they are important engagement tools that help a brand build and maintain relationships with the audience. It's not a risk-free zone but still a place where every brand should be active in order to reach and promote themselves to consumers at the most microscopic level. Customer communication collaterals that translate into customer mailers, campaigns, magazines and newsletters are also useful to any brand. These channels are affordable owned media properties that help the brand reach a large number of people with specific information at any given time.

Owned media helps reinforce key messages to the audience while giving absolute control to the brands over the messaging. While owned media properties may be comparatively inexpensive, maintaining accuracy of content and consistency across these channels is vital. It can effectively complement an organisation's overall brand-building efforts while providing support to the campaigns on paid and earned media. Earned media is considered trustworthy by customers and the first step to gaining earned media is to steadily grow owned media channels that customers instantly notice and engage with.

Rashmi Soni is the VP and Head of Corporate Communications at TATA SIA Airlines Limited

The opportunity in owned media

Today, consumer attention is costly but impossible to avert during a crisis. Owned media—brand websites, blogs, social media channels—has taken the spotlight in corporate communications. With such platforms, brands attempt to cut past the clutter at a time when information is abundant, misinformation is rampant and time and attention are precious.

Owned media lends brands the option of a one-stop source of information, allowing them to directly reach key stakeholders. During the pandemic, communications strategies saw a considerable pivot and the old playbook was thrown out of the window as brands navigated previously uncharted territory. Many met this challenge with great agility—from leveraging owned media assets, making company announcements or releasing instructional do-it-yourself videos to using their platforms to amplify important social messages. Communications by leadership eventually acquired a greater significance, both in times of crisis and business-as-usual. Stakeholders looked to leaders to cut through the inertia of uncertainty and provide trusted information.

In times of major crises, silence is not always golden. Failure to respond to consumer concerns leaves room for discontent and baseless speculation. Quick, transparent and clear communication imbued with accountability and sensitivity is essential. Owned media offers greater security and resilience around messaging, allowing brands to take control of narratives and enabling them to offer factual, evidence-based responses without the story spinning out of control.

Transparency tactics are multi-fold. For instance, an FAQ on a contentious tool created to alleviate concerns with simple, clear information can build consumer trust. Crises occur in stages, meaning that tactics must evolve with time—thus, communications should reflect prevailing stakeholder sentiment. FAQs can then give way to case studies of those benefitting from the brand's offerings or to a blog post that sheds clarity on the company's way forward. During a crisis, the option of dark sites or pre-built websites to 'turn on' as needed, equipped with relevant facts, also enables preparedness.

And for business as usual, owned media has its unique set of advantages, allowing brands to build a distinctive voice. Brand channels can fulfil what people want from leaders: fast communication, taking a stand and investing in their community. Making the most of owned media is a powerful, unparalleled strategy for reaffirming controlled messaging while ensuring brand presence and sustained resonance.

Rachana Panda is the VP and Country Group Head of Communications, Public Affairs and Sustainability at Bayer South Asia

∽

Owned media properties

I firmly believe that every company can be a media company. Every company needs to engage with various communities, its customers, employees and stakeholders. Owned media serves as the foundation of paid and earned media efforts. It's a misconception that such platforms are only particularly compelling for B2C companies as they need to build direct relationships with customers. For example, in the food segment, Godrej's Vikhroli Cucina has created a community of food lovers, chefs and content creators to engage with each other and effectively utilise conversations around food as a social currency.

B2B companies can also utilise owned media platforms effectively. For example, General Electric uses its pages to inject humanity and relatability into its complex projects. They focus on storytelling and creating content centred around how their services and products benefit their customers on a day-to-day basis.

There is no doubt that owned media strategies are complex and require a real commitment of time, energy and resources. I feel the future of such platforms is authentic, compelling content and not an explicit sale pitch.

These strategies must have an outside-in approach. Before we communicate, it's important to listen to and get involved in online discussions. Paid and earned media aren't going away. But if you want to truly be disruptive, it's time we rethink owned media and make it a more strategic part of the communications mix to craft inventive experiences for our target audience.

At Godrej, our platforms (Godrej L'Affaire, Vikhroli Cucina and Design Dekko) are based on three basic tenets:

❖ **Authentic content creation:** Investing in content pays dividends. To win new customers and earn greater loyalty from existing ones, we must invest in creating high-quality content.

❖ **Building communities of influencers and KOLs:** To drive thought leadership, we use audience insights and brand advocates to inform, entertain and inspire customer loyalty.

❖ **Authentic experiences:** The biggest limitation of paid and earned media is having a purely transactional relationship with customers. We aim to turn isolated interactions into a connected experience with cross-platform integrations and on-ground events to help create fulfilling experiences for the brand and its followers.

Our strategies help us create value for our consumers beyond just products being sold. And our community of loyalists is not just full of passive consumers—instead, it includes active co-creators of our platforms. Where most media strategies are about 'push', owned media strategies are about 'pull'—where you're not only building brand advocates but also building a digital safety net for your organisation.

Michelle Francis is AVP of Corporate Brand and Communications at Godrej Industries Limited and Associate Companies

14

TEN COMMANDMENTS OF CRISIS PREPAREDNESS

It was a beautiful evening celebration after the successful completion of a well-represented communications conclave in Mumbai. It was also the time when a few potentially damaging instances around some big known brands had come to the fore and the communications fraternity present was trying to put forth its own views on how these incidents could be rescued from becoming crises for the brands in contention. In hindsight, we can say that one of the situations was managed well and did not blow up into a crisis. However, the second one gave the CCO and the CEO a few weeks of sleepless nights, social media trolling and a substantial hit on the stock price.

Nothing can be more depressing (or for some, exhilarating) than a crisis. One of the most exciting parts of working in corporate communications or public relations is when there is a crisis. PR professionals won't admit to this publicly, but they thrive on a crisis because it is one of those times when they get to rise, call the shots and shine—if they manage it well, ethically and effectively.

Most large organisational crises evoke mental images of losses, fallen stocks, deaths, closures, brand carnage and a lot of emotional trauma for the management and employees—all while the world watches. The aftermath usually kills brands or changes organisations for good.

Visualise, and you will understand the same way as we did, that every issue starts as a small incident and, if not managed well, becomes a crisis.

An incident is an unplanned event that interrupts normal procedures with limited or no impact on people, the business or the environment. An incident that is not solved quickly often develops into a crisis. As a potential crisis, an incident must, therefore, be handled by the crisis management structure using the right tools as soon as possible.

A quick poll amongst young public relations professionals during a Zoom call laid out different descriptions of a crisis. Some of the common phrases used were 'disrupts organisation's profits', 'tampers with reputation', 'increases scrutiny by stakeholders', 'creates organisational stress', 'threatens organisation's sustainability' and so on. None of them is wrong.

Let us take a few moments to understand the life cycle of a crisis and arrive at a holistic definition. It is a given that just like everything else, a corporate or product brand is prone to risks. All risks remain dormant until there is an intervention that brings the risk to the fore, which is referred to as an issue. We have heard the term 'issue management'. An issue can go either way. It can be resolved and then go back to being a risk, or it can become a full-blown crisis. The difference between an issue and a crisis is that an issue is generally internal and only those impacted by it are aware of it. A crisis is when the information reaches those whom it does not impact and begins to have a bearing on the reputation of the brand. Information around a crisis is usually fodder for the media, for adversaries and for competitors. A crisis can also be detrimental to the mental and physical safety of stakeholders. When a crisis gets out of hand, it usually involves loss of life, property, money and reputation.

In a nutshell, a risk that is not contained ends up as an issue, an issue that gets out of hand becomes a crisis and a crisis that leads to loss of life and property is a disaster. There is nothing called a 'PR crisis', as it is sometimes referred to. There is a business crisis or a brand crisis. The brand may be the corporate or the product.

A crisis is any event that is going (or is expected) to lead to an unstable and dangerous situation affecting an individual, community or the whole society. Crises are deemed to be negative changes in security, economic, political, societal or environmental affairs, especially when they occur abruptly with little or no warning. More loosely, it is a term implying 'a testing time' or an 'emergency event'. It comes from the Greek κρίσις or 'krisis'—a decisive point.

Our definition is simple. An organisational crisis is anything which could:

* Threaten a major product line or business unit
* Damage an organisation's financial performance
* Harm the well-being of consumers, employees, surrounding communities or the environment
* Destroy the public's trust in an organisation and its reputation

If you try and consolidate all possibilities, there are broadly ten types of crises that lead to reputational loss. Of course, there could be many more, but these are predominantly omnipresent and a crisis manager should be prepared with plans and strategies to mitigate them effectively.

- ❖ People-related
- ❖ Financial
- ❖ Technological
- ❖ Environmental
- ❖ Contamination
- ❖ Media- and social media-linked
- ❖ Government-induced
- ❖ Geo-political
- ❖ Calamities
- ❖ Pandemics

Let us delve into some detail of these types of crises.

- ❖ A **people-related crisis** usually involves one or two individuals within the organisation who choose to follow a path that leads to the downfall of the brand. A people crisis is also referred to as a management crisis. Most often, founders and owners cause the most damage, stemming either from incompetency or greed. Abuse, violence or fraud are ways in which their actions are manifested. They get exposed either because of a whistle-blower or a victim who brings it to the attention of the authorities. It may also be the case where certain authorities find weak points during audits that lead to the problem getting uncovered. An extreme form of people-related crisis is when labourers go on strike or an important customer has pulled back and layoffs are the order of the day. At the smallest level, it may be because someone very low in the value chain took a wrong ethical call that would lead to a full-blown crisis. Suicide and death of an employee or leader can also be a crisis. The most common crises are linked to people and stems from bad governance or compliance.

❖ A **financial crisis** belongs most commonly to a few main categories: bankruptcy, losses, bribery, non-payment of dues and so on. A situation of bankruptcy is a nightmare for everyone. When companies make losses, both in terms of the balance sheet as well as if listed and the share price drops drastically, it is a financial crisis. When officials have used company resources to grease the palms of a third party—government officials or the media—it can be a crisis that reaches the court of law. And the most common crisis a company faces from its employees and vendors is non-payment of dues, such as fees, salaries or other items it owes for services provided. There could also be theft and robbery that involves missing cash, especially if the company is a banking or trading business. These all are crises that need deft handling.

❖ A **technological crisis** is usually one that affects companies that manufacture or market durables—for instance, automobiles or gadgets. These are typically categorised as glitches, faults, breakdowns and, in worst-case scenarios, can lead to recall or replacement. Recent examples of such a crisis are handsets or cars catching fire or blowing up. These are usually exceptions to the norm, but can bring the brand under immense scrutiny from consumers and courts.

- ❖ An **environmental crisis** is linked to emissions, violations and malpractices that affect the environment. Manufacturing companies that produce pollutants are usually pulled up. Industrial disasters such as major oil spills that harm the oceanic ecosystem are also a prominent example.

- ❖ A **contamination crisis** is one that usually affects food or beverage companies and drug manufacturers. This could include adulterations, sale of goods post the expiry date, food getting spoilt inside the packaging, tampering that takes place through planned human intervention or the packaging of items getting damaged.

- ❖ **Media and social media crises** are of two types. The first type takes place because one of the above five took place and the information has spilt into the social networking space. The second type can occur due to misinformation, incorrect spelling, rumour-mongering or a disgruntled stakeholder spreading a canard. It is this crisis that might be short-lived but can cause enough damage to affect stock price and hurt the brand.

- ❖ **Government-induced crises** are also broadly of two types. One is vendetta. The other is policy-driven. A political party with a certain ideology comes to power and passes populist policies that affect hiring, trading, manufacturing and taxation, among other things. This can be detrimental to some companies and can lead to a crisis.

- ❖ A **geo-political crisis** is self-explanatory. Such a crisis can be linked to turf wars between two or more nations or within a country between two or more states. Companies hire lot of locals in manufacturing and sales. Political manoeuvres can easily create major issues for a brand.

❖ A **calamity crisis** stems from natural or man-made disasters, such as floods, earthquakes, forest fires, arson, terrorism attacks, system failure or sabotage, leading to huge loss of life and property.

❖ We have all witnessed a **pandemic-linked crisis** and the multiple layers of misery that accompany it. Lives and livelihoods are at stake, and company and product brands are strongly affected across the spectrum.

There could be other types of crises that may not typically fit into these buckets, but most usually fall into one of the above categories.

If not managed well, crises can lead to permanent damage. Good PR is at the heart of any crisis management plan. It can reduce tension, demonstrate a corporate commitment to correct the problem and take control of the information flow. Crisis communications involves communicating with a variety of constituents: the media, employees, neighbours, investors, regulators and lawmakers.

It is said that public relations is 90 per cent behaviour and 10 per cent communication. This is apt when it comes to avoiding crises. A safety net, which we have discussed in earlier chapters, serves well in trying times and if you observe keenly, a lot of organisations are working on building a positive safety net that can hold them in good stead in case of adverse incidents. The table below gives an overview of the implication of both negative and positive safety nets on stakeholder behaviour during a crisis.

- **The social media crisis**

Today, because of social media, local is global. You face scrutiny not from your neighbourhood but from the entire

Stakeholder	Impact of negative safety net during a crisis	Impact of positive safety net during a crisis
Media	Media trial	Media support
Activists	Boycott	Positive advocacy
Investors	Value erosion	Value conservation
Employees	Disengagement	Support
Community	No licence to operate	Right to operate
Partners	Dissociation	Collaboration
Regulators	Legal actions	Benefit of doubt
Customers	Loss of trust	Loyalty
Academia	Blacklisting	Association
KOL/Influencers	Negative amplification	Positive amplification
NGOs	Protests	Support in initiatives

world. Consumers today are more aware; they demand answers and look for genuine dialogues. Today, Google or any of the search engines define who you are and how you deal with an adverse situation can immortalise your narrative on the world wide web.

After a lot of deliberations with multiple CCOs, getting our own experience on the table and studying multiple crises, we have arrived at the following top ten commandments for effective crisis communications. Chances are that if you follow them well, the success rate of your crisis management process may go northwards.

- **Map scenarios, understand and identify your key stakeholders—proactively**

Preparedness is of essence. Proactive mapping of potential issues and appropriate stakeholders is necessary for any crisis communication planning programme. In case of a social media crisis, mapping the right influencers, key opinion leaders and thought leaders to help set and own narratives can mitigate the issue. A brand may benefit immensely if it has significant goodwill and a positive digital safety net already in place.

- **Own up or clarify the issue early on—speed of response matters**

When an adverse incident occurs, organisations cannot afford to shift into denial mode. Acknowledging the issue and demonstrating the will to investigate it with agility helps showcase the responsible side of the organisation. Most often, an organisation is respected more for demonstrating ownership.

- **Buy time with an effective holding statement— empathy is key**

An effectively drafted holding statement helps buy time from the media to include the organisation's side of the story. An empathetic statement helps generate understanding of an organisation's intention and will to sort out a valid issue.

- **Understand that you cannot make something bad look good—be authentic**

Whitewashing or hiding facts has never helped any brand or organisation during a crisis. The focus should be on authenticity and being correct; this always helps. Avoid all forms of vulturism, more so during an adverse situation.

- **Keep internal stakeholders informed—ensure prompt escalations**

Keeping relevant internal stakeholders informed is vital. A blank response from an uninformed senior stakeholder can be seen as arrogant and non-empathetic. Employees should be sensitised to escalate the first instance of an incident upwards until the information reaches the right managers.

- **Protect the credibility of your brand—prioritise human safety first**

The first demonstration of empathy should be towards human impact like injury or death. There is no larger crisis than a casualty or mass casualties. A brand or an organisation will always be respected more for a human-centric approach.

- **Have a robust ORM strategy—enhance listening**

In today's digital world, enhancing your social listening and response capabilities can save an incident from spiralling into a full-blown crisis. Owning the narrative is important. It is imperative to invest in listening tools and the right ORM platforms.

- **Have trained spokespersons who are empathetic and calm in demeanour**

Critical competency during an ongoing crisis is when you respond holistically and with credibility. The message does not necessarily have to come from the highest authority of the organisation, but from someone who understands the nuances of the situation and can communicate with empathy. Proactively rehearsing via drills and crisis communication workshops help.

- **Be watchful—it's not over until it's truly over**

Efforts to mitigate a crisis should not end at the first evidence of it dying out. On social media platforms, a crisis can re-emerge anytime. Continuing to monitor your channels even after things have blown is an excellent practice to follow.

- **Document the learnings every time a crisis ends**

Every crisis leaves lessons in its wake. Apart from the changes it brings, document the steps taken, the statements, responses and experiences of the entire journey. This will ensure one does not reinvent the wheel during the next one.

~

The era of storytelling is over. Welcome to the era of story-shaping

As risk and reputation management professionals, we have seen threats and vulnerabilities against our organisations and brands go up significantly. Since 2020 alone, a lot of us have combated crises that we may not even have conceived of prior to that time, such as a pandemic, locust attacks, a Suez Canal blockage, a supply chain gridlock, not to mention an entire war—all events which have created uncertainty and impacted lives, trade and economies around the world.

My contention is that 2020 was the year when it was no longer enough for corporations to tell their story about their ambition and the world they wished to create.

After 2020, storytelling died. It is no longer just about one company's story.

Every corporation is now be shaped by how they fit into—and also affect—the story of the rest of the world.

The era of story-shaping encompasses the basic idea of how any business fits into the world we find ourselves in. A world with unmitigated pollution, violence, unpredictable climate, immense inequality and strident national sentiments.

Story-shaping means that it is less important what you say in your ads and marketing messages and more important how you respond to posts on social media handles.

Story-shaping means that it is less about how much inventory your sales team and field partners can move and more about how they go about representing your brand in front of the customers.

Story-shaping means that employees can no longer be considered resources who need to be trained and primed for performance; instead, they are viewed as true partners of the business and advocate for the firm's ethos.

Most importantly, story-shaping is about being aware of the changes to our stakeholder ecosystem and being able to prepare and act as per the need of the hour.

The 3Rs to building a story-shaper organisation

It's tough being a story-shaper. It requires prescience that borders on science fiction.

But I believe there are three organisational principles that could help define how companies insert themselves pre-emptively into relevant conversations, as well as defend in the event of crises that could otherwise have substantial negative brand impact.

- ❖ **Readiness:** Be prepared. It is not just about whether your organisation has a pandemic preparedness plan or a flood or forest fire emergency response plan to rely on. It is simply about whether the culture of the business is one that influences people with different functional responsibilities to come together as one to respond to the crisis. Of course, having a well-tested crisis or business continuity programme also ensures your partners and employees responsibly represent the brand during uncertain times.
- ❖ **Response:** Disruptions will be part of the story-shaping era as corporations worldwide navigate a changing economy. What matters is whether the company responds with empathy and agility. Executing a crisis response plan requires people to not just come together but also take decisions based on scant information and rapidly changing dynamics across all levels of the organisation, from an intern to the CEO.
- ❖ **Recovery:** The speed at which relief and rescue can

be affected, the pace of restoration of services or the swiftness with which a product can make its way back to store shelves defines the ability of the firm to be resilient in the face of chaos. Highly resilient organisations are those which can identify and adapt to change before it's too late—a skill that is referred to in risk management as 'resilience by design' and can only be acquired through constant improvement.

In essence, companies need to build trust with all their stakeholders, as well as promote a culture of situational awareness and preparedness to promptly identify, address and learn from incidents and risk factors.

Amit Narayan is the Partner of
India and South Asia at Control Risks

~

ORM and crisis management

ORM has become a major buzzword for PR professionals over the last few years. The combination of the internet, widespread technology access and global social media platforms has given every citizen a voice and an opportunity to comment on issues that impact them or society. Plus, brands are now expected to take a stand on various issues, which comes with its own set of challenges. As they do so, they also open themselves up to criticism from those who perceive the shift in brand narrative as whitewashing or hurtful towards their sentiments. Fake news, one of the most disturbing trends to take precedence in recent years, also muddies the waters. Most corporations have had to significantly expand their budgets and focus their attention on protecting their brands from product, marketing or corporate perception crises. Navigating such a space can be quite complex for any organisation, big or small.

A few simple tips:

* Social listening matters beyond your personal channels. Track conversations to find out growing positive or negative intent. Listening closely will also give you insights into what not to do.
* Know when to respond. The life of an online crisis is difficult to predict since it depends on the traction, the level of influencers engaging with the subject and crowd sentiment. It is also driven by brand love and previous engagement with online actors. When do you react? There is no perfect answer, but the brand must determine the time based on the rhetoric, sentiment and how the online narrative is evolving.
* Address fake news as soon as it appears. The impact on brand and sentiment is immense if not dealt with promptly. Good news never travels as fast as bad!
* And finally ... prepare, prepare and prepare through your crisis management and social listening teams. Today, crisis management protocol must include training and governance for social media crises and business leaders across all levels must be trained to respond and understand them. After all, this has a significant impact on trust, reputation and business performance.

Ophira Bhatia is the Senior Director of India and Lead of AMEA and Corporate and Government Affairs at Mondelēz International

The people-centricity of corporate reputation

You might be punctilious about the daily consumer feedback digests, with teams in place to address every complaint that rises to the surface by the end of the day. But two underlying aspects in those digests are perhaps under-acknowledged. If you trace back over the years, you will find product complaints reducing. Technology is becoming almost fail-safe. This is good news.

But the digests also reflect an increasingly discomforting reality. People behaviour-related complaints are increasing. The more global and visible an organisation is, the more serious is the fallout when people fall short.

People are emerging as the core reputation builders or destroyers for an organisation.

This is a worldwide phenomenon. Every year, PRovoke Media, which reports on and analyses public relations trends and issues, compiles the twenty most serious corporate crises. Of the sixty in the last three compilations, close to 60 per cent have been directly related to people behaviour. Interestingly, only 5 per cent have been product issues, the rest being due to either misinformation, process inadequacies business failures or political shenanigans.[*]

In summary, even a single careless action of one individual can and does become a national or international reputation corroding event, depending on who the entity is.

In my experience, there are two blind spots behind behaviour missteps.

The first blind spot is not taking into account the all-

---

[*] 'Crisis Review', PRovoke Media, https://www.provokemedia.com/focus/crisis-review.

seeing and all-knowing nature of social media and the way a situation can spiral out of control as a result. This ignorance is not always a factor of age or experience. This blind spot can, for instance, lead a young and relatively inexperienced staff member to drag a passenger through the aisle of an aircraft even as scores of phones were recording the act. It takes all of us to build reputation, but only one of us to ruin it.

The second blind spot is the different personae of a citizen. Being a customer is only one persona. Citizens are also very aware and articulate personae of diverse views—cultural, social and political. In a large country, these can vary across population strata and regions. The expression of these views has become far more resolute and persistent. This blind spot is increasingly leading to standoffs between corporations and citizens.

The remedy is continuous behaviour coaching. In large multinational organisations, this is an arduous task but must be methodically done. It is best achieved by making behaviour coaching a corporate governance agenda. ESG is becoming an accepted framework; the 'G' should encompass people behaviour. This people governance must be such that it fosters self-governed individuals. Reputed organisations stand out because people there do the right thing without a nudge.

The corporate communications practice has a crucial role in this interplay between a company and its consumers. Besides marketing and sales, communications is most poised to influence events both inside and outside a company, making communications practitioners natural agents of reputation-building.

Externally, effective communications teams and leaders nurture the context of a company. Context is simply the backdrop against which a company exists and operates. The backdrop, in turn, is dynamic, comprising ongoing social, cultural and political discourses. Making sense of shifting contexts is as important as insight into consumer needs. The greater the Information Quotient (what I call IQ) of a company, the deeper is its foundation inside the minds of communities. This foundation consolidates the right to exist.

Internally, the communications network supplements external radars and the signals that flow across all levels of the organisation. Signals that the radar grasps flow through the network from the apex to the base of the organisation. That is how people breathe in the context in which they act. Like breathing is to life, context awareness is to an organisation. Without context awareness, an organisation can be left fumbling in the dark during a rough patch.

But people and functions are often slow to respond to signals. It's usually the communications team that places pairs of shoes in front of people to step into and understand the context. Behavioural coaching can help people respond to signals faster, in appropriately informed ways, without fanning the flames higher. Behavioural coaching almost always results in more informed decisions. Call it the Empathy Quotient (EQ). The greater the EQ in a company's people interfaces, the stronger is its growth.

Younger associates nowadays are forthright and expressive. Communicators functioning as internal activists are well placed to lend voice to this expression, empathising objectively and on merit. Companies that are smart about their reputation are already placing value on this role. They realise that when people are ignored, simmering concerns can become a whistle blown from the rooftops, leading to a crisis of reputation.

So, for me, the top three reputation interventions are:

❖ Breathing in the context around you
❖ Behavioural coaching
❖ Communicators acting as internal activists

Debasis Ray is the former Head of Corporate
Communications at Tata Trusts

The best crisis management philosophy

In PR, all it takes is one bad day for a crisis to spiral out of control.

The nature of crises is that they often occur without warning. The last few years have taught us that there is no set playbook that can be uniformly applied to crisis management. Whether it was a global pandemic, a hostile takeover of a social media company or an invasion of a sovereign country, we saw leaders literally building the plane as they were learning to fly by adopting some basic fundamentals of crisis resolution.

Quick thinking, inclusive ideation and trust are the tenets of dealing with any crisis, whether it is a news leak, a spokesperson's tweet gone viral for the wrong reasons or a challenging political environment regulating your sector of business. We have to accept that a crisis is always around the corner, acknowledge the realities and think about how structures should be set up to handle tough situations as well as possible.

So, what options do companies have to prepare and what philosophy should a crisis plan follow?

❖ **Be on top of the news cycle:** The starting point of dealing with any crisis is to gather facts first and respond accordingly. The first thing we need is a flexible monitoring system that enables us to identify possible critical developments as early as possible. This must scan all relevant media in real time. At the same time, we also need a clear crisis protocol that gets triggered as soon as the first signs of a disaster are detected. The earlier we identify risks, the more options we have to eliminate the crisis in advance.

❖ **Have an escalation matrix:** Follow a RASCI (respond, approve, support, consult and inform) protocol for crisis situations to ensure key stakeholders within the company are poised to deal with the issue effectively.

❖ **Establish a comms strategy:** Establish a pre-aligned communications format for the relevant representatives to adhere to in order to present a clear, united front and a cohesive message across all levels of the company during a crisis.

❖ **Identify your primary stakeholders:** Crisis communication must be limited to people who are directly or indirectly impacted by it. It doesn't need a talk-to-all approach. Identify your primary stakeholders and offer them a clear narrative as soon as possible so they're in the know.

❖ **Own the narrative's destiny:** When dealing with a crisis, it is important to control the narrative via proactive media outreach and exclusive information sharing via social media posts from company handles, press statements, exclusive interviews while engaging with brand friends and advocates to build and maintain trust by association. It is critical to exert external control over the situation and secure the trust of broader stakeholders.

Remember, public memory has been kind to leaders and companies who have done the right thing in times of a crisis and have responded with honesty. There might not be one set playbook to handle a crisis. However, it might be useful to keep in mind the words of Ukrainian President Volodymyr Zelensky: 'People don't really believe in words. Or rather, people believe in words only for a stretch of time. Then they start to look for action.'

And in case of a major crisis, these actions are best implemented of the following three Es:

- ❖ **Engage:** Seek detailed information from those involved, from the lowest level to the highest, and lead by example.
- ❖ **Empathise:** Create a safe space for teams to own up to a mistake, a tech glitch, a social media crisis or an erroneous press release. An empathetic leader commands more truth and respect from their team, resulting in better team performance.
- ❖ **Empower:** Empower your team members to make the right decisions based on their abilities and facts at hand while following a clear crisis protocol.

Simran Kodesia is the Director of
International Communications at DoorDash

15

ROO: ONE SMALL STEP FOR MEASUREMENT, ONE GIANT LEAP FOR PR

Picture this: a glowing review of the PR team, excitement galore, a well-executed campaign, of course, as assumed by the communications specialists, great coverage, big turnout by the media, a flawless launch, amazing energy, super cool interactions.

The CEO is meanwhile thinking: How much will this event impact our sales? Can it increase footfall? Is the announcement a positive impact on stock? Will it raise the aura of the brand?

So, what are we trying to say?

Is the language of the communicators the same as the language of business folks? Are we limiting ourselves to efficiency parameters while the business is looking at efficacy?

The questions we keep hearing are: how does a PR consultancy demonstrate value for all the effort that they put in? How do we get bang for the buck? How do we convince management to invest more in PR? And so on.

However, the fact remains that even after so much expert commentary by so-called PR measurement gurus, measurement remains an enigma for most practitioners.

Today, PR significantly affects several areas within an organisation: corporate reputation, employee retention, crisis mitigation, sales, product brands, stock price, stakeholder engagement and much more. The PR community (as well as marketing, finance, strategy, sales and HR) know with conviction that PR works. Then why the constant need for validation?

While musing over this, another question comes to our mind. Do we generally have that posture and speak the language that is understood by our business leadership or the C-suite? The language used here is most often based on numbers and the general phrases that work for them are 'shift in perceptions', 'sales growth', 'brand preferences', 'stock performance' or 'ROI'. The disconnect happens when a hard-working PR practitioner talks only about headlines, photographs, a busy tradeshow or any other efficiency parameter which is a basic given today.

We would reckon that all the qualitative and quantitative measures that have been written about significantly are all important and necessary and need to be tracked together. However, to shift the needle, PR professionals need to also start speaking a language that resonates well with management and is outcomes-based.

Media relations is, as we all are aware, an important aspect of public relations. Please refer again to the framework of qualitative and quantitative metrics displayed below that would be useful in tracking a media relations campaign.

Qualitative measures	Quantitative measures
• Share of voice	• Press release hit ratio
• Coverage tonality	• Journalist hit ratio
• Coverage spread by geographies	• Industry stories participation hit-ratio
• Coverage contribution by journalists	• Key message analysis
• Measuring the reach	• Thought leadership analysis
• Headlines and photograph mentions	• Correlation with viewership data
• Presence in articles	• Correlation of PR data with footfalls/sales
• Content categorisation across themes	

Business Goal	PR Imperative
Sales and business development	Awareness and perception
Rise in market share	Brand preference
Build and sustain reputation	Bridge the gap between audience perception and desired reputation
No crisis	Crisis preparedness, crisis management and negative impacts reduction
Employee retention/talent attraction	Employer branding

Some of the examples of PR imperatives that can be connected to business goals across industry sectors are shown on page 309. These are imperatives that can be measured in multiple ways and may be tracked to form trends that can be used to improve business metrics.

While measuring them is possible, it is generally easier said than done. We see multiple impediments if you are trying to prove only PR effectiveness or contributions by quantifying such factors.

The outcomes-based approach becomes a bit ambiguous, as business outcomes are generally the result of efforts by multiple functions. It is also more and more evident that public relations work will transform more into earned, owned and paid media genres. PR professionals will find themselves increasingly doing work that transcends the traditionally rigid boundaries of earned, owned or paid media. Trying to pinpoint the contribution of one particular genre becomes impossible.

Lack of easily available statistical techniques and measurement models that can help drive PR strategy is another challenge. We reckon that the majority of PR folks do not have a statistical background and people who can do mathematical modelling do not have an orientation regarding the nuances and role of PR in an overall communication matrix.

Evaluating PR using purely quantitative methods also has its drawbacks. Parameters like perceptions, brand loyalty, feelings and engagement are best measured qualitatively. Quantifying something that is difficult to quantify is like trying to cut a tree with a shaving blade!

PR is a very dynamic process involving multiple variables

and most often, outcomes cannot be predetermined with a high level of confidence. Evaluating outcomes without any firm pre-determined goals (for instance, a sales target based on statistical forecasting) may just seem like a retrospective performance review of tasks carried out. And if there are no benchmarks, they are even more useless.

The PR business, hence, finds itself fumbling when it comes to establishing uniform, universally accepted measures, which translates into the larger question of how we demonstrate value addition towards the organisation's growth. It's quite like how the ROI of lakhs of rupees spent on advertising is never questioned the way the ROI on a fraction of that amount spent on PR is.

The Barcelona principles that have been recently updated have also made certain changes. At a time when the communications environment is becoming unified, it becomes even more important to integrate measurements across tactics and channels. The PR channel cannot flourish in a silo. The committee has also reinforced the focus on qualitative measures that add context towards understanding the reasons behind the quantification. Advertising value equivalent (AVE) is still quite prevalent across the profession, as it is a tool that creates the feeling that media relations is delivering. But truth be told, it does not measure the real value that PR can deliver. Some may not like to hear this, but AVE is an arbitrary and inaccurate scale—possibly the laziest way of convincing your boss, client or CEO that media relations is effective. The client may love it but it is still erroneous. It does not even consider actual content, nor does it look at the media outlets based on the audience. In today's digital world, it cannot even provide any metric for impressions! The Association for the Measurement and Evaluation of Communication (AMEC) even made a commitment in 2017 to eradicate AVE as a measure.

However, while we personally do not advocate AVEs, we acknowledge that it's going to take a lot of time for the profession to move away from it. Our recommendation is simple: stop using AVEs.

Barcelona Principles 3.0

* Setting goals is an absolute prerequisite to communications planning, measurement and evaluation.
* Measurement and evaluation should identify outputs, outcomes and potential impact.
* Outcomes and impact should be identified for stakeholders, society and the organisation.
* Communications measurement and evaluation should include both qualitative and quantitative analysis.
* AVEs cannot reflect the value of communication.
* Holistic communications measurement and evaluation must include all relevant online and offline channels.
* Communications measurement and evaluation must be rooted in integrity and transparency to drive learning and insights.

While we agree with all of these, our favourite principle is the first one. The question then is, how many of us do robust goal-setting before every campaign? Do we set objectives before every new media blitz? If we do, then we feel a return on objectives (ROO) approach would be a better measuring technique than a vague ROI for PR. How can one measure just the PR ROI when the final organisational achievement of your goal could have been on the basis of multiple approaches of varying functions? There is a need to change the terminology. And ROO can be that change that will raise the bar for PR.

We feel the adoption of the ROO approach should be undertaken for the following reasons:

❖ Crisp objectives are a strong foundation for any PR success story. Measurements are easy to use if one knows what success looks like, what the desired behavioural changes are and other well-articulated objectives. Measuring progress against each objective then becomes more realistic and believable. A good approach is to set clear PR objectives aligned to the corporate goals, perhaps in addition to qualitative and quantitative goals. Worked out in conjunction with business leaders, they become co-owned and get tracked regularly. Understanding overall corporate goals and figuring out how PR can help fulfil them also puts it in the strategic zone. The focus then shifts towards the outcomes (and not outputs) of the PR team. The good part is that there are techniques available to evaluate PR with respect to brand goals in terms of a shift in perception, reputation, brand tracks, leads and employer brand scores, to mention just a few.

❖ Course corrections, if needed, can be done at every step of the PR process if the objectives are known and measured. This can lead to a better quality of the final PR outcome. Monitoring and listening plays an important role in this. Many tools and agencies for tracking and monitoring traditional, online and new media are easily available.

❖ Measurement becomes easy, as each objective is a standalone one with respective measures; collectively, they lead to larger PR success. A robust increase in the ROOs (exceeding PR goals) would eventually lead to a larger ROI contribution from the overall PR campaign—be it corporate- or brand-related.

❖ Lastly, as PR ROI means effect of PR on increasing revenue or profits, we feel that calculating it in real terms is not a straight equation.

Perhaps the importance of a good communications department or a PR campaign is best understood by simply imagining what things would be like in its absence. We believe that large organisations are microcosms of a complex world full of diversity. With multiple stakeholders across multiple businesses and geographies, within and outside the organisation enabled by a global information landscape, the PR measurement conundrum can be complicated. Trying to quantify it could be even more so. Can one quantify the cost of reputation saved due to effective PR? Can we assign a monetary value to it, or to the frequent crises a PR team mitigates silently, and claim it as the ROI?

We feel the best way for a PR function to create and showcase value is to align its strategy to top organisational goals, articulate business/brand PR objectives in line with this strategy, set the expectations right with the C-suite by jointly agreeing on the objectives and measures of success, and then go all out in ensuring that the objectives are met, demonstrating maximum ROO.

Our way of looking at holistic measurement

We studied multiple organisations, spoke to about twenty-five practitioners and were amazed. The wide-ranging philosophies, measurement tactics and the sheer difference in the many ways that practitioners try and prove that PR works is astounding.

Of course, every organisation is at a different level of maturity and understanding of what PR can deliver. But it could be ideal if there are at least some common measurement principles that are easy to understand and present where they need to be in a lucid yet in-depth manner.

In the figure on the following page, we present our measurement philosophy and the richness it can bring to your PR and reputation-building process.

Seven key takeaways

- Crisp objectives linked to business imperatives are a strong foundation for any PR success story ... the rest is all noise.
- Measures are easy to attach if one knows what success looks like.
- Track progress using qualitative and quantitative measures.
- Numbers orientation for the PR team is a must.
- Do not stop at the first step—analyse outcomes.
- Educate leadership on the impact of PR.
- Invest in good measurement tools.

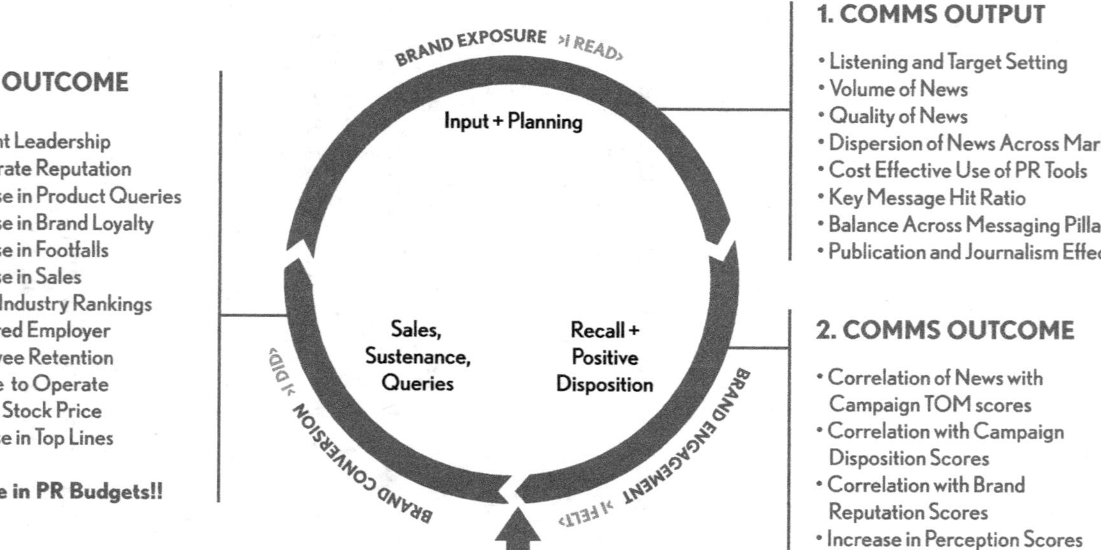
3. BIZ OUTCOME
• Thought Leadership
• Corporate Reputation
• Increase in Product Queries
• Increase in Brand Loyalty
• Increase in Footfalls
• Increase in Sales
• Rise in Industry Rankings
• Preferred Employer
• Employee Retention
• License to Operate
• Higher Stock Price
• Increase in Top Lines
Increase in PR Budgets!!
BRAND EXPOSURE ›I READ›
Input + Planning
Sales, Sustenance, Queries
Recall + Positive Disposition
BRAND CONVERSION ‹I DID‹
BRAND ENGAGEMENT ‹I FELT›
REPUTATION JOURNEY BEGINS HERE
1. COMMS OUTPUT
• Listening and Target Setting
• Volume of News
• Quality of News
• Dispersion of News Across Markets
• Cost Effective Use of PR Tools
• Key Message Hit Ratio
• Balance Across Messaging Pillars
• Publication and Journalism Effectiveness
2. COMMS OUTCOME
• Correlation of News with Campaign TOM scores
• Correlation with Campaign Disposition Scores
• Correlation with Brand Reputation Scores
• Increase in Perception Scores

The state of measurement business in India, issues and impediments

In 2005, we started our communications research and measurement journey at Impact. Coming from McKinsey & Co, I was keen to focus only on the qualitative part of communications measurement. We believed that it could provide strategic importance to the public relations function within a company's ecosystem. We aimed to ensure that each and every communications team that we worked with invests in, and benefits from, a high-quality communications measurement programme.

Here are a few reasons why communications measurement in India is not as mature as other countries.

❖ **Clients pushing back and discouraging measurement campaigns.** The most common reasons cited by them are:

- 'Why should we change? We have always done it this way.'
- 'Budgets are tight. Let's spend on execution rather than measurement.'
- 'We don't have people who are experts in this field and we can't afford to hire them.'
- 'We don't get access to the necessary data so what's the point?'

❖ **In most companies in India, there is no (or very little) incentive for communications heads to improve their game.** While there has been a big change in the importance of the communications function, most firms have not built incentives for their communications heads to take larger ownership in the overall success of their firm. In the absence of such incentives, communications heads are happy running their campaigns the way they have always been running it. There are some firms (like Google, GE, PwC, Microsoft, Godrej, etc.) who have got the formula right and the impact on their company's reputation and success is clearly visible.

❖ **Communications advisory firms (PR consultancies) prefer to conduct measurements in-house.** They do this so that they have better control over the cost as well as results. It helps ensure that their campaign is always shown in a good light. To add to this, most of the time, this analysis is done by interns or new joinees in the firm. This is evident in the quality of the research, as they fail to offer any actual benefit to the communications team or create an impact with the leadership.

❖ **Software-driven measurement firms take the easy route of providing automation-driven, cheaper measurement solutions to clients.** Such solutions do offer some analysis but are not good enough to guide the next steps. The only objective they achieve is in keeping the budgets low. These automated solutions are far away from a company's objectives and fall short of establishing the importance of the communications function and the benefits of communications measurement.

Things may have been difficult in the past but there are some positives too.

Today, more clients are asking about measurement. They may not be practising it yet, but they are eager to learn. Now, for us, every new business conversation starts with a discussion on measurement, which is encouraging.

We are hoping that this increased interest will soon convert into action.

Despite lack of appropriate incentives, some communications heads have risen to the occasion. They are demanding greater resources (both money and leadership time) for their communications campaigns. They are backing their demands with evidence of the impact created by their teams with the same transparency that is expected by leaders.

Communications advisory firms have realised that if they don't offer better measurement solutions to clients, they will move to one that does. More and more communications advisory firms have started employing specialised measurement firms.

Learning new measurement approaches and frameworks has never been as easy as it is today. Professional bodies, like the AMEC and the Institute for Public Relations, create new knowledge frameworks and guides every year. They offer these tools for free to the community and also organise educational events around the same. Teams that exhibit high levels of measurement maturity keep themselves up-to-date with the fresh knowledge created by such organisations.

Aseem Sood is CEO at Impact Research and Measurement

~

PR measurements can protect the balance sheet

PR balances the big picture for a brand. It manages business demand and also insulates the balance sheet. A scientific measurement framework should enable brand custodians to equate the effect of public relations to the balance sheet and protect it.

The state of PR measurement reflects the health of an organisation's brand and the overall state of the profession. It is a convergence point of an organisation's communication. If ERPs (efforts, resources and processes) are leveraged well, it can strengthen brand and business scores and possibly double the growth rate of the PR consulting business.

Initiatives to implement a conducive PR measurement ecosystem could include:

❖ **Changing boardroom mindset:** It has to be understood by all teams that PR impacts the boardroom and balance sheet, nothing less. This belief itself will catalyse the shift towards creating a scientific PR measurement arsenal.

❖ **Ownership and actions by stakeholders:** Mobilising deliverables from all stakeholders is essential. Very few firms in India currently practice PR measurement. For this to gain momentum, the following initiatives can be undertaken:

- Revise KRA–KPI framework of the PR machinery.
- Move beyond PR monitoring and explore measurement. The latter has the potential to showcase ROO.
- Stop the AVE cancer. It has caused enough damage to C-suite KRAs, brand health, budgets and the growth of the profession
- Move beyond news management (crisis, top management) to ROO, brand and business scores.
- Align yourself with the organisation's central business and brand objectives.

PR firms, as last-mile drivers, can position PR measurement within the work culture as a lifeline (not a liability), as well as deploy account and media planning to proliferate C-suite language. Measurement services providers can shift the mindset from mere PR monitoring to measurements, analytics, ROO, as well as upgrade the talent pool and balance the use of technology and manual intervention within the data assembly line, especially since an over-dependency on either end can lead to faulty client insights.

The formation of a joint professional body of key players will play a major role in education, expectation setting, uniform execution and last-mile implementation of the PR measurement culture. Communications industries outside PR have benefited using this cohesive approach.

Educational institutes should consider the inclusion of PR measurement within the brand management course curriculum, if not done already. This will create long-term efficiency for the profession. Business, media and communications management institutes will lay the foundation for a robust talent pool.

Measurement is our profession's lifeline! 'PR for PR' is lip service without it. It needs to be holistic and requires a conducive ecosystem. While initiatives are many, the onus is on PR firms, measurement service providers and academia to carry them out.

Siddhartha Mukherjee is the Founder of Brand Balance

Ride a trend or be ridden by it

The pace of change in media measurement and evaluation is poised to increase even more.

As the future beckons, it is vital to try and identify some trends that will overtake what is available today to change the media tracking and evaluation business.

The three trends that have changed the measurement and evaluation of PR campaigns are:

* **Goal setting:** Setting measurable goals is an absolute prerequisite to communications planning, measurement and evaluation. This is the reason why even AMEC endorses the fact that when it comes to effective evaluation of PR campaigns, the SMARTER template is an ideal place to start:

    * *Specific:* What do you want to do?
    * *Measurable:* How will you know you have done it?
    * *Attainable:* Is it possible?
    * *Realistic:* Can the results be achieved realistically?
    * *Timely:* When exactly do you want to accomplish it?
    * *Evaluated:* How much of your objective have you achieved?
    * *Reviewed:* Have you revisited and adjusted your approach to achieve your goal?

* **Input, output and outcome:** Gone are the days when judging the effectiveness of a PR campaign was akin to reading the entrails of an animal. The future of communications effectiveness and evaluation will be mapped on the template of input, output and outcome.

Input will involve all the efforts that go into defining the communications objectives and the preparations for a robust plan. Output will involve the qualitative and quantitative measure of exposure or visibility the brand has been able to achieve across media platforms. Outcome will include the behavioural or perceptional changes the brand communications campaign was able to create in the minds of the target audience. For many years now, our profession has been concentrating its efforts on input and output. The future will be about progressing into the evaluation of outcomes. Data from press releases, stock market, sales, brand perception audit reports, primary data, TV viewership, call centre details, etc., will be fused to achieve a robust outcome result.

❖ **Death of AVE:** AVE has been misguiding our profession for many decades now. The future is about a healthy mix of qualitative and quantitative parameters that can be weighted into an index score which ensures media planning and reduction in the wastage of PR efforts.

Ankoor Choudharri is the CEO at Concept BIU

~

The power of measurement, mindset and maintenance of the aim

As the practice of public relations has evolved over the years, the question of its impact has loomed over our heads. Every action we take as PR professionals in pursuit of success for our clients must tangibly contribute to their overarching goals. At the same time, the multitude of ways and means at our disposal has mushroomed.

With these changes comes the awareness that impact measurement is undeniably essential to everything we do. From boardrooms to pitch rooms, we regularly hear the same refrain, 'What does good measurement look like and how can I show returns on investment?'

We know that PR adds value to organisations in many ways: it builds awareness, prepares the market for conversation, engages stakeholders from employees to customers, helps maintain a licence to operate and, in most circumstances, directly drives sales. When it comes down to it, the quality and effectiveness of the effort paid toward reaching desired outcomes are only as good as their measurements because that is how success is ultimately judged. No single solution satisfies the multidimensional nature of that process. Rather, it requires a measurement mindset.

So, what is a measurement mindset and how do we cultivate it when planning and executing campaigns?

A measurement mindset simply means being intentional at every step of the campaign process, right from the early planning stage. From the initial briefing session through execution, our strategies and tactics always need to connect back to precise, achievable impacts. Whether this is reaching a certain audience and changing their perceptions or driving different behaviours, we need to be specific. Keeping this at the top of your mind throughout an entire engagement maintains a measurement mindset. Interrogate each step and tactic with how it achieves that aim.

To reach this mindset, PR practitioners need to keep three questions in mind:

❖ What am I trying to affect with my campaign and what does success look like?

❖ Who am I trying to reach and how will my campaign tactics affect them?

❖ What information do I have—either quantitative or qualitative—which shows that I reached my audience and that I drove the desired action?

To produce truly impactful results, it's not only about choosing the right metrics or having the optimal measurement tools but also about considering what impact means and designing campaigns targeted at specific goals. These questions may sound simple and straightforward, but this is exactly why they are important and useful. They encourage us be intentional in the way that we are designing campaigns and they remind us to think in the human terms of our audience.

To solve the measurement question for public relations, we simply need to practise applying the mindset to how we think, act and make meaningful impact on a daily basis.

Lynne Anne Davis is the former Asia Pacific President & Senior Partner of FleishmanHillard and Omnicom PR Group

16

COMPETENCIES THAT MATTER

Imagine you have the best of roads, the best of vehicles, the best fuel available and your destination is far but the ride is worth it. And now imagine that your ability to drive is questionable. How do you feel? The same is true for the PR profession. Most organisations today, and we say it with confidence, grapple with this conundrum—that of expecting the moon and lacking the means to achieve it.

The primary feeling we encountered when we spoke to numerous youngsters in the process of establishing themselves as communicators was that of excitement when it comes to the future of the profession and new-age media. However, there is an equal amount of confusion around how to own and effectively implement these areas of technology-based communications and navigate the nuances of such a fast-changing landscape. Worse so was the feel we got during our conversations with a few budding PR professionals who were either just a few years in the game or still studying in communications schools. Their anticipation and confusion were evident in equal measure. Considering the quality of the syllabus in most communication schools, the quality of the talent that emerges would possibly not match the expectations of this fast-evolving profession. Now that could pose a serious concern!

We do not mean to paint a bleak picture of the PR profession in India. It rocks. It has some of the best people calling the shots, there is energy and passion and, overall, it is quite an exciting profession to be in.

However, if we sit back and truly introspect ... has the profession been given the due it deserves?

Are we prepared to take on the challenges that the gig economy has thrown at it?

Do we keep up with developments in technology?

How are we going to be impacted by AI?

Are we building on our competencies to stay relevant?

Will we be able to clearly, in a measurable way, showcase the value we bring to the table?

Are we attracting the best talent?

How are we addressing the challenges of a talent crunch? (We have not met even one consultancy or corporate communications head who says they are sorted on the talent front!)

These may sound like random musings, but there is an enormous need to think in this direction.

We feel, going forward, one aspect that will make public relations bullish about its well-being is 'competence'. Competence, we believe, is the ability to solve problems in an organised way.

Expectations around the demonstrable competencies of PR and corporate communications professionals will continue to increase. Going forward, communicators will have to master a wide range of skill sets demanded by the nature of the industry they service. The old competencies of media relations, press release drafting or event management may not be sufficient. For example, many professionals are increasingly feeling the need to enhance their digital expertise or invest in learning big data analysis.

We have been working on a framework that would include aspects of the necessary competencies that are required at each level as professionals move up in their careers. While elements like ethics, engagement or strategy are useful, we firmly believe that in today's world and in the foreseeable future, competencies will be classified across five key verticals. We have listed out all the possible contemporary competencies and classified them under common themes: strategic thinking, stakeholder engagement, content curation, digital savviness and data analysis. Each vertical requires multiple abilities. They are the decisive factors that we believe will take our profession to the next level.

Strategic thinking

Strategy is a method or a plan chosen to execute a desired goal or to offer a solution to a problem. It is the art and science of planning and marshalling resources for their most efficient and effective use. This is the first set of competencies that can help a communicator be more strategic.

❖ **Business acumen and understanding:** Business acumen or sense is the competency that enables a PR professional to understand and cope with different business situations. It is all about market orientation and an ability to analyse competitive data—understanding the consumer's business needs, buying patterns, industry issues and the levers of the business that one represents. Understanding finance and being able to talk the language of the C-Suite (numbers, profitability, ROI, ROO) is quite useful.

❖ **Audience segmentation:** With multiple generations in the audience, each having different consumption patterns when it comes to information, the ability to segment and target consumers would be helpful. PR professionals having the ability to customise messages based on audience segments will have an edge.

❖ **Cultural empathy:** Cultural empathy is simply having an appreciation of and consideration for the differences and similarities in another culture in comparison to one's own. The internet has broken silos across geographies and messaging must be packaged in a way that it is not received poorly. A communicator needs to be respectful of diversity and equality, complying with ethical considerations to avoid stepping on anyone's toes.

❖ **Holistic campaign planning:** Campaign planning has evolved over the years and in today's world, which thrives on integrated communications, the respect for POEMS has gone up. Holistic thinking about impacts, reach, creativity and relevance must go into planning campaigns that are then enabled through multiple platforms. PR professionals need to start looking beyond traditional PR approaches.

❖ **Design thinking:** Design thinking implies resolving problems creatively. As a tool, it encourages organisations to focus on the people they're creating for, which leads to better solutions and processes. It's especially valuable for PR professionals who are trying to solve organisational issues. They must, going forward, master the design thinking stages: empathising, defining the issue, collaborative ideation, modelling and testing.

❖ **Ethics and governance:** In all they do, communications folks are expected to adhere to the highest standards of professional conduct, policies, standards and governance norms. This means that all communication must carried out in accordance with the law of the land, in line with any organisational regulations.

Stakeholder engagement

Availability of authentic, believable and relevant content has become a fundamental feature of a brand. The agility with which a brand can create content and stay relevant can define its success, but the content creation process can be time-consuming. Here's where influencers can play a significant role. They know the kind of content their followers want and if they can integrate your brand message well, your job is done!

Here's our second set of competencies or traits that are required by a PR professional to really build a good influencer network, engage with them meaningfully and build on earned social media potential.

❖ **Networking:** Most PR professionals are natural networkers. The success of a PR person is directly related to the kind of associations they have and the value they bring. In today's digital world, any and every person can be an influencer or micro-influencer. A constant focus on building these networks will only help increase the potential of connecting with thought leaders.

❖ **Industry connections:** Now more than ever, sectorial thought leaders, subject matter experts, academia, etc., are the real advocates of your brand. PR professionals need to up their game and get into relevant forums, even if it is just to network with industry experts. We have personally done this across industry platforms that are relevant to our organisations and it has helped us connect with some great people who are truly aligned to our brand purpose.

❖ **Social attributes:** Being social online is also important. Recently, during a communications conference, we asked over a hundred PR professionals in the audience about their presence on social media. Almost everyone raised their hands in affirmation, which was good. The embarrassing moment was when we asked the second question, 'How many of you have enough followers to really set narratives?' The general response was: 'We have never done enough for our own handles.' It is time PR professionals step up and expand their own reach. Regular conversations with the world help!

❖ **Influencer identification and management:** In your endeavour to build a network of influencers, it is important to know where you pitch. In an influencer pyramid, the top 10 per cent are going to be the massive social media sensations who have millions of followers. However, from an earned social media perspective, while they are good, they will charge! The bottom 60 per cent are what we call the wannabes, the not-so-serious ones who dabble with social media here and there and can be comfortably ignored. However, the real gig is with the remaining 30 per cent: serious content-producing, association-hungry bloggers and influencers who can really give reach and impressions. Try them, you will be amazed. But to get them on your network, research them, figure out their expertise objectively and rank them on the basis of their reach. It will need an in-depth understanding of metrics and realistic measures, but it will be one of the best investments of your time.

Content curation

One thing is certain: content is absolutely pivotal to an organisation's functioning. If data is the new oil, content is the output when the data is analysed and processed. One of the key roles that a communicator will have to play more often going forward is that of telling their organisation's story in a clear, consistent, creative and compelling manner. Good content is the bedrock of this endeavour.

Here are some traits that would be required by a PR professional to be an excellent content curator:

❖ **Articulation and creativity:** Gone are the times when a PR professional could just coordinate between management and the journalist, set up meetings or just be a courier! Today, excellent articulation, strong writing skills and the ability to present data in a lucid manner is what counts. Most importantly, content is most effective when it is relevant, fresh and can be shared easily across platforms. PR professionals need to polish this skill and become experts.

❖ **Video curation:** YouTube is said to be the world's second largest reputation engine. Videos spread faster than any other sort of content. There was a time when one needed an elaborate set-up for professional videos. Today, news is broadcasted using high-end smartphones. With cost pressures heading north, the onus is on communicators to be smart and churn out video-based communications in real time. Are we geared up for that? Do we still have the luxury of time to wait for a crew to come in, shoot and then take three days to send back the 'first cut' edits? Keep in mind that, at the moment, lo-fi content is performing better than polished, packaged content since the former is seen as more authentic.

❖ **Interviewing and podcasting:** Everyone with a smartphone and a knack for asking the right questions is a journalist today. Digital platforms enable amplification. Also, content is everywhere and it is up to us when and where to tap it. PR professionals can create testimonials for their brands at every appropriate opportunity. Third-party endorsements fly better and are more authentic. Podcasts have made a comeback and can be used effectively by PR professionals to frame narratives through thought leaders.

❖ **Packaging and repurposing:** The kind of opportunities that open up for a communications professional (once content and messaging is sorted) are amazing. Multiple platforms are available today, and each audience segment has a different consumption point. So, the trick is repurposing. An ability to present the same data in multiple ways across multiple platforms without losing its essence can create firmer narratives that are believable and will reach a greater number of people. The Indian PR scene is so rich and the work being done across varying regions is phenomenal. However, are we good at packaging it? Probably not. No wonder, internationally, our share of the awards pie is dismal! Packaging of content or our work can be beneficial in terms of 'PR for PR'.

Digital savviness

PR professionals have taken some time to recognise the power that digital tools add to their practice. An inertia towards adopting a complete digital approach when it comes to earned media can hold one back. But it's not too late. Social media platforms have demonstrated beyond a doubt that authenticity, third-party endorsements, testimonials and subtle integrations are more effective than advertising. Embracing them is the base of any PR strategy.

❖ **Mastering SEO:** SEO refers to the process by which search engines crawl through content to see how effective it will be to attract traffic. Search engines evaluate tags, keywords, titles, etc., on a site and rank them for their capacity to attract organic traffic based on multiple factors. Your ability to optimise your content in a way that the traction is high is very important. Your entire digital strategy could collapse if SEO is not done well. Understanding the basics of SEO and search engine marketing (SEM) is an absolute must for public relations professionals.

❖ **Managing social media handles:** How many public relations professionals today are adept at managing social media? Digital platforms have become major areas for discourse and socialisation. Narrative setting, enhancing brand love, responding to crisis situations, lead generation and many other important business imperatives are possible on these platforms and one can't ignore that. It has become critical to master the art and science of creating content that works, has the potential to become organically viral and is relevant to the audience for whom it has been made.

❖ **Blogging, digital publishing:** Blogging and digital publishing for your clients or for your own business will enhance your presence on social media and further help you get discovered. Every new content piece can be repurposed for multiple handles that helps expose your brand's products to various audiences. Well-written blogs can help build thought leadership and increase the positive disposition towards your organisation—a much better means than advertising. A public relations professional can create an owned media platform where the brand can interact directly with the stakeholders. Today's consumers want to be part of a brand's journey, and if a brand has its own media platform, the conversations can be more effective.

❖ **Webinar curation and hosting:** The pandemic ensured that platforms like Zoom and MS Teams became the new ballrooms. Their widespread acceptance by organisations worldwide has opened new vistas for communications. Press conferences, seminars, product launches and knowledge-sharing events are taking place online. As a public relations professional, it has become necessary to adapt to online event management. A deep understanding of what works and what can enhance engagement on these online platforms will be useful. The ability to curate these sessions effectively also helps.

Data analysis

As we've discussed in the previous chapter, AVE needs to be phased out as a metric used to demonstrate the effectiveness of a PR campaign. Today, there are many more ways to demonstrate campaign effectiveness, and one needs to have the right skills to derive insights from the data that is all around us, such as:

- ❖ **ORM:** Previous chapters have established the value and power of social listening and how it can help public relations professionals by alerting them to potential crisis situations, which can be mitigated with strategic interventions on the basis of real-time input. PR teams have to take the lead in combating inappropriate narratives by constantly listening to rants on social platforms and accordingly fine-tuning their crisis and response plans.

- ❖ **Research and analysis:** Looking back, the basis for the successful campaigns that we have had the good fortune to be a part of or lead has always been research. Especially now, research provides a strong opportunity to understand the beliefs and needs of our audience and to gain insights that can help appropriate messaging that is precise, targeted and error-free. With research, you also gain the ability to demonstrate results, help measure impact, track changing opinions and generally gauge the pulse of the public, making it an excellent competency to cultivate.

❖ **Data science:** Data is now essential in almost every aspect of business and data science combined with PR can forge a powerful interdisciplinary union that could entail producing, managing and understanding vast volumes of data, offering us useful insights. We reckon that it will become increasingly critical for public relations and communications professionals to have a firm understanding of data science techniques to deliver strong results.

❖ **CommsTech:** CommsTech is the umbrella term for all tech tools and platforms that communications professionals have to leverage in order to plan, execute and measure their campaigns. An understanding of how the tools work and, most importantly, how data can be used to execute good decisions is critical.

Indian PR's talent problem

Smart CXOs rely on their PR consultants for reputation counsel, and the quality of that counsel depends on the training that the counsellors undergo. When it comes to talent-building in PR, a lot remains to be done. For most HR leaders in India, the biggest pain point in talent management is usually the challenge of finding the right kind of professionals.

The tenets of PR

When the talent isn't right, it's visible in several areas, from engagement to job satisfaction. The most prominent area is attrition. A significant number of these young professionals don't just leave their first job but leave the profession altogether. Now why would they do that? Let's look at a hypothetical situation. It could be possible that during higher education, students are exposed to a number of communications disciplines, but not so much to PR. They learn how advertising agencies work, they know what copywriting is and they aspire to be a part of a creative team but are not given clear direction on the tenets of PR. Consequently, when the time comes to choose a career, PR is not high on their list of considerations, and those who do choose it do so with little understanding of what PR is, what it entails and what it demands. It is unsurprising then that many of them experience friction, confusion and unmet expectations in their first few years, and leave.

Who's to blame?

Reputation management is formidably dynamic today. Educational institutions with archaic curricula and outdated pedagogies are no place to train professionals for a field that is undergoing rapid shifts. On the other hand, PR firms have no choice but to recruit fresh graduates from such institutions.

This is at the core of Indian PR's talent problem. And therein lies the solution as well. If the professional community wants world-class PR counsel, it must invest in where it is created. They must work with institutions that are flexible and willing to cooperate with the professional community.

How can this be addressed?

There are three ways in which this can be handled:

❖ **Greater participation in institutional boards:** CXOs have constituted boards of business institutions for over a century—boards which govern philosophies, modus operandi and the value created by those institutions. This has strengthened the business management discipline as a whole and created immense wealth. It is time for the profession to proactively govern the creation of the single biggest asset that organisations can cultivate: reputation. This must be done by placing leaders of PR firms in academic councils and boards of institutions where PR talent is created. With such placements, the curricula and pedagogies of these institutions should evolve to address Indian PR's talent problem.

❖ **Enhanced interface with communications students:** The next generation of PR consultants need role models. They need to be inspired to join the wonderful world of reputation management. Business and communications leaders must increase their interaction with communications students. There is a need for business leaders to outline the value of reputation to students. Real-time projects (sponsored case study contests, for example) can be resource-intensive but highly rewarding from an employer branding perspective.

❖ **Fund action research with communications institutions:** Involving academia in business by putting them at the centre of the work that organisations do is a great way for both parties to become familiar with their respective ecosystems. Organisations must fund and/or facilitate research to work with institutions and address key reputational challenges faced by them. Such higher engagement will also help researchers and faculty members of institutions understand how the professional community thinks and what they need.

Smart CXOs appreciate that PR is a strategic function. It's about time that there is strategic investment made in it.

Hemant Gaule is the Dean of the
School of Communications and Reputation

~

Competency gaps—and how education can bridge the divide

The most disheartening remark for a teacher to hear from a senior professional is, 'These students do not have the right skills.' It would be equally frustrating for business leaders to hear from experts in academia that the profession lacks creativity or innovation. This clearly shows a huge gap between the profession and academia. Both can contribute immensely to each other's work, yet there is a lack of interaction, engagement and collaboration, especially in the field of media. If a student has to join the profession after the completion of a course, it becomes critical that the right skills are imparted which can help them do their job well. This can only happen when institutes are in constant touch with senior professionals and involve them in all stages of the teaching process, from curriculum development to evaluation. Since the profession is in constant flux, the curriculum should also be reviewed and revised more frequently, keeping in mind any changing requirements. Universities, colleges and other institutes should reject inflexibility and embrace innovative pedagogies.

Steps PR and academia need to take together to solve the competency gap problem:

- ❖ **Invite senior professionals as adjunct professors:** There are clearly laid out rules and regulations regarding the selection of teaching staff in universities wherein even senior professionals can join the academic institutes. Experts with rich experience are teaching in many colleges/institutes and universities, but educational institutes should also have the autonomy to hire experts as adjunct professors for a specific duration.
- ❖ **Senior professionals should mentor students:** Established professionals should consider mentoring a few students every year. This means offering students professional exposure via internships, involving them in research and writing, taking them to meetings or inviting them to events. This will not only show the students how the professional PR space works but will also help them build their own network.

❖ **Collaborate for media research:** An academician's expertise lies in teaching, training and research. Practitioners should take advantage of that expertise by involving them in audience research, product research, media monitoring, etc.

❖ **Keep up with consulting firms:** To keep themselves abreast of what is happening in the profession, academicians should undertake secondments. Though teachers are expected to attend faculty development programmes to upskill themselves from time to time, there should be flexibility in the system where teachers can choose classroom-based learning or practice-based learning.

❖ **Co-creation of content:** The pandemic has shown how bricks were replaced by clicks. Learning can now happen anywhere, at any time. Content for online courses should be prepared and offered by academicians and practitioners.

❖ **Organise seminars and conferences together:** In the past, academicians and professionals have hosted several webinars, seminars and conferences to keep themselves engaged and discuss new learnings, albeit separately. And in a few exciting instances, practitioners and teachers teamed up with each other to host an event. There is a need for more such collaborative events where academicians and practitioners join hands to deliberate and discuss issues related to PR so as to create dynamic and exciting experiences for students to learn from.

Professor (Dr) Anubhuti Yadav is the Head of the Department of New Media and Information Technology, and Course Director of Advertising and Public Relations at the Indian Institute of Mass Communication, New Delhi

∽

Shaping the competencies of a budding PR professional

With an area as specialised as public relations, the role of an institution becomes more significant. In an educational institution, it's possible to undergo the kind of focused training and structured pedagogy that a PR professional would need to navigate a VUCA world. Institutes have a significant role to play in skill-building, strategy- and planning-oriented inputs, and training- and application-oriented learning. Apart from strong communication skills (verbal and written) and proficiency in strategic networking and media relations management, PR professionals need to develop the ability to cope with dynamic and fluid environments without losing focus. This is where, as educational institutes, we have to create simulations of real-life cases in collaboration with the professional bodies. As an educational institute, we have realised that students have to become a part of social media and be up-to-date with digital analytics, which have become an integral part of our offerings.

PR competencies that recruiters look for in entry-level candidates

While creativity and writing remain core, digital PR literacy, communications and relationship management and understanding of strategic elements in PR competencies have also emerged as primary expectations by recruiters. A solid understanding of the digital and social media ecology and a sharp data-centric mindset are the contemporary competencies expected from polished PR professionals.

Gaps that communications institutes should fill

PR is all about helping shape the right narratives in the world and the right narratives require the right voice and right expression. This is what we, the educators, strive to teach the next generation of professionals. In India, there is still a gap between the academic institutes teaching PR and the profession practising the same. The interaction between the academic institutes and the profession should be broadened for the benefit of exposing students to practical issues, live projects, etc. Here, what we also require are proactive initiatives from corporate organisations to provide real-time data for young students to work on and learn from. Additionally, academia and professional associations should engage in collaborative conversations to discuss the future of the domain and revisit opportunities and growth in terms of possible career paths.

Dr Ruchi Kher Jaggi is the Director of the Symbiosis Institute of Media and Communication, Pune

~

Thoughts on learning and development

The tumult of recent years has highlighted the need for adaptability and resilience in order to cope and grow with new, stressful challenges. Essentially, adaptability entails managing your own well-being, cultivating a learning mindset and nurturing relationships that promote happiness and learning for all. Resilience helps us respond to external events by bouncing back, but adaptability helps us bounce forward by evolving further and changing in response to the environment.

For any organisation to develop resilience, one of the strategic priorities has to be a focus on their people and developing the skills, capabilities and culture needed today and in the future. Learning and adaptability are fundamental to growth. The ever-changing environment requires recalibration of our knowledge and skills. Besides technology skills, what will be important are human skills that cannot be fully automated, such as being emotionally intelligent, being collaborative and human communication. People with adaptability and the ability to learn quickly as well as being open-minded, flexible and versatile in their roles will be in high demand.

An attitude towards learning has to be developed. When I was the Head of Learning and Development at Tata Group Corporate Communications, my role was to develop global best practices and embed them within the corporate communications teams of the group companies. For all the events and training organised, the response of the corporate communicators was terrific. Crisis communication protocols were also embedded across the group and a three-hour customised digital simulation was developed to train leaders to respond accurately to crises escalating.

In order to learn, humility is very important. Respecting your guru is the basis of real learning. In the army, as commissioned officers, we are imparted weapons training by our instructors, who are usually junior non-commissioned officers. When we join their classes, as a part of our training, we are required to remove our shoulder rank epaulettes so that, symbolically, our officer ranks are set aside and we ready ourselves to imbibe learning from juniors who are experts. In the corporate world, high ego levels can prove to be a barrier to learning, and senior professionals often deprive themselves of learning opportunities in the process of trying to seem superior. As Epictetus said, 'It is impossible for a man to learn what he thinks he already knows.' Shift your mindset from 'I know it all' to 'I will learn it all'. When we shed our egos, our minds become open to new ideas, methods, concepts and innovation. Constructive and fearless debate must be encouraged to allow for deep learning.

While every individual is primarily responsible for their own personal and professional development, organisational processes must be established to review their skills, aspirations and expectations to assist them in aligning their individual interests with organisational needs and investing in learning that is meaningful.

Organisations must offer mentoring to communicators, coaching them and offering feedback to encourage learning. Reward systems must also exist to recognise the acquisition of new skills and standards.

To set global standards in business communication, the International Association of Business Communicators (IABC) created the Global Communication Certification Council (GCCC) some years ago. As vice-chair of the inaugural council, I know that intense care was taken to chart the career path of communicators and the competencies required at different stages of one's career. The GCCC offers certification for communicators that meets international standards. It is a significant benchmark for use by all in the communications profession. A self-assessment tool for communicators has also been developed to help mark the level of competency achieved so far.

People at the top get there because they work harder than anybody else. Talent helps, but what is important is the aptitude for hard work and a commitment to learn and better yourself. My advice would be to be curious and passionate about your craft for your own satisfaction and confidence. At the end of each day, you should know something you did not know before. Keep striving to know more. There is really no end to learning.

Dr (Col.) Rajeev Kumar is a consultant in strategic communication management with The Communicologist

17

CCO: A CATALYST FOR ORGANISATIONAL ENGAGEMENT

Once, while researching some data online, we attempted to see the kind of results an online search throws up when the query is 'CCO'.

To our amusement, some of the top results were, 'Chief Compliance Officer', 'Chief Content Officer', 'Chief Commercial Officer', 'Chief Customer Officer' and even 'Clinical Care Options', just to name a few. 'Chief Communications Officer' finally appeared on the fourth page. But when we combined the search with the term 'reputation management', 'Chief Communications Officer' appeared first. It would seem that only when the subject concerns reputation is the CCO remembered. And for good reason. A CCO holds immense power and sway over reputation and it is in the organisation's interest to recognise this and reap the benefits.

We asked a lot of communication heads, PR firm founders, CEOs and upcoming stars of the PR profession as to what they think could be the true role of a CCO in an organisation. The word cloud below sums it up.

CORPORATE REPUTATION

CORPORATE PR

MEDIA RELATIONS CORPORATE COMMUNICATIONS
COMMUNITY RELATIONS

INTERNAL COMMUNICATIONS

EXECUTIVE COMMUNICATIONS PUBLIC POLICY

MARKETING EVENT MANAGEMENT

CSR CORPORATE PHILANTHROPY

CRISIS MANAGEMENT INVESTOR RELATIONS

GOVERNMENT RELATIONS SOCIAL MEDIA STRATEGY

The need for a consummate CCO

Today, we feel the role of the CCO is at an inflection point. Unprecedented challenges, risk to reputation, growing vulnerability to crises and changing macro indicators are just a few of the nuances of the business environment. Other issues—the need to reinvent business models, uncertain socio-political conditions, hybrid ways of working and a higher dependence on technology—have shaken up business set-ups. Leaders today have had to navigate the new environment and, at the same time, build organisations that can endure such onslaughts. And there is no simple solution or precedent to learn from. Could robust communications, structured the right way, bordered by clearly defined responsibilities and led by a consummate CCO be the answer? We believe so.

According to the 'Future of Corporate Communications' study released by Edelman in 2021, the message from nearly 250 of the world's most senior communicators is clear: 'To meet the challenge of this moment, the corporate communication function must advance from operating as a transactional cost centre delivering on a communications agenda to being an indispensable partner generating measurable business value.'[*]

Some notable insights from the Edelman study

❖ The role of communications has become more materially important to CEOs, boards and the C-Suite.

❖ The modern corporate communications function is agile, multidisciplinary and insights-driven.

❖ CommsTech is already ushering in a new era and communicators can use it to deliver quantifiable value to the business.

❖ An increased focus on the workplace, workforce and well-being of employees isn't a temporary fad.

❖ Expectations around social issues have shifted the agenda—and there is no turning back.

❖ A modern organisational structure only gets you so far.

❖ Communicators are increasingly acting as change agents, enabling ongoing transformation.

---

[*] 'The Future of Corporate Communications', Edelman, 29 September 2021, https://www.edelman.com/sites/g/files/aatuss191/files/2021-10/Future%20of%20Corporate%20Communications_FINAL_FULL_REPORT.pdf.

- ❖ The lines between communications and marketing will continue to blur, creating new challenges and opportunities.
- ❖ In an increasingly complex multi-stakeholder world, the corporate brand matters now more than ever.
- ❖ While the importance of the communications function is increasing, resources to deliver are lagging.

Obviously, CCOs have years of experience under their belt in putting out fires. But in current times, they should also be adept at proactively managing their brand narrative in a digital environment where organisations don't have control over what's been said about them online. They need to be bold, vocal about the company culture and values and to double as spokespersons and trusted advisors to their CEOs.

However, if you scan the landscape, CCOs are a relatively new addition to a corporate or business organogram. Broadly speaking, the role is meant for guarding and enhancing the company reputation and being custodians of brands, culture and corporate behaviour. Organisations serious about building reputation consider CCOs as valuable and strategic business partners.

The CCO role has been evolving much before the global COVID-19 pandemic. The pandemic, however, brought to the fore multiple nuances of communication that were probably ignored earlier. Communications in organisations to inform and stay connected with stakeholders, retain customers, engage employees and drive financial performance started to be seen in a new light.

Of course, times have changed and the CCO role grew beyond the previously defined scope, and for good reason.

The world today has demonstrated ample evidence of a much deeper need for communications as an organisational elixir for success.

And if the trends we've discussed in this book are here to stay, the way organisations look at communication needs to change. Our multiple conversations with PR professionals, CEOs and many organisational agents across industry sectors all came back to the same point: a communications structure that is predominantly based on a traditional PR mindset of media relations will not be able to cope with the ambiguities of the world today.

We put in a lot of thinking and studied a few organisations that we feel have managed to break the traditional mould of doing PR and evolved significantly in terms of their processes and outcomes. Based on these learnings, we are presenting our model of the five non-negotiable roles of a contemporary CCO.

The Aligner: *Aligns communications strategy to tie back to objectives and business goals; not just communications based on 'look-and-feel'.*

The contemporary CCO must be a business-oriented person. Impact on business will earn them a seat at the decision-making table. We found that the top teams consistently characterised themselves with a very intricate alignment between organisational business goals and communications and objectives.[*]

Alignment and integration of messages across platforms

---

[*] '30 Top Corp Comm Teams', *Reputation Today*, https://reputationtoday.in/30-top-corporate-communications-teams/.

is a key strength expected of a CCO and this calls for the critical ability to collaborate smoothly with multiple stakeholders. CEOs also expect CCOs to act as strategic business advisors rather than just messengers of news. They expect them to be the eyes, ears and mouthpieces of the organisation and to ensure that communication is transparent and effective across all audiences.

According to Gallup, less than 50 per cent of employees feel connected to their organisation's mission.[*] Organisations with effective CCOs as partners for organisational alignment enjoy better outcomes on employee satisfaction and engagement. Further, according to the Korn Ferry Institute, 67 per cent of the Fortune 500 organisations say that CCOs are expected to anticipate future opportunities and convert them into effective strategies for organisational success.[†]

The Coach: *Guides leaders to communicate and be comfortable with social media and new-age technologies.*

How many professionals can boast of having a significant part of their organisational leadership be familiar with communications? How many top leaders do you find on social media taking decisive stances or owning narratives that the organisation believes in? Some leaders are better

---

[*] Jim Harter, 'Employee Engagement vs. Employee Satisfaction and Organizational Culture', Gallup, 12 April 2017, https://www.gallup.com/workplace/236366/right-culture-not-employee-satisfaction.aspx.

[†] 'Chief Communications Officers Grow Influence, Responsibilities, and Team Size—and In Turn, Compensation', Korn Ferry, 1 June 2023, https://www.kornferry.com/about-us/press/chief-communications-officers-grow-influence-responsibilities-and-team-size.

writers than they are speakers. Some are flippant on social media but are unsure about responding to a Twitter comment or a LinkedIn post. Our chats with multiple CEOs revealed one thing: they need a bit of handholding. They are on the fence, ready to take the plunge, but need that nudge from someone who will sustain the presence. We feel the entire C-suite can benefit from a CCO's perspective on building a personal brand and engaging with stakeholders through traditional and social media.

In the true sense, a good CCO builds and educates the organisation on the benefits of segment-wise communication, facilitates platforms for higher engagement and creates opportunities to constantly keep the corporate brand in the realms of conducive narratives.

The Scout: *Finds and influences people internally and externally to write about issues that the organisation advocates in order to showcase the brand in the right light.*

CCOs are in a unique position. They are privileged to have direct access and working relations across stakeholder groups and set the context. Taking a stand on societal issues, thought leadership, inclusion, and diversity, ESG and many others is no longer optional. The role of the CCO is useful for creating an ambience that enables transparent communications within and outside the organisation. Understanding the nuances of and the potential risks related to governance, ethics, corporate citizenship, etc., is a high priority.

CCOs also need to be creative storytellers. They need to be able to locate stories that are authentic, inspiring, relatable and easy to amplify. Clear, effective storytelling also requires a profound understanding of the business levers, the legacy and the external environment. If the CCO is able to get such stories written and told by advocates of the organisation, it would be the icing on the cake.

The Builder: *Builds reputation, is aware of reputation levers, is an expert in branding, understands stakeholders, is media-savvy and does not bend during crisis situations.*

Corporate reputation and the whole idea of corporate purpose has today become a sort of currency that decides an organisation's ability to operate, raise funds, retain staff and gain customers.

A fair ask is to ensure equilibrium and coherence of all internal and external communications across touchpoints. An ability to constantly build external relations across stakeholders and enhance the positive digital safety net for the organisation is a must. The contemporary CCO is actively engaged with all the key players and is in the best position to uphold and enhance the brand's reputation. A strong connection in relevant social circles, influencer groups and engagement with key opinion leaders only helps keep the brand narratives live in the right circles.

The Insights Junkie: *Relies on CommsTech, uses research, is data-driven and insights-based, works like a data scientist and is a measurement expert.*

Use of data in the PR and communications space has been very limited. Given that everyone agrees on the value of data and with so many tools to acquire it, data can be put to better use when it comes to PR, such as using it to measure and demonstrate the direct impact of communications on business—a major challenge every CCO today faces, especially with leadership beginning to prefer measurement as a way to gauge effectiveness over simply having a few pictures published on the front page.

The contemporary CCO is expected to have a fair degree of comfort with data analysis and generating workable insights that can enhance the strength of organisational communications. As use of analytics grows throughout enterprises, CCOs will have to establish metrics that are worth tracking and create processes that will help them action the insights accrued. Effective CCOs will have to work on dashboards that have trackable KPIs and a real-time data feed that constantly showcases the pulse of overall reputation. The good news is that all this is possible.

Final words

The CCO can never affect change alone. Organisations need to take notice, recognise the vastness and potential impact of this role and prep infrastructure so as to set the CCO up for success.

While CCOs do have direct access to all senior stakeholders, how much of it translates into strategic conversations and expectation settings that have an impact on business objectives? When asked this, a majority of the CCOs said the trend is changing and that expectations comprise a lot more than just getting leadership featured in publications or running brand campaigns. Many CCOs also spoke about how CEOs have started sharing larger organisational concerns, which was not the case before the pandemic.

We believe that a conducive ambience, resources,

trust and transparency in terms of the CCO's roles and responsibilities will be the keys to success, no matter how smart the CCO is. The level of commitment must match from both sides.

It has been proven on multiple occasions that this function, which probably has not got the due it deserves, can be called a 'mission-critical' function, impacting reputation, employees and financial levers for any organisation. We believe that the CCO's role will evolve further. Now is the perfect time for CCOs to engage and make their presence felt as a strategic ally of the C-suite.

~

Attributes of an effective CCO

Business acumen

Woe to the CCO who does not comprehend the business and its core products, services and value proposition. There is no way to develop a communications strategy that delivers on business priorities without knowing what the business stands for. If communications has to have a seat at the CXO table, it needs to surpass its remit and extend itself to a deep and wide understanding of the organisation, the dynamics of the industry it operates within and the global and regional environment (legal, tax, financial) that applies to it.

Marketing mindset

A communications specialisation is insufficient without a sharp appreciation for and thorough application of marketing thinking. Fundamentals such as market segmentation, marketing mix and targeted messaging cross over into the communications realm and build the foundation for a firmer communications strategy than PR or media relations skills alone.

Top three roles a contemporary CCO plays in building reputation

Functional qualification is more or less a given when someone makes it to the role of a reputation builder. Here's what is less obvious:

❖ **Mind-reading:** Know your audience's minds. Who is your customer and who are your internal and external stakeholders? Where do they consume information? What is it that they want to see and hear about your brand and your products? Audience segmentation, profiling and meaningful media plans are made when you read your audience's minds well.

❖ **Mindfulness:** Being creative and disruptive without respect usually backfires. Mindfulness about culture and context is important but is often forgotten in the race to catch attention or to be different. Having a say in the marketing principles of the company and being respectful of culture and context is necessary when building a reputation to last.

❖ **Relationship management:** I say relationships, and not media relations, because relationships are and need to be more human to be effective. In the give-and-take of information, if you are not forthcoming and respectful of people's time, it is not possible to manage reputation only via influence or tactical media relations. Honesty in media relationships or communications, of course, does not imply providing all the answers all the time, but also simply the ability to say that sometimes, you don't have one.

Madhavi Jha is the Director of Communications,
India at Boeing

~

Credibility has become paramount and needs to be micromanaged

Corporate communications has evolved considerably in recent times, making the CCO's job even more challenging in navigating complex environments while anticipating and mitigating risk.

Credibility has become paramount and needs to be micromanaged. The company's intrinsic value and purpose must be woven into the matrix of sophistication and creativity in messaging. This is critical so as to define the playing field and positioning of brands. Brands and reputation need to be managed cohesively to create awareness and reduce risks.

CCOs need to create and manage messages that support their company's mission, values and vision, and deliver them to internal and external audiences with differing needs, triggers and perspectives. The need to align and integrate messaging across the organisation requires collaboration with various stakeholders. Organisations that view communications professionals as partners in driving organisational alignment with the core company values see much better business results and more engaged stakeholders. Telling the story of how an organisation delivers on its purpose and promise is what offers a competitive edge.

In closure, reputation is a great asset for businesses and there is a compelling need for communications teams, directors and external consultancies to be able to incorporate superior integration, consistency, coordination, collaboration and alignment for a successful outcome. The task ahead is to shape the organisation's narrative, build advocacy and drive authentic conversations with stakeholder groups.

The scope of the CCO is broadening and the mandate is to be a business strategist and advisor, helping organisations shape strategy, manage reputation and problem-solve. The time for the CCO to have a seat at the table is now.

Rakhee Lalvani is a consultant with IHCL, handling their Diversity and Inclusion; she is also the Founder of RLA (Rakhee Lalvani and Associates) Communications

~

The CCO is the guardian of reputation

Just about five years into my career when I gave up a promising future in journalism to explore the challenging terrain of corporate communication, it was like venturing into the unknown.

There were just about two or three very senior journalists before me in the country who had made the successful transition from media to communications by setting up their own consultancies. At that time, I didn't personally know any of them to be able to reach out and seek their guidance.

It was the turn of the century, and terms such as 'public relations' or 'corporate communications' were not yet part of the common lingo in corporate or media corridors in India. It was a profession still in its nascency and, if I have to be honest, even looked down upon by some in the media.

It was at a time like this that I took the decision to leave the news agency, Press Trust of India (PTI), and join the India operations of PepsiCo, first as a media consultant, and then as corporate communications manager. When word got around in the office about my resignation and the move to join a corporate, one of the most senior editors in the PTI bureau asked me, quite condescendingly, 'So you will now just be stopping negative stories from appearing, eh?'

Nothing could have probably prepared me for the initial experience that I had at the new organisation. It was the proverbial baptism by fire and yet, the happy beginning of a massive learning curve that has stood me in good stead till date.

I was fortunate to have landed my first communications job at an iconic company that had already realised the critical role of communications and PR—a foresight that was, at that time, quite rare.

About a couple of decades later, the role of the CCO has come to define the face and character of the organisation. Now, the CCO is the chief custodian of the values, reputation and image of the corporate brand. This role, over the years, has developed to a point where it is not just important 'who' you know but also 'what' you know. This becomes critical in a knowledge-based environment for the CCO to be able to claim a rightful seat at the high table of organisational decision-making hierarchy.

Today, therefore, it is not simply about aligning your communications strategy with the overall organisational agenda. It's also about setting the agenda itself and driving it beyond. It is about shaping organisational behavior in terms of business results and corporate reputation. Organisations that have understood this are today at the peak of the pecking order when it comes to their corporate value, reputation and image.

And yet, there is a long way to go.

Well into the third decade of the twenty-first century,

I find it hard to believe that innumerable organisations (including large corporates) both within India and globally still continue to look at and treat PR and communication as an extension of marketing and advertising—which is clearly a complete lack of understanding of the role of CCO.

I guess the problem lies on both sides, as some of us also aspire for PR and communications to replace advertising—which, in my view, is a misplaced aspiration born out of a gross misunderstanding of the role of corporate communications vis-à-vis advertising/marketing.

We live in an era of highly proliferated digital and social media and increasingly integrated communications. While some of the folks cite this to justify the integration of communications with that of marketing, I would stick my neck out to say that this is exactly (and more so) the reason why the role of the CCO has to remain distinct. Else, we are diluting the very philosophy and ethos of that role.

Bharatendu Kabi is the Head of Corporate Communication and Corporate Social Responsibility at Hero MotoCorp

~

CCO—seat on the high table

All CCOs want a seat at the high table. Few get it. Fewer still deserve it.

Here are nine ideas to assist you, the CCO by any name, to get there—and stand the trial:

* ❖ Get comfortable with the fact that the company's owner—or the P&L owner, at the very least—is the real CCO. They do not wear the title with bells and whistles,

but each time a stakeholder thinks of the reputation of your business entity, it is this person, not you, who will and must occupy centre space on the reputational radar.

❖ Stakeholders remember stories. Think Steve Jobs at the Stanford commencement. Think Azim Premji stepping out of a three-wheeler autorickshaw. Think Dhirubhai Ambani addressing an entire stadium. Think Mukesh Ambani walking into an open office.

❖ Only a profound understanding of the reason why customers love your company will give you the ability to curate ideas and stories that resonate. Once identified, these stories must pass the test of compelling narration and sophisticated proliferation. Think video, think discoverability, think scale.

❖ Next comes the 'return path'. Storytelling is only one way of saying it. A lot more rewarding is the journey in discovery and humility. Obsess over ways to hear what the recipient has to say. Provoke, but respectfully. A critic is an ally. Ensure that internal critics are more talented than you, that they are fired up about the company and that they feel safe enough to point out red flags.

❖ The measure of your reputation messaging is a fair ask. But leaderships are used to seeing indisputable zeroes and ones like sales figures or stock prices. Help them discover the shades of grey. It might take them time and credibility to accept metrics like sentiment analysis and cultural hot buttons. They may come back to column centimetres, messaging misfires and misquotes. Respect that.

❖ While on credibilty, a tip on media meetings. A free-wheeling conversation, even on tape, is hard to navigate.

The interviewer may ask questions that have nothing to do with the story they have in mind. The actual storyline may be tucked in an aside. On their part, your CXO may be opening up in trust, saying things 'off-the-record' here and there, without switching back to 'on-the-record'. This is a recipe for misunderstandings. A conversation on '100 per cent background' followed by a written Q&A has better outcomes.

❖ Your personal social media is a resource. Use it, albeit sparingly and constructively. The number of 'influencers' in touch with your social media, tacitly in most cases, might surprise. Here, don't endlessly plug your company. Nor even your vacation. Differentiate. As 101, you might want to post on LinkedIn differently than what you would on Twitter. Resist putting Instagram or Facebook on a LinkedIn autofeed and vice versa!

❖ There are those I know who find it cooler to stay away from social media. To each their own. But if your entity is in any business where real human beings are involved, it is hard to argue that social media is an outright time-suck.

❖ Finally, something on a scale of 1–10. Read: 10/10. Meet: 10/10. Listen: 10/10. Write: 2/10. Speak: 1/10. Repeat.

Rohit Bansal is the Group Head of
Corporate Communications at Reliance Industries

AFTERWORD

We hope you enjoyed reading our thoughts on the various nuances of contemporary public relations practices presented in the book.

The curation of the chapters is based on our daily work experience, engagement with professional leaders and youngsters who are training to be public relations professionals. Each topic has been carefully chosen to provide insights and practical tips that are much needed to address the nuances of contemporary public relations for building organisational reputation.

Our endeavour has been to elucidate the practices that many of us follow and bring them together in one place. In our daily grind of planning campaigns and affecting PR, we sometimes miss out on the true sense of what a holistic application of PR processes in your arsenal can do to raise the effectiveness of your overall campaigns.

The year 2022, we feel, was the year of 'systemic renaissance' for PR and corporate communications and a new beginning for many practitioners as they went back to their drawing boards to redefine public relations in the post-pandemic era. Of course, barring a few trends that have emerged stronger, most of them have been sacrosanct over many years now. Our intention was to bring them to the fore, recognise the importance of each one of them and how their interplay can enhance your PR outcomes. Demand for data and research-driven narratives, focus on measurement, rise in regional media relevance and authenticity and empathy in narratives were some of the emerging trends for the year.

To sum up, going forward, some of the key trends, and most covered in the book, that we see being followed by serious public relation practitioners are:

Data and analytics to drive effectiveness of PR

Data and analytics will help professionals measure results against goals and channelise their efforts to help improve outcomes. The ability to use data to make informed decisions around content that resonates with audiences, change tactics during a campaign and respond during a crisis will elevate the stature of the PR profession.

Cause, purpose and values would be the base for storytelling

Recent years have brought to the fore authenticity, empathy and an enhanced relevance of purpose of a brand or an organisation. PR programmes designed around causes that serve public interests will see a huge rise. Done in an authentic and transparent manner, corporates stand to generate a lot of positive reputation and a superior connection with customers. We'll see a lot of action in this space.

Owned media properties will become more popular

There is a visible trend of media houses charging for their content. This is fair and will only grow. However, many cannot afford to pay for content. This (and many other reasons, namely, building communities, direct-to-consumer communication, etc.) has propelled organisations and brands to launch their own media properties. The objectives of owned media are to reach the desired audiences organically, build communities, provide experiences and express its purpose on its own terms. The bottom line is if your customers feel included, they remain loyal to your brand.

'Lo-Fi' unfiltered content will rule the roost

We can assure you that this word will be heard very frequently in the future! Consumers are interested in authentic, behind-the-scenes footage of a brand's journey. The term covers all forms of raw content that is refreshing, relatable and real.

Digital PR and influencer engagement will get sharper, regional and niche-based

Today, influencers continue to emerge from every nook and corner of our country. In many cases, brands are moving away from celebrities in favour of these influencers. In 2024 and beyond, we see a significant trend of engagement with regional influencers and content creators. Focus on traditional as well as digital PR in regional languages is on a rise. We also see a shift in priority from quantity to quality of content from influencers/creators. PR teams will have to have a better understanding of the influencer's audiences, their niche and the type of content they dabble with. Fortunately, tools are available to evaluate reach and potential impact.

PR around ESG will offer competitive advantage and will build strong employer brands

It is a no-brainer that employees are more engaged, satisfied and productive when they bring their whole self to the workplaces. Diversity, equity and inclusion are today seen as key objectives by organisations. Research has also demonstrated that employees prefer working with organisations that demonstrate concern for the environment, are socially responsible and have good status. As more and more employees, consumers and other stakeholders raise their expectations of brands on ESG and demonstration of diversity, inclusion and equality at workplaces, PR professionals will certainly use the opportunity to build a strong employer brand through more focused PR campaigns around these themes.

Use of creativity and emotions in PR to rise

In this world of dwindling attention spans and clutter, what remains top of the mind is not the brand signage or colour scheme or the USP. It is that ubiquitous phenomena called 'emotion'. We think many organisations have raised the bar when it comes to use of creativity and emotions in PR. Being a part of multiple juries for awards platform, we can tell you most of the winning campaigns have an element of emotion rendered creatively. Data is, of course, very important. It fortifies the emotions. We strongly feel that brands will use PR to cultivate an emotional aura as part of their everyday manifestations.

AI and the rise of Web 3.0 will enable direct interactions between brands and their audiences

We believe that Web 3.0 will offer enormous opportunity for brands to experiment and adopt new forms of engagement: gamification, immersive experiences and direct consumer communication. Our belief is that driving awareness around virtual worlds can position brands as dependable partners across internal and external audiences. The modern-day consumer likes to be heard, engaged and given centrality. We all agree that the AI, VR, AR and the metaverse are in early stages but also have the potential of opening the doors to a new level of doing business that will certainly transform the way PR professionals operate.

This book has been a collaborative effort and that stands for our readers too. We loved writing this book for you and would be delighted to know your thoughts so we can continue to improve it and raise the bar of this wonderful profession, together.

ACKNOWLEDGEMENTS

First and foremost, we want to express our heartfelt gratitude to the man who pushed us to get started on this book. There was a time we were contemplating writing one but not adopting the correct structure. We were nudged in the right direction which led us to think of a format and the appropriate chapters subsequently emerged. Unfortunately, due to his untimely demise in May 2022, he is not around to see the published work. We are indebted to the late Anant Rangaswami for his encouragement. We know we have his blessings.

Our heartfelt gratitude to Julia Joseph for volunteering many weekend hours assisting us with research and fusing the various chapters and expert commentaries together in a logical manner.

When we completed all the chapters, we needed someone who could go through the manuscript using a fine-tooth comb. A special appreciation goes to Pradyuman Maheshwari for being the one who ensured that the manuscript was worthy of being sent to potential publishers.

We are grateful to Anish Chandy, Founder at Labyrinth Literary Agency, for being our trusted advisor and for helping us find the right publisher.

Much gratitude to the lovely team at Westland. We're grateful to Karthika V.K. and Sonia Madan for their clear guidance on this project. Many, many thanks to Sanjana Tiwari for a superb job done in finely editing the copy and working so closely with us every step of the way. Special shout-out to Saurabh Garge for an absolutely fantastic job with the cover—we could not have asked for a better designer! And to Amrita Talwar, Shivani Kaul and Divya Shah from the marketing department for doing our book justice.

Many thanks also to Rajinder Ganju for the fabulous work done with the typesetting.

To Shivani Patil for helping conceptualise the book design and creating emblems for each chapter.

A special thanks to Mr Adi Godrej for taking time out of his busy schedule to pen the foreword for the book.

From Sujit

To my parents, Mrs Meena and Dr M.S. Patil, for having believed in me every step of the way throughout my career and through the ups and downs of life.

To Shubhangi and Shivani for allowing me to devote the time to embark on this project and constantly cheering me on.

To my wonderful colleagues at work at Godrej Industries Limited and Associate Companies, the corporate brand and communications team—Michelle, Usha, Nitin, Gaurav, Deepak, Anurag, Meenakshi, Ayumi, Zeba, Ankit, Shreyoshee and all brand and marketing managers as well as functional and business heads.

To Nitin Shimpi and Vishnu G. Haarinath for the

professional job done in clicking and editing my picture for the book.

To Tanya Dubash for always encouraging me to raise the performance bar of the communications profession.

From Amith

My parents—the late Ethel and Prof. Sukhdeep Prabhu. Thank you for being with me every step of the way in my life and my work.

To Suchetha and Swara for their support in allowing me to devote myself to this book.

To my wonderful colleagues at work at The Promise Foundation: Roshan, Anubhuti, Ameeta and the first cohort of the Fellows. At SCoRe, thank you, Hemant.

From the both of us

We believe this book is a community project. We have seventy-five leaders who have shared insights that feature at the end of each chapter. Some of them have been our personal role models from whom we have learnt a lot. We are grateful to them.

The list below is in alphabetical order:

Abhilasha Padhy, Ajita Shashidhar, Aman Gupta, Ameer Ismail, Amit Misra, Amit Narayan, Aniisu Verghese, Aniruddha Bhagwat, Ankoor Chaudhary, Anubhuti Yadav, Anup Sharma, Aparna Thomas, Archana Jain, Aseem Sood, Ashwani Singla, Babita Baruah, Bharatendu Kabi, Chaavi Leekha, Debasis Ray, Dilip Cherian, Dilip Yadav, Faiza Kapoor, Gabriela Lungu, Gaurav Bhaskar, Girish Balachandran, Harshil Karia, Hemant Gaule, Karthik Srinivasan, Komal Lath, Kunal Sinha, Madan Bahal, Madhavi

Jha, Madhu Chibber, Manisha Kapoor, Melissa Waggner-Zorkin, Michelle Francis, Mihir Karkare, Minari Shah, Mukesh Kharbanda, Mukund Rajan, Nandini Chatterjee, Nandita Lakshmanan, Nitin Mantri, Ophira Bhatia, Pragnya Ram, Pranshu Sikka, Prasad Sangameshwaran, Prema Sagar, Rachana Chowdhury, Rachana Panda, Rajeev Kumar, Rakesh Thukral, Rakhee Lalvani, Rashmi Soni, Ritesh Singh, Roger Darashah, Roger Pereira, Rohit Bansal, Ruchi Jaggi, Seema Ahuja, Senjam Rajasekhar, Siddhartha Mukherjee, Simran Kodesia, Stuart Bruce, Sunanda Rao-Erdem, Sunil Gautam, Tejal Daftary, Tuhina Pandey, Valerie Pinto, Varghese Thomas and Varsha Chainani.

To all who have invested in and bought this book, a part of the proceeds will go towards the education of deserving young candidates who aspire to make a space for themselves in the wonderful profession of public relations. We thank you for enabling that.

Words are not enough to express what we feel in terms of gratitude towards all who have, directly and indirectly, played a role in shaping our thinking and enabling us to create this book.

Cheers!
Amith and Sujit